THE AMERICAN WEST

A spacious log ranch house in southern Dakota Territory, 1888. Even today, such a house would attract buyers. At center is a days-old colt. (US Library of Congress)

THE AMERICAN WEST
Living the Frontier Dream

JAMES R. ARNOLD AND ROBERTA WIENER

BLANDFORD

ACKNOWLEDGEMENTS

The authors extend their heartfelt thanks to Mother and Father (Joyce and Robert Arnold) for research assistance in far-flung libraries, and dear old Dad (Bernard Wiener) for buying us some really good reference books. Just wait until they find out about our next project. Also: the Rockbridge County, Virginia Public Library for prompt interlibrary loans; the University of Virginia and Washington & Lee University for extending library privileges to two strangers; the Museum of New Mexico, the Arizona Historical Society, and the Museum of American Frontier Culture for opening their collections to us; the National Archives picture research staff for going above and beyond; and the U.S. Library of Congress Photoduplication Service for processing our orders so efficiently even during the government's 'shutdown.' Finally, thank you to Rod Dymott for ideas and inspiration, and for having faith in us.

AUTHORS' NOTE

In all quotations from old diaries and letters, we usually retain the original phrasing, spelling, and punctuation. The only exceptions we make are for words that are so badly misspelled as to be incomprehensible. We also make unapologetic use of what is today known as sexist language. If we are writing about tasks that, two hundred years ago, were as a rule performed by women, or by men, the pronouns will reflect the rule without regard to the possible exception.

Blandford Press
An Imprint of the Cassell Group
Wellington House, 125 Strand, London WC2R 0BB

British Library Cataloguing-in-Publication Data:
a catalogue record for this book is available from
the British Library

ISBN 0-7137-2548-6

Designed and edited by DAG Publications Ltd.
Designed by David Gibbons; layout by Anthony A. Evans;
edited by John Gilbert; indexed by Maureen Charters;
printed and bound in Great Britain.

CONTENTS

PROLOGUE

The American West has long held the imagination. To most pioneers it represented freedom and opportunity, to natural drifters simply the chance to keep moving. To outlaws it offered easy victims and easier escapes. To entrepreneurs the West promised untapped wealth for the taking. After the frontier had disappeared, fiction writers and then Hollywood created the West anew and offered it for sale. Theirs was the fantastic West where crack gunslingers and outlaws, homesteaders and Indians played at life and death in front of frontier façades and scenic backdrops. More recently the owners of Hollywood fortunes have bought their own fantasy in the form of palatial ranch houses sitting on great tracts of western land. Here, for a few weeks a year, they act out on set a new version of pioneer life. Meanwhile, Californians from all walks of life are nowadays heading eastward to the enduring mountain heartland – to Colorado, Wyoming, New Mexico – in search of the qualities still associated with the West: clean air, wide open spaces, freedom, a fresh start in life. In 1795 or 1995, to dream of the West is to dream of change.

We look beyond the dream and ask, how did the pioneer settlers of the American West actually spend each day? On the one hand we have the image of the handsome cowboy tall in the saddle, his plucky woman bravely gazing to the horizon, the children clustered at her skirts. On the other, we have historical accounts of great danger, backbreaking labor, numbing isolation, and youngsters dying one after the other. But those do not provide the whole story. The words of the pioneers themselves present some of the truth, but they left much unsaid.

We will describe how the pioneer family undertook the leap into the unknown that was their journey west; what they found when they arrived; how they gathered the necessities of life, the food, clothing, and shelter needed to survive. If they decided to stay – and many turned back when they understood the practical reality of establishing a life on the frontier – how did the settlers build and manage their farms, conduct trade, and form villages and towns? How did they coexist with their neighbors, raise and educate their children, tend to their health, maintain order, and defend their lives and property in the years before civilization overtook them?

One of the reasons people then and today dreamed about the West was the gnawing suspicion that if only they could somehow settle in the West, life would instantly become better. Such thinking persists. Some modern people believe that if they could return society to the values practiced by the western settlers it would be a very good thing indeed. In reality, did America's westward pioneers have greater freedom than we have today? To what extent did government regulate their lives? Did random acts of violence fall upon them with greater frequency? Did they live in a world that had more respect for life, or less? Lacking in material comforts, did they reap intangible rewards?

The idea of the American West encompasses a vast area and a century of time. The American frontier began at the Allegheny Mountains in the late eighteenth century, rolled to the edge of the continent by the 1840s, broke on the shore and rolled back to the arid Great Plains toward the end of the nineteenth century.

In what follows, we open a window on Kentucky in the 1780s, where pioneers labored under the new nation's most primitive frontier conditions to carve out productive farms and bring the first American territory to statehood; Oregon in the 1840s, where pioneers tended lush and abundant fields at the far end of a grueling six-month journey; New Mexico in the 1850s and 1860s, a territory won in war, where Americans settled among the adobe towns and irrigated fields of Mexicans and the pueblos of southwestern Indians; and South Dakota in the 1870s and 1880s, where homesteaders seized a last chance to own land, no matter how arid and treeless.

* * *

Look elsewhere for the lives of legendary cowboys, outlaws, fur traders, and miners, and for the histories of the Indian nations. They are amply covered by other authors. This book is about the daily lives of American pioneer families of European origin, ordinary people of average means.

Many of these ordinary people made the same beginning. A journey west to start a race against the seasons: find a claim; erect a one-room dwelling of logs or earth; clear a few acres; plant corn around the stumps or in slashes in the sod; pray that the crops prospered to provide food for the first, lean winter. Everyone worked according to their strength, the young side by side with their elders. Perhaps winter would provide time to educate the children, if all chores were done first!

For the overwhelming majority of first settlers in a new territory, life's work was farm work. Indeed, in 1790, ninety percent of the entire nation's population farmed. But those in established communities on the eastern seaboard had tremendous advantages. If the plow broke, there were local blacksmiths to repair it. If floods washed out the first crop there were stores selling food, and seeds to start again. Most importantly, there were nearby friends and family to help in times of need. None of this was true for the pioneers. The frontier rewarded hard work, resourcefulness, and makeshift...by giving the settlers a new year for more of the same. Only after a settlement had proven its viability, did tradesmen and professionals appear and farmers branch out into new occupations.

Beyond this common experience, American pioneers of different times and places also encountered resources and privations unique to each frontier. The location, the climate, and the available farming technology all governed their daily lives. But the settlement of the West began with a journey – on foot, on horseback, by wagon, or by steamer and rail – and that is where we too will begin.

I

'A STRANGE FEVER RAGING'

'The past winter there has been a strange fever raging here (it is the Oregon fever) it seems to be contagious and it is raging terribly, nothing seems to stop it but to tear up and take a six months trip across the plains with ox teams to the Pacific Ocean.' — Keturah Belknap, 1847[1]

OVER THE MOUNTAINS TO KENTUCKY

The year 1740 found many colonial Americans feeling the burdens of too many people living too close together. They saw their farmland becoming less productive and wild game dwindling. The land beyond the mountains beckoned, a land of reputed abundance, a land supposedly without winter. The reality of Kentucky turned out to be quite different, but even hard winters and food short-

ages, an unrelenting campaign of terror by the Shawnees, and tenuous and disputed land claims failed to quench the hunger for new territory.

So it was that in 1750 a land speculation company sent the first known white explorer, Dr. Thomas Walker, into the Kentucky territory. Walker discovered and named the Cumberland Gap, a pass that would become one of the two main portals into Kentucky. But the land remained cloaked in mystery for a while longer as the British and the French fought a war for control of the wilderness between the Appalachian Mountains and the Mississippi River. Once the British emerged victorious in the French and Indian War in 1763, the way was open for parties of men to embark on 'long hunts,' leaving their farms in North Carolina to spend months or years gathering animal skins in eastern Kentucky.

The station at Boonesborough, Kentucky in 1775. One-room dwellings line the inside of the stockade. In the early years, pioneers left the shelter of station walls at their peril. (In Lewis Collins, History of Kentucky, *Covington, KY, 1878)*

10

The first permanent settlements of Kentucky grew out of forts established in 1775 at Harrodsburg and Boonesborough. The trickle of settlers swelled to a flood in 1780, the year in which the Virginia legislature officially opened Kentucky to settlement. Hundreds of families, perhaps 3,000 people in all, crossed the mountains, only to find the settlements ill-prepared to absorb the onrush of new pioneers. The previous winter of 1779–80 had been exceptionally cold. Settlers had starved, frozen, or succumbed to illnesses. With the ground frozen solid, some could not even bury their dead. Livestock died in great number, and even wild animals starved or froze to death.

> '[We'd] go through the cane and see cattle laying with their heads to their side, as if
> they were asleep; just literally froze to death.... A great country for turkeys, and they
> had like to have starved to death; a heap! a heap! of them died.'[2]

Spring found food in short supply. New arrivals who had counted on being able to purchase corn from established settlers were forced instead to eat the thawing carcasses of long-dead animals.

The Kentucky pioneers lived within the walls of forted stations. Stockades with heavy gates surrounded the small log dwellings, and fields and gardens surrounded the stations. Each venture outside the station to work the land, draw water, or tend the livestock was taken at peril of Indian attack. As the frontier moved westward across Kentucky, forted stations remained at the leading edge. Only as the risk of Indian attack subsided did settlers live outside the walls, although they still clustered their cabins together for security. Slowly, as confidence increased, people spread out to till as much prime land as possible. The countryside became dotted with isolated farmsteads.

To establish a farmstead on the Kentucky frontier required more than blood and toil: it required cunning, legal knowledge, and the ability to turn the law to advantage. The first settlers claimed the land they desired by making 'tomahawk improvements.' This consisted of using a tomahawk to girdle a few trees around the claim's boundary. These marks served as signs to hold the claim in one's absence. Pioneers, by general agreement, honored such marks and ejected anyone who didn't. Not so speculators, latecomers, and their lawyers.

Soldiers of the Revolution had won the nation's independence with their blood. The new nation, as penniless as any pioneer, paid its liberators with warrants for land west of the mountains. Many veterans, needing cash, sold their warrants to speculators. The speculators in turn hired surveyors to mark off the huge tracts they thus accumulated. In this they were abetted by the lack of a central registry, oddly shaped tracts, and vague survey descriptions.

Speculators and newer settlers rushed to register their claims. Many of these claims came into conflict with those of earlier settlers, who had endured hardship and the wrath of Indians to carve out their farms. Like flies to honey, lawyers swarmed into Kentucky to take up the fight, representing the side that paid them best. Virginia set up a special land court to handle the resulting lawsuits. In these battles fell pioneers who had successfully fought off Indians and survived to make substantial improvements to their land. Subsequent claimants, sometimes decades later, had the law, and lawyers, on their side. Even Daniel Boone, first among the first to win Kentucky, lost title to his land because he had neglected to follow all the required steps to register it. Kentucky alone among the states established after Independence, practiced this haphazard and disastrous approach to land ownership.

* * *

The land for which so many hungered was a land of heavy forests rising from fertile untapped soil. Canebrakes – dense thickets of brambles climbing to 20 or 30 feet in height – covered much of the ground beneath the trees. Such thickets were passable only through trails already beaten by wild animals. Kentucky's wooded valleys promised a generous living to the first arrivals, while the high-

DATELINE TO KENTUCKY

1768: In the Treaty of Fort Stanwix, the Iroquois nation cedes to Britain its claim to a vast land area that includes Kentucky. The Shawnees, however, who live to the north of Kentucky, are not party to this treaty. The Shawnees recognize that British dominion will ultimately bring permanent settlement to their traditional hunting grounds. Unless they drive back the white settlers, they will lose their hunting grounds.

1773–1774: The Shawnees succeed twice in repulsing the tide of white settlement. The first parties of settlers move westward, and then flee eastward to save their lives. In the town now known as Harrodsburg, emigrants clear land, plant corn, and build log cabins in the spring of 1774. Shawnee raiding parties force the settlers back east, but in 1775, in the wake of Lord Dunmore's campaign, Harrod and his party return and build a fort. This time, the English have come to stay.

1775: Daniel Boone marks and clears the Wilderness Road through the Cumberland Gap to Boonesborough.

1776: The Virginia legislature creates the county of Kentucky. Its population, centered around three forts, rises to 280 by 1777.

1782: The final battle of the American Revolution takes place on Kentucky soil at Blue Licks.

1783: More than 12,000 settlers inhabit Kentucky.

1792: Kentucky, population 100,000, becomes the first new state to join the United States.

lands offered rocky soil of lesser quality. The climate was mild: warmer than that of the northeast, not as oppressively hot as that of the south Atlantic. Most years saw sufficient rainfall to water the crops that sprang abundantly from the rich soil.

The distance from Philadelphia to Harrodsburg, down the Shenandoah Valley of Virginia, through the Cumberland Gap into Tennessee, and over the Wilderness Road, covered more than 600 miles. This was the route most frequently taken by the early emigrants. They began the journey in the east with horse-drawn wagons, but in the Appalachian mountains the trail narrowed to a track where only pack animals could go. There remained ahead hundreds of miles for the emigrants to walk. They forded rivers on foot or horseback, and they slept out on the trail, wrapped in blankets that were often soaked by rain. They survived on a diet of meat and little else. They carried with them hard biscuit, bacon, some flour, dried beef and pork, live chickens, and whiskey. When all went smoothly, the overland trek took five or six weeks. Too often, it did not, and people perished. The emigrants,

A typical flatboat, with horses and cow aboard, bearing emigrants by river to a new territory. The long oars were known as 'sweeps.' (Library of Congress)

frequently quite ignorant of how to survive in the wilderness, ate poorly, succumbed to disease and exposure, drowned in swollen rivers, or fell to Indian raids.

The earliest emigrant parties came from Virginia and North Carolina. The end of the Revolution saw an increase in settlers from Pennsylvania, Maryland, and New Jersey. They assembled into larger parties of 300 or 400 for the 130-mile trip through the Wilderness. The trail was well marked by 1785, but the Wilderness remained a fearful passage shrouded in dark forest and prowled by hostile Cherokee raiders. By 1800, most Kentucky-bound settlers evaded the Wilderness by traveling through Maryland to

A PLANTER GOES WEST

Wealthy slaveholding planters migrated from the southeastern seaboard states, first to Kentucky and Tennessee, then finally to Alabama, Mississippi, and Louisiana. Soil depletion and falling tobacco prices encouraged them to seek their fortunes by growing cotton on vast and rich new lands. Slaves came to Kentucky with the first pioneers. By 1777, slaves constituted ten percent of Harrodsburg's population. By the year 1800, slaves made up half the non-Indian population in Mississippi.

Members of the planter class could afford to take a scouting trip west to select and purchase acreage. Returning, they sent their overseers and slaves west to the new property to clear land, build houses, and plant crops in preparation for the master's arrival. The treatment of slaves during the westward migration veered from cruel to humane. Some slaves made the march on foot, carrying heavy loads on their backs, chained together, and under guard. Others went in loosely formed caravan, with house slaves riding in wagons while field slaves walked. One master let his slaves shop in a town along the route and bought them presents, while another had his overseers awaken the slaves several times a night for roll call. In contrast to the less wealthy emigrant with his one cart of earthly goods, planter households moved in cavalcades of wagons and horses. However, their wealth did not shield them from accidents, deaths, and loss of possessions along the way.

Wheeling, in present-day West Virginia, and from there down the Ohio River. This route was faster but not without danger. The river passage took only days when the current was swift, but the boats were vulnerable to Indian attack.

Whether by wagon, pack horse, or flatboat, settlers tried to bring everything they would need for their first couple of years on the frontier: metal tools and utensils, clothing, bedding, household goods, seeds and root stock, farm animals, extra iron for making and repairing tools, powder, lead for making shot, whatever money they could scrape together, and even extra goods to sell to other pioneers. More than a few brought their fiddles, those essential instruments for brightening up an evening. They outfitted their pack horses with saddles made from a single piece of white oak, a forked limb of the right shape carved to fit the horse. Small children sometimes rode in packs borne by horses.

Men frequently made this journey in reverse, returning east to conduct business or escort their families west. Groups gathered at Crab Orchard, at set intervals or in response to public notices, so they could enjoy the safety of numbers as they traveled. Women and children almost never ventured a return journey east in the hazardous early days. They literally left their past lives behind when they began the exodus west.

Some pioneers sought solitude and independence but most emigrated in organized groups: extended families, entire neighborhoods, whole congregations or communities who wished to have familiar company in a new land. They wanted not solitude, but land ownership, and the opportunity to amass wealth. Throughout America's pioneer history, groups organized on the basis of family, nationality, religion, business interest, or colonization scheme traveled westward alongside or behind the rugged individualists striking out alone. One such group set out in 1788. It consisted of five New Jersey families, including the family of the famous future doctor, Daniel Drake. The Drake party comprised mother and father, two children (including Daniel, age two, who grew up to tell this story), and an unmarried aunt.

They first traveled some 400 miles across Pennsylvania by horse-drawn wagon. They spent the nights sleeping in their wagons, and purchased some of their food from taverns. The taverns of the day did not provide beds, so travelers slept on the floor, wrapped in their own blankets. Later taverns offered beds, but tavern-keepers only rarely changed the vermin-ridden bedsheets. Guests also shared their beds with fellow-travelers, a practice that persisted into the 1850s. Eventually, a number of flatboats brought the Drake party down the Ohio River to Limestone, Kentucky, today known as Maysville. Since leaving Pittsburgh they had traveled more than 350 river miles. The Drakes were like many emigrant groups who either built or purchased flatboats, also called 'arks,' and hired a pilot. A typical flatboat measured less than 15 feet wide by about 50 feet long. Properly built, it could carry numerous people and all their possessions, wagons, and livestock. Most sold the boats at half cost when they arrived at their destination, though a few ventured to break up the boats and haul the lumber to their land.

The Drake party arrived on the Kentucky shore in June. Since they had not yet purchased land, there was no time to clear and plant that year. Whereas such a predicament could be fatal in the early days, the Drakes benefited from the growth Kentucky had experienced over more than a decade of settlement. Drake senior took on work hauling goods and harvesting crops in order to be able to purchase provisions. The family first stayed in Washington, a village four miles from Limestone, in a lean-to built for sheep, adjoining somebody's cabin. They pooled their resources with those of several relatives and other New Jersey settlers to buy 1,400 acres located eight miles from Washington. Of this purchase, the Drakes acquired 38 acres. These families clustered their cabins together for mutual defense, and named their community Mays Lick, after the original owner and the salt lick on the premises, a name that persists today.

Most settlers aimed for a late spring or early summer arrival, hoping to get a first crop in the ground. Fear of Indian attack, however, caused many to migrate late in the fall when the Indians stayed closer to their homes. These settlers tried to beat the onset of winter, arriving with just enough time to build a cabin. They survived on game and purchased food, and spent the winter clearing land. Sometimes miscalculation or just bad luck intervened. One well-equipped group of several hundred, an entire congregation, tried this in 1781 and got overtaken on the trail by an early winter. Their pack animals stumbled and fell on the slick, half-frozen mud. Rivers swept away possessions and people drowned in attempted crossings of swollen fords. Foul weather so slowed their progress that they took three weeks to make thirty miles.[3] Bedraggled and depleted, they arrived late and lacking the things with which they had expected to begin a new life.

The white population of Kentucky in early 1780 numbered only in the hundreds. By 1783 it had grown to 12,000. By the time Kentucky attained statehood, in 1792, close to 100,000 Americans – including 12,000 slaves – lived there. They inhabited a land that would have been all but unrecognizable to the first settlers. The frontier had disappeared in fewer than twenty years.

In its place rose a society stratified into landed slave-holding elite and subsistence farmers, often merely tenants on a wealthy man's land. Brick houses and coaches soon shone in resplendent contrast to log cabins and horse-carts. Wealthy men moved their households in convoys of wagons and coaches, while their slaves walked, chained together. Some sent their slaves and livestock ahead under command of the overseer. Only after the slaves built a house, cleared and fenced the fields, and planted crops did the owners venture west.

THE LAND OFFICE BUSINESS

By 1815, migrations to the old northwest began to surge across Ohio from east to west, and across the Ohio River from south to north. Those coming from the east traveled by road across Pennsylvania to Pittsburgh. While people of means sent their belongings ahead in Conestoga freight wagons and rode in stagecoaches, most migrants traveled in their own horse-drawn wagons. Those who lacked wagons or horses carried packs on their backs or pushed wheelbarrows piled high with possessions. Such labors notwithstanding, they traveled an easier and safer road than had the pioneers to Kentucky, and held a more certain title to their land.

The Northwest Ordinance of 1787 set forth the procedure to be followed from initial white settlement to statehood. It applied to the five territories of the Old Northwest – Ohio, Indiana, Illinois, Michigan, and Wisconsin – but became the model for all subsequent states. Under the new law, each territory received an appointed governor and three judges. Upon attaining a population of 5,000, a territory elected a legislature. A territory with a population of 60,000 was permitted to draft a constitution and apply for statehood. While the 1787 law prohibited slavery in the Old Northwest, future territories became battle grounds for the slavery issue. The ordinance also prohibited entail and primogeniture laws, which in Europe had fostered a landed aristocracy by requiring that all properties pass intact to the eldest son. This last prohibition reserved to American farmers the right to divide up their property at will.

THIN ON THE GROUND 1810 POPULATION *			
State/Territory	Area	Population	Density
Ohio	43,860 sq. mi.	230,760	5/sq. mi.
Indiana	39,000 sq. mi.	24,520	less than 1
Illinois Terr.	52,000 sq. mi.	12,282	less than 1
Michigan Terr.	34,820 sq. mi	4,762	less than 1
Kentucky	40,110 sq. mi	406,511	10/sq. mi.
Tennessee	43,200 sq. mi	261,727	6/sq. mi.
Mississippi. Terr.	88,680 sq. mi	40,352	less than 1
Missouri Terr.	985,250 sq. mi	20,845	less than 1

1995 U.S. population density: 70 persons per square mile

* From John Bradbury, 'Travels in the interior of America in the years 1809, 1810, and 1811,' in Reuben Gold Thwaites, *Early Western Travels, 1748–1846* (New York, 1966), vol. 5, p. 287.

Once Indian title to a parcel of land was extinguished, the U.S. government had it surveyed in rectangular lots, set up land offices, and offered quarter sections of land at auction. Land not sold at the initial auction could be bought later at the set minimum price: for cash at $1.64/acre, or for $2/acre on credit, with 50 cents down payment. A quarter section consisted of 160 acres, or one-quarter square mile.

In the weeks leading up to a sale, prospective buyers toured the parcels. As the opening day of the sale approached, strangers flooded into the area and camped out around the land office. Sales lasted several weeks, with parcels sold off in order, section by section, township by township. Prospective bidders milled about waiting for their desired section to come up, and purveyors of whiskey rolled out their barrels.

The federal government intended, with the passage of early laws for the sale of public land, both to place land in the hands of farmers and to enrich the national treasury. Because the government offered land on credit, it actually promoted speculation and encouraged settlers to overextend their financial resources. Widespread defaults deprived the federal treasury of funds, causing Congress to abolish the credit system in 1820. The same legislation reduced the price to $1.25 per acre in cash and reduced the minimum allowable purchase to 80 acres.

Backwoodsmen, eager to stay ahead of the encroaching population, willingly sold their clearings and improvements, but the buyer still had to purchase the land itself from the government. Settlers who squatted on Indian land before the government acquired it, or on government land before it was offered for sale, faced the threat of being ejected by the government or bid off the land by a cash-rich speculator. A series of pre-emption acts recognized squatters' rights, allowing squatters on public land to purchase the nearest quarter section at auction. Prior to these acts, some squatters successfully cooperated to intimidate speculators from bidding, or failing that, to drive them off at gunpoint.

Much of the land intended for public sale never got past the obstacle of collusion and price-fixing among speculators and the wealthy. Speculators agreed not to bid against one another and thus helped themselves to land at minimum price. This corruption of the public distribution process contributed to the social stratification of the frontier. Collusion by land office officials also worked to shut men of modest means out of land ownership.

This state of affairs spurred Congress to pass a new pre-emption act in 1841. The act secured to permanent settlers the right to buy public land, at minimum price, prior to auction – up to 160 acres per adult – by improving and living on it. They still needed to have the money in hand when the government was ready to sell it. The law simply forced speculators to reach a little further into their bag of tricks. Soon they colluded with phony settlers, who made a slight pretense of improving and occupying public land and then disappeared after the sale. In fact, in the years to come, Congress never did succeed in passing a land law that prevented speculators from using it to amass acreage at bargain prices.

CROSSING THE RIVER

The first decade of the nineteenth century propelled American settlers across the Mississippi River. The Louisiana Purchase of 1803 represented a huge addition of territory to the United States. Meriwether Lewis and William Clark crossed this territory to explore the Pacific northwest, and fur traders ranged across the continent.

Lower Louisiana was a mixed settlement of French, Spanish, and Americans, with about one-third of the population slaves. During Spanish rule, the governor had granted land to selected Americans because of their purported antipathy to the British. The abundantly rich soil of the river bottoms supported planters in style, but the same climate that provided such good crops brought mosquitos and malaria.

The French preceded Americans into Upper Louisiana, a land of alternating woods and prairies boasting rich soil and adequate rainfall. They founded settlements on the eastern shore of the Mississippi River, in present-day Illinois, during the late 1600s. On the west side in present-day Missouri were settlements such as Ste. Genevieve and Carondelet, dating back to the early 1700s, and St. Louis, founded in 1764. The French had laid out the villages in squares, with houses built on the streets, and long strips of land, a mile or longer, allotted in the communal fields for farming. Following the Louisiana Purchase, U.S. examiners approved the allotments as claims for the original settlers.

French settlers made up about a third of the population at the time of the purchase. Many still subsisted on hunting and Indian trade, although farming was becoming more prevalent in the face of the rapid depletion of wild game. The French allowed their livestock to run free on the prairies, established apple and peach orchards, and raised much the same crops as did American settlers in Kentucky: corn, wheat, pumpkins, melons, potatoes and vegetables, and small tobacco and cotton patches.

In 1803, Upper Louisiana also held relatively peaceful and prosperous log-cabin villages of Delaware, Shawnee, and Cherokee Indians who traded with white travelers and settlers. At the same time, outlaw groups of Creeks, Choctaws, and Chickasaws conducted sporadic raids on white settlers. As they always had, and would in the future, whites viewed with distrust any Indians encountered on road or river.

American settlers had begun crossing the river in the late 1790s, a few years in advance of the Louisiana Purchase, but large-scale American emigration to the area did not begin until after the War of 1812. Many Kentuckians and Virginians migrated to Missouri, once again seeking new land and opportunities. Among the earliest, in 1798, were Daniel Boone and several of his sons, ousted from their Kentucky holdings for lack of clear titles.

St. Louis, the capital of Upper Louisiana, contained about 180 houses, the best of them built of stone. The town lay about 1,300 miles by river from Pittsburgh. Soon, the Rocky Mountain fur traders would use St. Louis as their base of operations. Decades later, wagon trains heading across the continent to Santa Fe or Oregon would congregate in the towns lining the western shore of the Mississippi and outfit themselves in the stores of St. Louis.

STE. GENEVIEVE, MISSOURI

First settled by French-Canadians and Creoles in the mid-1700s, the village was laid out in squares, with houses built along the streets. Each family farmed a long strip of land, a mile or longer, allotted to them from the commonly held village field of some 7,000 acres. Located along the Mississippi River, the field had a perimeter fence with each section maintained by the family farming the adjacent plot. The inhabitants grew wheat, corn, and tobacco, exported flour downriver to New Orleans, and raised cattle, which they turned out into the field after the harvest. They relied upon the floods to renew the soil, and used no fertilizer beyond what the cattle deposited.

When, at the turn of the nineteenth century, Americans began to settle the area in large numbers, they planted crops on the uplands instead of relying on the floodplain. They also introduced water mills, which made a better quality of flour than the horse mills used by the early French inhabitants.

By the 1830s, steamboats and canal boats had brought white settlement to all of the lands east of the Mississippi. The U.S. Army had either subdued the Indians or driven them across the river. Perhaps the government believed that settlers would not follow them there. The trans-Mississippi climate was, and is, more severe than that of the east coast, the summers hotter and the winters colder. This discouraged settlement to some degree. Even more discouraging, much of the territory across the river was treeless prairie. Many Americans believed that land without trees could not produce crops. Thus arose the idea that an uninhabitable Great American Desert separated the Mississippi from the verdant Pacific coast. Yet the tools that would help settlers conquer that seeming desert, the reaper and the steel plow, had just emerged from their inventors' workshops. A far-seeing English visitor wrote, 'My own opinion is, that it can be cultivated; and that, in process of time, it will not only be peopled and cultivated, but that it will be one of the most Beautiful countries in the world.'[4]

ACROSS THE CONTINENT TO OREGON

By the close of the 1780s, both British and Spanish mariners had explored the Northwest Pacific coast and taken away sea otter pelts. Englishman George Vancouver made a detailed survey of the coast in the early 1790s. The as yet unclaimed Oregon Country, an entity that extended from the coast to the Rocky Mountains, and from northern California to Alaska, possessed untapped riches that beckoned to all.

Hard on the heels of the Louisiana Purchase, the famed Lewis and Clark expedition sought and found an overland route to Oregon. The explorers returned to the States in 1806 bringing with them the first detailed maps and information about a vast area of the continent. American fur trappers and traders made immediate use of this new-found knowledge to set out in the explorers' footsteps. John Jacob Astor tried to establish a beaver pelt empire based at Astoria, but plagued by assorted disasters, his men sold the post to British traders in 1813. Although Britain and the United States had signed a joint occupation treaty in 1818, they continued to vie for domination of the northwest fur trade. However, the St. Louis based American traders failed to mount a significant challenge to the British-backed Hudson's Bay Company and its chief factor, Dr John McLoughlin. During the heyday of the beaver trade, from the mid-

1820s to 1830s, McLoughlin and his company dominated every aspect of society in the Pacific northwest.

From Company headquarters at Fort Vancouver, at the confluence of the Columbia and Willamette rivers, McLoughlin presided over thirteen posts, a shipyard, farms, and a trade that extended to Hawaii, Alaska, California, and South America. He attempted to halt American traders at the Snake River watershed by sending his trappers to wipe out the beaver population in the region. However, when a party of Methodist missionaries arrived from the United States in 1836, two women among them, McLoughlin extended every courtesy. The Company enjoyed the fruits of well-established farms, mills, and dairies and their long years in trade. They ate varied and well-balanced meals on fine china, and offered the missionaries hospitality, seeds, root stock, and household goods.

The missionaries' goal was to bring salvation to the Cayuse, Nez Perce, and Walla Walla Indians. They walked a line between competing Hudson's Bay Company traders and American traders. They relied on American fur traders to escort them across the Rocky Mountains and then depended on the Hudson's Bay Company to provide supplies once they arrived. McLoughlin did not see in the missionaries any threat to his dominion, nor did he object to any force that would help keep order in the territory. His benevolence was perhaps misguided. Although the Methodists ultimately retired defeated from the battleground for Indian souls, word spread that families could make the arduous cross-continent journey, and that an Eden waited for the taking. During the decade the missions spent at their task, thousands of settlers flooded into Oregon Territory and made it American.

First these thousands had to traverse the Oregon Trail, a journey of 2,000 miles taking four to six months. More so than previous American pioneers, those who ventured on the Oregon Trail had to forsake their prior lives. A single exchange of letters with the folks back home took two years. Friends and relatives did not come for a visit. So eager were some to claim a piece of Oregon that they left their business affairs back home in the hands of trusted neighbors. Inevitably, anxious letters rolled eastward across the plains, demanding to know whether the old farm had been sold yet, and where the money was!

> 'Instead of the funds which I have been long expecting from Missouri I have received letters from Cynthia's brother Sidney that my agent Joseph Story is dead.'[5]

Still, many Oregon settlers believed the sacrifice well worth it and wrote back east to encourage additional emigration:

> 'Just say (for me) to the young men of old Milton, Don't live & die in sight of your Father's house, but take a trip to Oregon! you can perform the journey in two years & I am sure you will never regret spending the time. But, if they should come to settle here, I would advise them, to bring a wife along, as ladies are (like the specie) very scarce. And if you have any maiden ladies about dying in despair, just fit up their teeth well, & send them to Oregon.'[6]

Presumably the writer believed that the rough and sometimes raw diet of the Oregon Trail required strong teeth!

* * *

Keturah Belknap emigrated to Oregon from Iowa in 1848 with her husband and child and five neighboring families. She was twenty-eight years old at the time. Like many women, she did not favor the move, especially after struggling for seven years to get established in Iowa. She knew as well that few people would make the long journey to Oregon more than once in a lifetime. On her final visit to her family in Ohio, she wrote in her journal:

'I knew it would be the last visit I would make there whether I lived or not, but I kept all these thots buried in my own breast and never told them.'[7]

Back in Iowa, and having just buried a child, she wrote, 'So now I will spend what little strength I have left getting ready to cross the Rockies.'[8]

In fact, with six months to prepare for the April departure, Mrs. Belknap performed a Herculean labor of weaving, sewing, and packing with the help of her neighbors:

'The neighbors are all very kind to come in to see me so I don't feel lonely like I would and they don't bring any work, but just pick up my sewing.... I try not to think of the parting time but look forward to the time when we shall meet to part no more.'[9]

Meanwhile the men traded for oxen, carved ox yokes, and made bows to support the wagon covers. They practiced driving the ox teams, and put all the stock to pasture together so they could bond as a new herd. The women cooperated to produce muslin and linen wagon covers, some women spinning, others weaving. Mrs. Belknap made clothing and candles enough to last a year, and sold excess household goods, exchanging them for time spent doing her sewing. She cooked enough food for the first several days on the trail.

The ever democratic Americans typically held meetings before embarking upon the Oregon Trail. They passed resolutions governing the journey. One such meeting in 1843 specified the provisions to be carried by each individual: '100 pounds of flour, 30 pounds of bacon, 1 peck salt, 3 pounds powder, in horns or canteens, 15 pounds lead or shot, and one good tent cloth to every six persons; every man well armed and equipped with gun, tomahawk, knife.'[10]

In Mrs. Belknap's case, it fell to the wife to organize the packing and loading of the wagon. Filling the front of the wagon stood a large box that served as storage, a seat for the driver, and a dining table. Wooden cleats nailed to the wagon bed kept things from sliding around. Next in was a chest of older clothes to wear on the trail and a medicine chest, followed by a space for the wife's chair and a play area for the boy. A large crate with goods they would need upon their arrival went in next, and then linen sacks full of flour, cornmeal, dried apples and peaches, beans, rice, sugar, and coffee beans. At the rear stood the washtub with the lunch basket and dishes nested in it, and a box of cookware for the trail. The feather bed was folded over (many settlers carried their precious china inside the feather bed) and, strapped on top of the food sacks along with pillows and blankets.[11]

Mrs. Belknap's account ended along the Oregon Trail as events overtook her. Her son became gravely ill, and another son was born to her on the trail. The family arrived in southwestern Oregon in October, where both children survived to adulthood. Their descendants report that Keturah Belknap lived to the age of ninety-three.

* * *

In the 1840s, Independence, Missouri, St. Joseph, and other river towns served as outfitting and jumping-off points for both the Oregon and Santa Fe Trails. Many emigrants had been lured west by overly sanguine accounts of the paradise that awaited them. One typical booster published the information in eastern papers that the only serious hazard along certain portions of the Oregon Trail 'is the propensity to sleep in the daytime' because the air was so pleasant and the route so smooth.[12] At any given time during the travel season, a thousand emigrants camped in the prairies surrounding a Missouri staging point while waiting to assemble a wagon train. They made their way across the country by train to a river port on the Ohio or Mississippi, then by steamboat up the Missouri. In 1850, the Colby family of Massachusetts traveled by wagon, then by rail to Cincin-

*An emigrant wagon train crossing the Platte, en route to Oregon. Every river crossing imperiled the wagons and their occupants. (*Harper's Weekly, *13 August 1859)*

nati, then spent two weeks on a steamboat to Missouri. They then camped out for several weeks among the hundreds of other emigrants waiting for the grass to green up for the cattle. Planning a May departure, they expected the overland trek to take about five months. Meanwhile, the family bided their time '...in an old log cabbin where we go to bed on the [floor]. At night the big norway rats run and caper over you so you can not sleep.'[13] Emigrants endured more than rats as they waited to depart. Missouri River port towns presented a chaotic aspect to families fresh from the civilized east. One eastern gentleman observed, 'Whiskey, by the way, circulates more freely...than is altogether safe in a place where every man carries a loaded pistol in his pocket.'[14]

When a sufficiently large party had assembled to make the crossing to Oregon, the emigrants elected officers and enacted laws to govern the wagon train. Strife on the trail caused leaders to be deposed and replaced, and some caravans even split in two to follow opposing leaders. The necessity of forced togetherness for months at a time under primitive conditions fostered all manner of personality conflict. Mary Richardson Walker, a missionary traveling the Oregon Trail in 1838, regularly noted such tensions in her diary:

> 'I never saw such a cross company before.'
>
> 'Our company still have a good deal of unpleasantness among them.'
>
> 'Mr. Smith short as pie crust. Mr. W. begins to see how things are.'[15]

Once they reached the point where wagons could go no further, the Oregon pioneers rode 20 to 40 miles a day on horseback, first enduring heat and thirst across the plains, then cold and rain in the mountains. In later years, when the entire trail became passable by wagon, the parties made about 25 miles a day.

The high altitude made it more difficult to cook over open fires. Later in the trek, food ran low and the hunt for wild game grew more important. Scurvy afflicted those who failed to bring dried fruit or other appropriate food supplies to supplement their bread and salt pork. Accidents and illnesses took their toll, and those of uncertain health were the first to succumb. Graves lined the trail, some disturbed by wolves.

With each successive migration, the trail itself grew smoother but trailside resources dwindled. The large numbers of people used up the firewood and buffalo chips, polluted the watering holes, and drove away or killed the wild game while their livestock depleted the grazing and forage.

During the months on the trail, pioneers mastered skills they had not acquired in their previous lives. Men managed livestock, yoked oxen, drove wagons, forded rivers, and hunted. Women had to do all their familiar tasks under unfamiliar conditions. Many had never cooked over open fires nor washed clothing and dishes under dusty trail conditions. Sudden bursts of wind singed the dresses of women laboring over cooking fires or flung sand into the food. Children fell under wagon wheels or regularly wandered off the trail. Those few who brought servants along often found themselves dispossessed and forced to acquire basic housekeeping skills when another traveler lured the servants away with better offers. Women servants quickly got snatched up by offers of marriage. If a husband or wife took ill or died, the survivor had either to take over the work of both or prevail upon the other travelers for help. When a child was to be born, generally one wagon or the whole wagon train might lay over for a few days or a few hours, depending on whether they had come to a suitable camp. Then there were the routine arguments over whether to wait for slower wagons and livestock, and who had to bring up the rear and breathe the dust kicked up by the leaders.

On the flat plains there were no natural barriers to prevent storms from acquiring tremendous energy. Downpours and hailstorms came on with appalling suddenness, surprising people who were used to the more gentle storms back east. Typically, following even moderate amounts of rain, wagons got stuck in the mud several times daily. At night people found themselves sleeping in puddles. Horses and mules varied in temperament, and emigrants met their full complement of animals determined to have their own way. Like many, Frances Parkman could never be sure he had won the battle of wills with his horse, Pontiac. Parkman wanted to travel west, but Pontiac wanted to return to the States. One day as Parkman ate, suddenly:

> 'we saw the whole band of animals, twenty-three in number, filing off for the settlements, the incorrigible Pontiac at their head, jumping along with hobbled feet, at a gait much more rapid than graceful.'[16]

Dogs presented a unique problem on the trail. Pioneers treasured their dogs as guard animals at home, but on the trail, some dogs stampeded the livestock. Parties nearly broke up arguing over motions to slaughter all the dogs. Wolves as well stampeded the livestock, and if the draft animals could not be recovered, pioneers had to abandon nonessential goods. Fine tables and dressers sat forlornly at trailside. Another difficulty was attributed to wolves' fondness for chewing on rawhide, just like dogs do today. But instead of chewing on pieces of rawhide bought for them by loving owners, canines crept into camp at night and chewed through the rawhide trail ropes that secured the horses. Dawn found the unfortunate traveler chasing his animals instead of packing to depart.

The six-month trek to Oregon country was at first considered an insurmountable obstacle to settlement, because it seemed too great an ordeal for white women to endure. Wagons could not pass over the mountains or down the Columbia River, forcing all travelers to abandon their wagons and make a large part of the journey on horseback. For women, this meant riding sidesaddle, a much more uncomfortable enterprise than riding astride. However, in 1836, Narcissa Whitman and Eliza Spalding proved the nay-sayers wrong by being the first white women to cross the Rockies thereby setting an example that helped open wide the floodgates of emigration. In 1841, twenty-four overland migrants came to Oregon from the United States. The year 1842 brought another hundred, also on horseback and without wagons. The first large immigration to Oregon took place in 1843: it consisted of close to 1,000 men, women, and children plus 5,000 animals, but still no wagons.

Invariably, each year's emigrants arrived with far less than they had owned when they set off from the States. Stampedes, theft, and river crossings all took their toll from the settlers' cargo.

An 1843 party left their wagons and livestock in the care of the Hudson's Bay Company at Fort Walla Walla, on the Columbia about 200 miles from the mouth of the Willamette. They plied their whipsaws to build boats, loaded up their possessions, and headed down the Columbia River. Disaster struck at the falls of the Dalles, about 80 miles short of their goal. A boat capsized, people drowned – two children among them – and possessions were lost. A survivor recalled:

> 'Much of the furniture, cooking utensils and bedding had been lost in the disaster on the Columbia River. The families had reached the place where they were to pass the winter almost destitute of furnishing goods or food supplies.... I remember that mother did her baking all that winter on a skillet lid found in the house.'[17]

The survivors vowed to cut a road to outflank the treacherous river to make the trek easier for future emigrants. This they did three years later, on their own initiative and at their own expense. The new route, however, did not eliminate all the hardships of the passage. Weather still delayed numerous parties and caused them suffering.

With what little they still possessed, the arriving Americans claimed the reward for all their travails, a piece of land in the verdant Willamette Valley, a 100-mile long basin extending southward from the Columbia River between the Cascades and Coast ranges. In a few short years, more than 100 households each farmed 100 to 500 acres apiece in the Willamette valley. Towns had begun to flourish, and fourteen water-powered grist and saw mills served a total of 4,000 white Americans, plus about 1,000 British and Canadian farmers. The majority came from the midwestern states and the Ohio and Mississippi valleys. Unlike other newly settled U.S. territories, Oregon attracted a high proportion of law-abiding citizens in family groups. They were a surprisingly orderly bunch who did not want to escape civilization; they wanted more settlers to come join them.

As orderly as they were, Oregon settlers too had to contend with poorly surveyed land, overlapping claims, claim-jumpers, and speculators before land distribution became regularized. They organized into protective associations and resorted to gunpoint confrontations when pressed. It was the need to regularize land ownership that caused them to form a provisional government in 1843. Three years later, Oregon became officially American by treaty with Britain.

By 1850, a much smoother Oregon Trail had brought 12,000 American settlers to Oregon Territory. Under the Oregon Donation Land Act of 1850, Oregon settlers received free land from the government – 320 acres for a man and another 320 acres for his wife, 640 acres – one square mile – for a married couple. This generous policy set the pattern for future federal land law. The Homestead Act of 1862 continued the precedent of offering free land, but limited it to 160 acres per household and one claim per lifetime. In addition, that 160 acres could not be claimed by a person who already owned 160 acres. A homesteading claimant had to reside on and farm the land for five years.

The Willamette Valley was mostly open, with scattered groves of ash, oak, fir, maple, and cottonwood trees. The wooded areas had little undergrowth and therefore were easier to clear than woodland in the east. The open grasslands tended to flood and remain swampy most of each winter and spring, impeding travel. Settlers found a mild climate and reported that February and March in Oregon were like April in New York. The winters brought plentiful rain, as much as 50 inches a year, and twice that in the surrounding mountains, but it snowed only rarely. The constant winter rainfall discouraged the newcomers at first, until they came to appreciate the bounties it bestowed. Farmers could sow wheat any time from October to June. The grass remained green all winter. Summers were cooler and more pleasant than in the east.

Many a wife who had been reluctant to emigrate found, on arrival, that life in Oregon could be sweet: 'I know when one gets comfortably fixed here they can live as well as they can any where else and with one half of the labour that you do in the States you can rais all you want to live on and have a good lot to sell.'[18]

After two years on their Oregon claim of a full section, one couple had managed to fence 140 acres and break the sod on 40 of them. Twenty acres had been planted to wheat and they had started an orchard. Their land was all prairie but for the timber along two streams that crossed the property. They lived in a two-room log cabin and owned a yoke of oxen, seven cows, six calves, fifteen hogs, and twenty-four hens. They planned to supplement their income by raising chickens and making butter and cheese.

Such glowing reports convinced thousands of Americans that they could better their lot in life by emigrating. On arrival they could live and farm much as they had before, in Kentucky or Missouri, but with less labor, on richer land, in a milder climate. A nationwide depression in the late 1830s that had dashed the hopes of many farmers drove the poverty-stricken westward to try again. As overland traffic and settlement rapidly increased, the hardships imposed by isolation from the States and the expense of trade goods gave way to a thriving community, eager for statehood.

DOWN THE SANTA FE TRAIL

The arid southwest, part of the enormous area won from Mexico in 1848, had a long European history prior to American settlement. The first Europeans – Spaniards – entered what is now known as New Mexico in 1598. They founded the dusty village they called Santa Fe de San Francisco in 1610. The Indians succeeded just once in driving out the Spanish but inevitably they returned. A group of 800 Spanish colonists came to stay in 1693.

The first Americans entered New Mexico as traders, down the Santa Fe Trail from Missouri. Some of the trail's ruts are still visible today. The nearly 1,000-mile trail began its service as the principal trade route in 1821, when newly independent Mexico opened her doors to traders and goods from the United States. The Spanish colonists had lived in isolation, separated from the distant cities of Mexico by miles of desert patrolled by hostile tribes. When American traders arrived with their wagon-loads of merchandise, the colonists welcomed them with open arms, the customs officials with open palms.

Like the pueblo-dwelling Indians, the Spanish had settled along the rivers, particularly the Rio Grande, which they tapped for irrigation water. Like the early Kentucky and Tennessee settlers, they had followed the European tradition of clustering their houses together for defense from the hostile tribes and going out each day to work their farms and ranches. Both the Spanish communities and the pueblos maintained reservoirs and gravity-fed irrigation ditches, called *acequias*. The Spaniards enacted controls on water use based on irrigation techniques derived from pueblo Indian, Spanish, and Moorish methods. Prior to American occupation, they had put about one percent of the territory's land area under irrigation.

Such irrigation systems required a great deal of central control and citizen cooperation. Elected officials in pueblo and village supervised *acequia* construction and maintenance and regulated water distribution. Each farmer or landowner had to provide labor, namely backbreaking ditch-digging. The main canal, about 15 feet wide and 2 to 6 feet deep, ran from the water source through the acreage to be watered. From the main canals ran networks of smaller ditches, controlled by floodgates. Each system contained miles of ditches that could water up to several thousand acres of field. Several times each growing season, the communities flooded their fields. During the winter, they closed off the ditches.

American traders entering this foreign land found the Mexicans to be a baffling people whose finely made gold and silver jewelry contrasted with their crude cart wheels made from rounded cross sections of cottonwood trunk. All buildings were constructed of adobe bricks. Thick walls kept the houses cool in summer and warm in winter. Most houses had one story, and each house formed a square around a central courtyard. Covered galleries ran along the inside walls, and the small windows faced away from the road. Mexicans kept their adobe houses clean by watering down the dirt floors and covering them with mats or carpets. They whitewashed the walls and then covered the lower portions with fabric to keep the whitewash from rubbing off on their clothing. Red geraniums decorated deep window sills and strings of dried red peppers hung by the door. The parents occupied the solitary bed, topped by a corn husk mattress, and all the others slept on the floor, wrapped in blankets. They kept sheep and Angora goats, which they sheared with knives, and wove blankets from their fleeces. Goats, because they are thriftier keepers and require less food than cattle, also served as dairy animals.

The Mexican diet included goat meat, mutton, antelope, venison, buffalo, and tortillas and cornmeal mush, supplemented by the blue corn, peppers, beans, and squash that they grew. The men rode out onto the prairies and hunted buffalo with bow and arrow from horseback. The women cooked both at their hearths and in beehive-shaped adobe ovens outside. The wood of mesquite and piñon trees fueled the fires, and the nuts of the piñon were widely enjoyed by all races. Isolated in New Mexico, the Spanish colonists borrowed many of their dietary habits from the Indians. They used Indian-made earthenware dishes and took their meals seated on the floor.

Mexican farming methods resembled those of eighteenth-century Kentucky. Farmers used ox-drawn wooden single-furrow plows, one man driving the animal, and one guiding the plow. They still used the hoe to cultivate, the sickle to harvest wheat and corn, and animals' hooves on the threshing floor. They grew many of the usual fruits and garden vegetables, plus abundant peppers and tobacco. American settlers, recent beneficiaries of such inventions as the iron plow, the cradle scythe, and the threshing machine, scorned Mexican agriculture as primitive.

Rather than fence their fields against livestock, Mexican ranchers relied on herdsmen to keep animals off the fields. The livestock survived almost entirely on the prairie grass pasture, which dried out into hay each winter. The small sheep of New Mexico's ranches possessed inferior wool, several sets of horns, and delicious meat. They were much hardier and thriftier than sheep raised in the United States. Mexicans skillfully trained and rode the wild mustangs, and men learned from earliest youth the use of lasso and lariat (from the Spanish *lazo* and *la reata*) for roping livestock and game. They bred mules for pack animals, although the poorer farmers had to content themselves with the smaller burros.

The New Mexico landscape and climate excited comment from American newcomers. They enthused about the dryness, clarity, and healthfulness of the air. The air was so dry that one could air-cure meat in the summer sun with no interference from flies. In the mountains, August days and nights were cool, freshened by regular brief rains. Most of the region's scanty rainfall occurred from July to October. The cold and snowy days of winter in Santa Fe gave way to frequent warm clear days. Only in some areas where constant high winds flung clouds of dust through the air did the climate seem unkind.

The mix of Spanish and pueblo Indian settlement in such an arid land had produced a distinct southwestern culture unique in its architecture, diet, ranch management, and water use patterns. Incoming Americans, while embracing some aspects of this culture, quickly asserted dominance over New Mexican society.

Mexico had permitted Americans to immigrate but did not encourage them. A few dozen American traders had settled in New Mexico, taking Mexican citizenship in the process. In the decade immediately prior to the American conquest, the Mexican government offered some land grants to Canadians and Americans who were married to Mexican women or were in partnership with Mexicans. By so doing, they hoped to throw up a bulwark against hostile Indians and annexation by Texas.

New Mexico at the time of the American conquest was home to around 50,000 Mexicans, 10,000 pueblo Indians (in about twenty villages of around 500 inhabitants each), 30,000 nomadic

Zuni Pueblo, New Mexico. About 1,500 people inhabited the pueblo at the time the United States conquered the territory. Today, the population of New Mexico is about one-tenth Indian and one-third Hispanic. (U.S. National Archives)

Indians (Navajo, Apache, and Cheyenne), and several hundred American immigrants and traders. A few of the wealthier Mexicans had adopted American ways and sent their children to schools in the United States. They were prepared for the coming Americans and established amicable relations with them. Most of the Mexican inhabitants, however, spoke only Spanish, adhered to Catholicism, and were illiterate. To them, the arrival of the Americans represented only the replacement of one set of wealthy masters with another. American settlers generally viewed Mexicans with contempt. Frances Parkman described them as 'swarthy ignoble Mexicans' with 'brutish faces.'[19] Only a handful of 1850s Americans accepted the Mexicans they encountered as individuals.

When the United States conquered the Spanish southwest, the resident Mexicans owned the best and most productive land. Unlike in other territories, the U.S. government had little public land to offer as a draw for settlers. Therefore, the non-military American population grew little at first: by 1856, it numbered only about 500. Americans desiring land had to purchase it from a willing Mexican. Some used counterfeit Mexican land deeds to secure title to the land they wanted. The U.S. government, in 1855, charged its first Surveyor General with the task of surveying land that was suitable for growing crops. The officer soon realized that there was little arable land to survey, so he expanded his definition to include good pasture land. His job was a challenging one, as he had first to determine that each tract of land was not privately owned by an absentee owner. As in Oregon, emigrants to New Mexico could receive free land under a donation land act, provided they had not already received a Spanish or Mexican land grant. The law provided 160 acres to any adult male who held or intended to acquire American citizenship and who resided on his claim. Not until 1858 did an American apply for free land in accordance with all the legal requirements. However, he abandoned the claim, and only in 1870 did an American succeed in proving up a donation claim. Few Americans tried to claim land prior to the cattle boom of the 1880s; those who did often tried to make multiple claims.

More than vacant land was required, however, to establish a farm. Access to water had to be secured, whether for crops or for livestock. The aridity of the climate, as little as 8 inches of annual rainfall, required a different approach to farming. Therefore, wealthy Mexicans and Americans strove to accumulate large holdings in the few flood plains, leaving little or nothing for the smallholder. In the regions lying far from rivers, large-scale ranching was viable; farming was not.

Americans took up sheep ranching alongside the Mexican ranchers. Together they profited from huge drives of hundreds of thousands of animals to California to feed the gold miners. The fewer than one million sheep of the Mexican period grew to five million under American rule. Americans crossbred Merino sheep with the Mexican animals, producing a strong animal with better and more plentiful wool. A handful of wealthy Mexican families had dominated sheep ranching, supported by the debt-based peonage system that had prevailed under Mexican rule. This system of virtual lifelong slavery continued under American governance for decades to come, as did government by patronage. The peonage system served ranchers so well that Americans brought very few Negro slaves to New Mexico after the conquest. However, in addition to the legion of peons, more than 3,000 Indian slaves, captured from the hostile nomadic tribes, labored under Mexican and American masters. One American woman received a captive Indian boy as a gift but, unsatisfied with him as a worker, returned him to his family. The boy's inefficiency, not his enslavement, troubled her.

* * *

Unlike previous pioneers, American settlers who traveled the Santa Fe Trail took a well-established trade route to a thriving community with a long history. From Independence, Missouri, they faced a journey of one or two months. Traders and soldiers had gone before them and often went with them, as they had to organize into large parties for defense. In 1853, a well-armed mule-drawn mail wagon operated monthly throughout the year between Missouri and New Mexico and accepted paying passengers. It could make about 40 miles a day in good weather.

The first 150 miles, from Independence to Council Grove, Kansas, passed through an area populated by friendly Indians and widely scattered pioneer cabins. Council Grove consisted of a trading post, a few log cabins, and an Indian agency for the Caws. In November 1853:

> 'Many of the tribe were there, awaiting the distribution of their annuities. They number about a thousand in all, and were among the most miserable set of human beings I have ever seen. They are said to have been in a fine condition at one time, but have sadly degenerated from their intercourse with the whites. They are great drunkards....'[20]

Bent's Fort, Colorado. A fur trading post that also served as a popular stopping place for traders and travelers on the Santa Fe Trail. The structure features a window through which the fort conducted trade with Indians who remained outside; with the gate securely closed, the occupants could trade in safety. Charles Bent, one of the fort's founders, became the first governor of newly captured New Mexico and was killed in a rebellion at Taos.

The 600 miles from Council Grove, to Fort Union, New Mexico traversed arid open prairies occupied by hostile Indians and large herds of buffalo and antelope. Santa Fe lay 110 miles beyond Fort Union.

Hostile Indians raided small parties along the trail but hesitated to make direct attacks on large parties. The wagon trains posted sentries through the night, but sometimes failed to prevent Indians from stampeding off the livestock. In 1852, a nighttime raiding party made off with 200 horses intended for U.S. Army garrisons in New Mexico. By day, Indians hung about the wagon trains and traded with the travelers. The latter were forbidden from trading guns or powder to Indians. By 1860, white criminals presented the greatest danger to small parties of travelers. By that time the chain of army forts along the trail had greatly reduced the Indian threat.

Like their brethren on the Oregon Trail, settlers en route to the southwest drove oxen, made camp, cooked, cleaned, conserved water, braved dust storms, and sought grazing and water for the animals. They sometimes had to urge their draft animals onward for days through long stretches of trail without water. Dry river beds concealed quicksands to trap the unwary. Unlike the common run of settlers, the families of officers and wealthy traders were largely buffered from these tasks.

Nineteen-year-old Susan Shelby Magoffin was a Kentucky governor's daughter, newly married to a wealthy older man engaged in the Santa Fe trade. She is commonly credited with being the first white woman to travel the Santa Fe Trail in 1846. In fact, she must share that distinction with her personal maid, Jane, who makes several appearances in Susan's journal. Sheltered by her husband's wealth from having to cook and make camp on the trail, she enjoyed the journey immensely: 'It is the life of a wandering princess, mine. When I do not wish to get out myself to pick flowers the Mexican servants riding on mules busy themselves picking them for me.'[21]

Lydia Spencer Lane, an army wife, traveled the Santa Fe Trail several times over the course of the 1850s and 1860s. Like other army wives, she rode in a mule-drawn army 'ambulance,' though at times the ride was so rough that she got out and went on horseback. The soldiers pitched her tent for her at night and donated their wagon space to carry her excess household goods. She brought with her two carpets, chintz for curtains, six wooden chairs, a bedstead, a table, a cookstove, china, glassware, silverware, and linens. Mrs Lane identified the usual trailside meal as bread or hardtack, bacon or salt pork, and coffee. No milk or butter was available. Both women reported that whenever they made camp near friendly Indians, the Indians crowded close and stared through the tent flaps at the white women as though they had never seen any in their lives.

In contrast to the married women, Marian Sloan Russell tells of making the trip at age seven, as the child of a nearly penniless widow. No servants or soldiers tended to their needs. The widow Sloan's courage and enterprise in taking her small children west was far from atypical. What little money the mother had was stolen one night as their wagon train camped, making her position in life even more tenuous. She abandoned her plans to take her family to California, and instead sold her few pieces of jewelry to pay the rent on a six-room adobe house in Albuquerque. The family survived on the $40 per month that five Indian scouts paid her for room and board.

THROUGH THE PRAIRIE TO DAKOTA

The Louisiana Purchase gave the young United States vast new lands for settlement. Few people paid any attention to one remote part of the acquisition, a little-known region called the Dakota Territory. Here the Sioux Indians, also known as the Dakota, hunted buffalo across windswept prairies. The French first explored the territory in 1742 but their arrival had small impact on the land and its people. For more than 100 years, the only Americans to venture into this seemingly bleak land were trappers and traders. The US Army built its first fort in South Dakota in 1856, with the sole purpose of protecting travel to Oregon. It was a land to hurry across, no place to loiter. Settlement of the surrounding arid plains seemed inconceivable.

By 1859, when the United States purchased land from the Yankton Sioux, in the southeast portion of present-day South Dakota, nearly 1,000 settlers were clamoring to enter. As the best lands to the east got taken up, this corner of the arid Dakotas began to look more promising. The army tried to perform the thankless task of ejecting the 'sooners' who slipped in before the official opening. Farmers from the adjacent states, and European immigrants arrived by covered wagon or Missouri River steamer. In this first wave of white settlement, the area east of the Missouri River, known as 'East River,' attracted farmers, and 'West River' drew ranchers. Even though steamboats plied the river, some pioneers chose to emigrate by covered wagon because it was more economical. They did not have to pay passage and freight, and they could live in the wagons while building their new homes.

A Sioux uprising in 1862, followed by a series of droughts and grasshopper plagues, drove many settlers back to the east and warned off others from even trying to settle. Yet memory of these threats subsided with time while the hunger for land grew unabated. So crowded had the east become, that by 1870 some 10,000 settlers had come to make their homes in South Dakota. Both the Homestead Act of 1862 and the Timber Culture Act of 1873 – a federal scheme to promote forestation of the Great Plains – now offered avenues to acquire land free of charge. The arrival of the railroad in 1873 also encouraged expanded settlement. Would-be land owners failed to reckon with grasshoppers, however. Their raids leveled entire crops in 1873, 1874, and 1876 and gave Dakota a bad name once again.

Then, the U.S. Army reported gold in the Black Hills in 1874. The land belonged to the Sioux by treaty, and the army tried to keep the thousands of arriving white prospectors out. Failing that, the government tried to buy the Black Hills or lease mining rights, but the Sioux held the area sacred and refused. By making war, systematically eradicating the buffalo, and forging signatures on land purchase agreements, Americans subdued or drove out the Sioux between 1876 and 1890. Most were consigned to reservations. Today, the Sioux still comprise seven percent of the state population.

By 1876, more than 10,000 miners had come to the Black Hills. Simultaneously, cattle ranchers were driving their herds to western South Dakota in large numbers. They supplied meat to the miners and to the Indian agencies. The removal of the Sioux and their buffalo eliminated competition for grazing land. Having unscrupulously established themselves as sole tenants, ranchers were able to expand their cattle herds to three-quarters of a million animals by 1884.

A second wave of settlement by American and immigrant farmers crested between 1878 and 1887, raising the population to 81,000 in 1880, and almost 250,000 by 1885. Most of the population increase occurred east of the Missouri. Isolated settlers saw houses spring up around them virtually overnight. In the spring of 1884, after a hard and lonely winter, a homesteader wrote, 'It hardly seems like the same place here now that it did last winter thare are so many more people here now.'[22]

Families settling Dakota Territory during the boom years came from as near as Minnesota, and as far away as the Old World. A surprising number of the homesteaders were unmarried women, with estimates ranging up to one-third of the total. The women sought either independent lives as landowners or to acquire an asset to sell later to fund another venture. They reportedly succeeded as farmers at about as high a rate as men or families did.

The territorial government did its part to attract settlers. Those settlers who began their journeys in Europe – from Russia, Bohemia, Scandinavia, Germany, or England – were bewildered by the bustling, teeming life of the eastern cities where they came ashore. Some fell victim to a criminal element that strove to part them from their money and possessions either by theft or deceit. They must have considered themselves fortunate to meet the Dakota Territory immigration agents sent to east coast seaports and to the Chicago railroad stations to persuade immigrants to come to Dakota.

By the 1880s, those emigrants who could afford it made their journey to Dakota by rail, several families and their livestock sharing a boxcar. Although trains carried people to their destinations much faster than the wagons of old, the trip offered a new set of discomforts, particularly for emigrants. For his money, the emigrant got crowded conditions, foul air, poor food, limited water, and squalid sanitation facilities. However, the ability to travel by relying upon mechanical power, as opposed to the animal power used by earlier settlers, made a large difference in what and how much the emigrants could bring with them for their journey west. They brought cookstoves, furniture, food, clothes, utensils, and farm equipment, including plows and horse teams. Unlike the pioneers of a hundred years earlier, some also brought a sewing machine or a piano. Since emigrants could not afford to ship everything, some came to regret their choices. A farmer who rued the purchase of a piano lamented, 'I think the musick from a good Reaper is far better and more money in it than all the Pianoes ever made.'[23]

They arrived on the treeless, windswept, semi-arid plains as a last resort, a last chance to own a productive piece of American land. Said Dakota settler Isreal Trumbo in 1861, 'I do not much like the idea of living out in the prairie but others do it and we will get ust to it. I know you all want to leave there and I don't know of any place where there is government land that is as good as this place.'[24] Homesteading in the Dakotas continued well into the twentieth century. Regardless of when they came, Dakota greeted emigrants with extremes of climate, intense summer heat, death-dealing winter storms and bitter cold, and cycles of drought. Annual rainfall varied from 14 inches in the west to 24 inches in the east. When it fell reliably during the growing season, it could sustain agriculture on the fertile soil. But if it did not:

> 'When there was a dark cloud we would look at it hopefully. Then we would see the flashes of lightning and hear the claps of thunder and feel sure that rain must follow. Then would come a heavy wind accompanied only by the dust, and that was all.'[25]

People did not venture to settle the treeless prairies in large numbers until railroads existed to bring in lumber and get crops to market. Advances in plow design and the invention of barbed-wire fencing also encouraged people to settle this late frontier. Inexorably, settlement changed the face of the plains, turning it from open-range land to a patchwork of private holdings.

Experts foresaw that conventional agriculture on 160-acre farms could not succeed in a semi-arid environment, but an extended period of unusually steady rainfall caused people to ignore them. Railroads, town boosters, and land speculators all did their part to convince farmers that they could prosper in Dakota. Over a dozen years, from 1878 to 1890, millions of acres were put under the plow, and wheat and corn replaced the native grass. A belief prevailed during the period that putting large tracts of land under cultivation actually changed the climate and brought increased rains.

Drought returned in 1887 and persisted into the 1890s, ruining thousands of farmers. Government aid in the form of seed wheat, and private donations of food and clothing kept many from perishing. Survivors fled the Dakotas in droves. Those that remained turned their attention first to deep well irrigation, and second, to more drought-resistant crops, livestock, and larger farms.

The promise of free land often lured people westward who were grossly unprepared or unqualified for farming. Lacking cash or equipment, they were unable to survive until their farms produced a living. Having not paid for the land in the first place, they returned east, or tried their luck on another claim rather than persevere on the original claim. The railroads, which had been granted huge tracts along their routes by the federal government, preferred to sell the acreage to those who could afford to pay. Lacking such well-heeled customers, they recruited whole communities from Europe and the eastern United States, offering generous credit and moving settlers and their possessions westward without charge. Thus they assured themselves that future customers would live along the railway.

In the effort to attract lenders and capital to the Dakotas, the territorial government set the maximum interest rate at 24%. Speculators took advantage of the 1873 Timber Culture Act, as they had the 1862 Homestead Act, to make false claims for free land. False claimants who had no intention of ever living on the land employed inventive ruses to acquire legal title. They set four corner posts to represent a cabin or dug a 3-foot hole to symbolize a well. Some even mounted small shacks on wheels to move them from tract to tract. Once they became legal owners, they commonly sold the land, at a tidy profit, to the people for whom the law was actually intended. The settlers who bought such claims from speculators often borrowed the purchase price. Debt was much more widespread than on the earlier frontiers. Many a struggling Dakota farmer lost his property to foreclosure, for lack of $250 to pay off a 24% mortgage. So abused was the Timber Culture Act that Congress finally saw fit to repeal it.

Like generations of pioneers before them, Dakota pioneers journeyed westward to begin new lives with far more hope than money. All would owe their success or failure to a host of factors, but the most important one was how hard they worked to develop their farmsteads. Too often, in spite of diligent hard work, uncontrollable environmental factors thwarted the Dakota farmer.

[1] Kenneth L. Holmes, ed., *Covered Wagon Women: Diaries & Letters from the Western Trails, 1840–1890* (Glendale, CA, 1983) vol. 1, pp. 209–10.

[2] John D. Shane, 'Interview with pioneer William Clinkenbeard,' *Filson Club History Quarterly*, II: 3 (April 1928) p. 112.

[3] Helen Deiss Irvin, *Women in Kentucky* (Lexington, KY, 1979), p. 4.

[4] John Bradbury, 'Travels in the interior of America in the years 1809, 1810, and 1811,' in Reuben Gold Thwaites, *Early Western Travels, 1748–1846* (New York, 1966), vol. 5, p. 267.

[5] Maude A. Rucker, *The Oregon Trail and Some of its Blazers* (New York, 1930), p. 243.

[6] 'Documents,' *Quarterly of the Oregon Historical Society*, III: 4 (December 1902) p. 398.

[7] *Covered Wagon Women*, vol. 1, p. 211.

[8] Ibid., p. 213.

[9] Ibid., p. 213.

[10] 'Documents,' *Quarterly of the Oregon Historical Society,* III:4 (December 1902) p. 391.

[11] *Covered Wagon Women*, vol. 1, pp. 214-218.

[12] 'Documents,' *Quarterly of the Oregon Historical Society*, III:4 (December 1902) p. 419.

[13] *Covered Wagon Women*, vol. 2, p 47.

[14] Francis Parkman, *The Oregon Trail* (New York, 1949), p. 9.

[15] Cathy Luchetti, *Women of the West*, (St. George, Utah, 1982), p. 64.

[16] Parkman, p. 42.

[17] Rucker, p. 171.

[18] *Covered Wagon Women*, vol. 2, p. 50.

[19] Parkman, pp. 67–68.

[20] W.W.H. Davis, *El Gringo: New Mexico and her People* (New York, 1857), p. 22.

[21] Stella M. Drumm, ed., *Down the Santa Fe Trail and Into Mexico: The Diary of Susan Shelby Magoffin, 1846–1847* (New Haven, 1926), p. 11.

[22] Ruth Seymour Burmeister, ed., 'Jeffries letters,' *South Dakota History,* VI:3 (Summer 1976) p. 320.

[23] Ibid., p. 318.

[24] Isreal Trumbo, 'A pioneer's letter home,' *South Dakota Historical Collections*, VI (1912) p. 203.

[25] Ruth Cook Frajola, ed., 'They went west,' *South Dakota History*, VI:3 (Summer 1976) p. 286.

II

'WORK THE TEAM ALL DAY'

Whether a lone backwoodsman fleeing ahead of civilization or one of a horde of home-steaders looking for a better chance at riches, the new settler hurried to put a roof over his family's heads and see to his first crop. In 1788, the settler built a log cabin and cleared a few acres out of the woods. The settler of 1878 built a sod house on the Dakota prairie and laid claim to a vast homestead. All the same, survival was the first order of business, comfort and prosperity the second.

Arriving on the much longed-for new land, the settler had to find a temporary roof to shelter his family while he built a more lasting home. This might be a hastily assembled 'camp,' – a shed of four poles and a brush roof – a cave, the wagon in which the family drove westward, a tent made of blankets, a neighbor's house or outbuilding, or, if such a thing existed, a hotel in the nearest town. In already settled areas, some camped in the church or schoolhouse.

In most American pioneer settlements, neighboring families cooperated in building their cabins. Understand, however, that the word 'neighbor' included anyone living within a radius of miles, not the suburban blocks of today's world. A family began by felling the trees and shaping

the logs into useful timber. The size of the logs depended on the number of hands available to shift them. It did no good for a man working alone to fell a mighty tree if he could not then haul the logs. Logs for houses ranged from 1 to 2 feet in diameter, and from 10 to 30 feet long, depending on the house dimensions. A log cabin required about twenty logs per side. To saw logs to length with the two-person crosscut saw, one placed them on a scaffold or over a pit. The man working down in the pit soon became covered with sawdust as it fell and clung to his sweat. His was a miserable lot. Next, the home builder, using hatchet, axe, or chisel, notched the ends of the logs so they could interlock at the corners.

Settlers built their cabins out of various kinds of logs, but

'Sawing Into Logs.' A whipsaw team at work. These logs appear too large to be used for a log cabin. (Library of Congress)

they preferred poplar, cedar, or chestnut because of their water resistant properties. Oak was too heavy, pine too flammable, and hickory too prone to decay. As a rule, the settler used only one kind of tree for the entire log cabin. Logs could be used round, hewed (squared off) on four sides with a broad-axe, or hewed only on the two horizontal surfaces. However, few early pioneers could spare the time to hew their logs at all. Finally, the neighbors arrived to build the cabin. Raising a small cabin took about three days as a group effort: a skilled man could build the cabin alone over the course of several weeks. The helpers exacted no payment at the time, but expected help in turn at some future date. Thus was laid the cornerstone of relations among neighboring farmers: they would exchange work at every task that required many hands.

Modern log cabin builders use a variety of methods and materials to accommodate logs' natural tendency to shrink and swell. The pioneers, using unseasoned logs, did not enjoy such luxury. Consequently, their log cabins had wide gaps between the logs and this required chinking. If one accepted that whatever was outside could live inside as well, the mud and grass chinking between the logs could be left out until winter approached. Farther south, occupants chinked their log cabins with Spanish moss, and knocked the chinking out when warm weather arrived so that air could circulate. Where available, pioneers hung buffalo skins around the inside walls to cut down the wind blowing through the gaps. All of these measures were literally 'stop gaps,' and by modern standards they did not do a very good job. Even with the chinking in place, log cabins were drafty and cold. Dust blew in through the chinks. Mice, snakes, and insects entered freely. The gaps admitted blowing snow. Depending on the season, people awoke to find themselves cloaked in snow or dust, or with unwanted animal and insect sleeping companions.

The log cabins of Mays Lick were typical of eighteenth-century Kentucky: windowless, the door facing south and equipped with a strongbar, with a porthole for shooting at attacking Indians. The floors were of split logs, called puncheons, as sawmills were not readily available for making sawn floorboards. Skins covered some floors. The roof was commonly of wood shingles or overlapping boards held in place by weight poles laid across them. Wood roofing, rather than the thatch or slate of Europe, became popular in the New World because of the plentiful trees.

A 16 by 20-foot one-room cabin was considered

Hand-hewing logs to construct a post and beam cabin in the late eighteenth century. (Arizona Historical Society, Tucson)

large. Reflect upon this for a moment and consider that modern Americans view these dimensions as far less than what is necessary for two bedrooms, let alone a sufficient size to house an entire family. After some time, a cabin might acquire a board floor over the puncheons, and even a small window or two, usually without glass. Door and window frames were fastened in place with wooden pegs. Windows were covered by hinged wooden shutters, deer skins scraped thin to admit light, or paper soaked in bear grease. Those who could afford it could purchase panes of glass from the general store. To attain a measure of privacy inside the cabin, occupants strung up blankets as partitions.

Some built their cabins on foundations of stone or log, with floors a few feet off the ground so that they could store food in a cool place, or so that sheep could take shelter beneath the house. They added sleeping lofts, lean-tos, and sheds as the farm and family grew. Among the unexpected consequences of incremental building was the challenge to heat the home. During the winter, families found, to their disappointment, that all the heat rose to the level of the new sleeping loft, leaving the ground floor frigid. A more satisfactory way of adding on to the original cabin, prevalent in the old southwest, was the 'dogtrot,' two small cabins, each with its own fireplace, connected by a covered or enclosed walkway – the dogtrot from which the whole arrangement took its name. The dogtrot and second cabin appeared only after the family had been in residence for a couple of years. Also in the deep south, extensive porches helped to keep the interiors cooler.

The tall fireplace, as much as 12 feet wide, served as cooking center and heat source. Stone-cutting skills were more common among pioneers than they are today, so hearths and chimneys were built either of stone or of sticks embedded in clay, known as 'cats and clay.' The clay in a 'cats and clay' chimney served to keep the sticks from igniting. The chimney vented smoke, but also

An idealized image of a frontier log cabin. Note the picket fence, the rain barrel at the corner, the crude plank roof, and the 'cats and clay' chimney. (National Archives)

served as an escape hatch for the home's core heat due to the fact that hot air rises. It was a horribly inefficient way to heat a home, requiring vast amounts of firewood to create a barely satisfactory level of comfort. In the winter, pioneers lived at a temperature far below what modern man considers acceptable.

IN THE FIELD

Most pioneers prior to the 1840s settled on wooded land. Woodland took more time to clear, and the stumps and roots left behind took up to twenty years to decay. But the land, once cleared, was fertile, the trees provided both fuel and building material, and the rainfall was ample for agriculture. The most fortunate, like the settlers of Oregon's Willamette Valley, selected land that encompassed both forest and prairie. On the prairie, sod provided the building material and prairie grass the fuel, both unfamiliar to settlers accustomed to the forests of the east. The prairie frontier also confronted the farmer with much lower annual rainfall than he had known in the east.

A pioneer farmer, with the help of his sons, used axe, grubbing hoe, and mattock to clear his wooded fields, burning the brush as he went. The Kentuckian felled such trees as buckeye, blue ash, hickory, and walnut. He killed the largest trees by girdling: soon the leaves fell off the girdled trees and let sunlight reach the soil. Each year he cleared another parcel of land, at the rate of about one to two wooded acres per man. Another method of felling large trees, used in Oregon, was to cut through the bark and the outer layer of wood, then apply hot coals. The coals burned through the trunk far enough to make the tree fall. To fell a large tree is extremely hazardous work in any era. The impact of the axe can cause a large, rotten branch to come down on the wood chopper's head. Even an experienced woodsman can fatally miscalculate which way a tree will fall. That is why the term 'widow-maker,' long applied to timber, so chills the blood.

The all-important axe weighed 3–4 pounds, with a handle of shellbark hickory 2–4 feet long. The axe handle was marked off in 1-foot intervals so it could double as a ruler. The end of the han-

A farmer at work clearing land, working around stumps. An unconfined sow and piglets are in the background. (National Archives)

THE PLOW

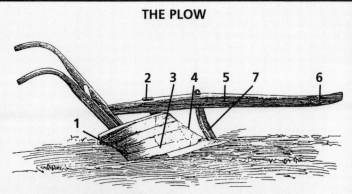

An early American plow. (National Archive)

1. Landside – flat back side of plow, away from furrow, runs on unplowed land
2. Standard – attaches moldboard to beam of plow
3. Moldboard – curved part that receives and turns over loosened soil
4. Share – the part that cuts the soil
5. Beam – main piece of plow, to which handles and colter are attached
6. Drawbar – the part by which the horse pulls the plow
7. Colter – blade or sharp wheel attached to beam to make vertical cuts in soil and ease work of plowshare

The plow of the 1700s weighed relatively little but produced a lot of drag. The moldboard was unevenly plated with sheet iron or tin, and the share was of wrought iron. The wooden parts were crude and homemade. Thomas Jefferson pioneered the idea of a scientifically designed moldboard. Others built on his ideas and made less resistant moldboards. In 1839, inventors first patented a moldboard that not only cut, but turned over and broke up the soil. Inventors patented more than 100 plow improvements between 1800 and 1830. *

The use of cast iron for a single-piece moldboard, share, and landside also constituted a major advance, beginning in the 1790s. However, farmers shunned it because a broken share necessitated replacing the entire apparatus. The most important advance was the introduction in 1819 of separate and replaceable cast-iron components. A pivoting moldboard facilitated plowing on hillsides. Cast-iron plows quickly grew in popularity east of the Mississippi after 1820. The stickier soil of the prairie west of the Mississippi required the more polished steel plow, invented by John Deere in 1837. Until steel plows came to be more widely used in the 1850s, farmers had to stop every few feet to scrape off the plow.

* Percy W. Bidwell and John I. Falconer, *History of Agriculture in the Northern United States, 1620–1860* (Washington, 1925), p. 209.

dle was narrowed for flexibility, providing built-in shock absorption. The owner of a well-balanced axe performed astounding feats. Two axe-wielding men felled a 14-inch diameter pine in six minutes. It was known that the blade had to be warmed before use in winter months, or it could break. Every farmer owned a whetstone for sharpening axes and hoes. In the absence of a nearby blacksmith, farmers sharpened their own plows as well, using anvil, hammer, and file. The farmer's anvil consisted of an iron slab fastened to a wooden block.

With the hammer and anvil, plus a chisel, a frontiersman was able to cut nails from rods of iron. While one could substitute wooden pegs for nails in house-building, iron nails were essential for shoeing horses. A farmer who wanted to be self-sufficient in making and mending his own metal tools had to own a bellows, cooling tub, vise, tongs, files, wedges, and punches. Branding irons, shovels, hoes, and logging chains were all essential to farm life and costly because they contained metal.

Having cleared the trees and brush off the land, the farmer then had to hitch horse to the plow and break up the soil. In the exceptionally root-filled soil of newly cleared fields, one person guided the horse while the other held the plow to keep it in the soil.

Plows underwent many improvements after 1800. The most important advance was the introduction of replaceable cast-iron components. The steel plow, invented by John Deere in 1837, saw wide use in the prairies by the 1850s; and other inventors tested steam plows later in the decade. Even though improved plows increased the acreage a farmer could prepare for planting, plowing was

Above: In background, scythe and plow; on the right, harrow, hoe, and axe; in foreground, shovel, rake, fork, sickle, and ox yoke. (National Archives).

Left: Plowing, circa 1867, with three yoke of oxen. (Library of Congress)

only the initial step. A farmer's crop was still limited by how much he could sow, cultivate, and harvest.

Then as now, farming was hard work and not all pioneers were up to the labor required. An early Oregon pioneer recalls that some neighbors 'were not at first pleased with the hard work and drudgery of farming.' They applied repeatedly to Dr McLoughlin of the Hudson's Bay Company to purchase supplies on credit. Uncharacteristically, he refused. Finally they asked the doctor what they should do. 'He replied in a loud voice: "Go to work! go to work! go to work!"'[1] The applicants sheepishly acknowledged that this was exactly what they did not wish to do.

Sowing grain. First the harrow to smooth the soil and break up the clods, followed by hand-broadcasting of seed. (Library of Congress)

In Kentucky, the pioneer farmer planted newly cleared land to corn: virgin soil was too rich for wheat. Most farmers planted corn four seeds to a 'hill.' They created the hills, actually only slight mounds, by plowing 'check rows.' First they plowed parallel furrows in one direction, and then crossed them with furrows running perpendicular to the first set, spacing them to permit cultivation. Finally, they dropped the seeds at all intersections of the rows and covered them by hand, thereby forming hills. The growing corn presented quite a different picture from today's long parallel rows of closely spaced stalks marching from horizon to horizon.

The early nineteenth-century farmer planted all seeds by hand: he broadcast wheat and harrowed the field – that is, raked it smooth, – or dropped corn into furrows and covered it using a hoe. Hand-operated or horse-drawn seed planters emerged in the east by 1850, but did not appear west of the Mississippi until a decade later. Even so, if the ground was too wet for machinery, a farmer had to revert to hand seeding. One Dakota farmer made a hand seeder out of a grain sack with a rope attached. He slung the bag from his shoulder by the rope, so the seed trickled from the opening into his right hand. Today's farm stores sell seeders that are very similar, being little more than canvas bags hung from the shoulder. The only improvement is a hand crank that controls the flow and spread of the seeds.

Farmers controlled weeds by cultivating between the rows several times each growing season with a hoe or a light horse-drawn plow. Inventors introduced horse-drawn cultivators during the 1840s and continued to improve them over the next two decades. During the first cultivation of the season, corn seedlings lost to crows and other pests had to be replanted.

At harvest time, the neighbors gathered to cut down hay, wheat, and other crops with sickle and scythe. Repetitive motion, hour after hour, led to accidents, and harvesters often ended up with cut hands. Over time, technologies emerged to reduce risk and improve efficiency. The cradle scythe [see illustration] represented a major advance because it laid the grain out all in one direction for ease of binding. The cradle appeared in the late 1700s and continued in use into the 1860s.[2] Experienced reapers could cut and bind at most an acre of grain in a day with sickle or scythe, or three acres with a cradle scythe. The grain was cut, bound, and stood up in shocks in the field until cured.

In Virginia's Shenandoah Valley a twenty-two-year-old wizard-inventor named Cyrus McCormick pondered the nature of the farm harvest. His solution, a horse-drawn reaper, forever changed farming. McCormick introduced his mechanical reaper in 1831 and patented his design three years later. His first reapers were so noisy that someone had to walk beside the horse team to reassure the frightened equines that doom was not imminent. McCormick's reaper underwent a series of improvements over the next two decades before farmers widely adopted it. The mechanical reaper cut about 12 acres a day. Not only did it offer a twelve-fold gain in efficiency, but it eliminated one more back-breaking farm chore. Nonetheless, a considerable amount of hand labor still remained. The mechanical reaper cut the grain onto a platform. A man raked it off, and then another person grabbed several strands and twisted them into a makeshift piece of twine to encircle the sheaf of grain. First the raking, then the binding became automated as inventors developed machines to reduce hand labor on the farm.

To separate the grain heads from the stalk, a man beat out the grain with a hinged stick called a flail. One man with a flail could thresh 5 to 6 bushels of wheat a day. To accomplish the same work, horses could trample the grain off the stalk on a threshing floor, thereby daily producing 20 to 40 bushels. In Oregon, a farmer first prepared a threshing floor out in the field by fencing a

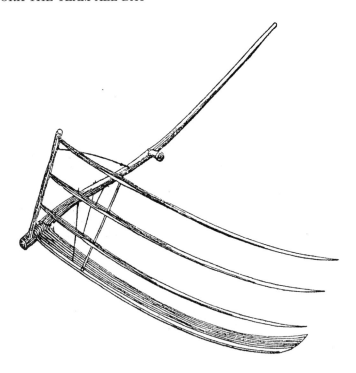

Above: A cradle scythe, which in the hands of an experienced reaper could cut three acres of grain in a day.
Below: Mechanical reaper. Behind the mowing bar is the platform which receives the grain. A hand rake, necessary for clearing off the grain, lies across the platform. (National Archives)

Slaves threshing grain with flails. (Library of Congress)

small area with rails and turning animals in to trample and compact the earth. Then he placed bound sheaves in the pen and set his livestock to walking over them. Naturally the animals preferred to stand around eating the grain. A girl of ten contrived a risky solution:

> 'I would go into the corral, catch a young heifer by the tail and while she would bawl and try to get away I would hold on like grim death and as she sailed around the corral trying to escape I would be taking steps ten feet long. This would start all the rest of the stock going full tilt so the grain got well trampled.'[3]

By the 1840s, inventors addressed this problem as well by creating horse-powered threshing machines with a capacity of 100 bushels a day. The first such machines appeared in Ohio and began

Machine threshing powered by a two-horse treadmill. (Library of Congress)

PEST MANAGEMENT

FIELD

As soon as the farmer put kernels of corn in the ground, the feast began...for crows, blackbirds, squirrels, opossum, raccoons, moles, and mice, plus gophers and cranes on the prairies. The feast continued as the surviving seeds put up tender shoots. Boys hunted the squirrels and birds with shotguns. Whole neighborhoods competed to see who could shoot the most animals. Settlers put out traps and encouraged cats to hunt rodents, but the pests grew ever more populous as they throve on whatever the struggling farmer could produce.

The abundant wild geese of Oregon country descended upon young wheat fields and ate the shoots to the ground. Shooting barely made a dent in their numbers, so farmers resorted to the effort-intensive 'twining.' They laboriously set out stakes at short intervals and strung twine between them in two directions to form a grid. The descending geese struck the twine and most were repelled. A few birds got entangled in the twine and ended up becoming a meal instead of having one. *

Wolves, bears, and wildcats preyed on sheep and other young livestock on every frontier. Local governments offered bounties, paid out of public funds, for killing wolves. Foxes and minks ate poultry. An Oregon farmer reported poisoning wolves with nux vomica (an East Indian plant containing strychnine) concealed in meat. Strychnine itself could be purchased freely, at a low price and in several forms, and sent through the mail without raising comment. All predator populations decreased dramatically as each area grew more populous and settled. Until that occurred, most farmers had no recourse but to keep their most valued animals in corrals or barns near the house.

Along with birds and rodents, deer also liked to dine on young shoots of wheat. Later in its life cycle, wheat fell to rust, a form of fungus, and such pests as the larva of the Hessian fly, the grain worm, weevils, and the chinch bug. These pests grew more numerous with each successive crop of wheat, until increasing numbers of farmers began to rotate their crops. Farmers also tried to time the plantings for periods when the pests were less active. By so doing, they sometimes lost their crops to frosts. As a last resort, some farmers turned cattle out to graze the wheat fields, hoping they would also kill some pests.

Caterpillars devoured the leaves of fruit trees and sugar maples. Sulphur had some effect in keeping caterpillars off fruit trees, but it did not work on maples. An especially fierce infestation killed many trees in 1791. Insect larvae attacked peaches and caused them to fall before they ripened. Farmers let the hogs into the orchard to eat the fallen peaches, at the same time killing the worms.

An 1800 essay on the control of hornworms on tobacco plants illustrates the sum total of pest control knowledge of the time:

'The act of destroying these worms is termed worming the tobacco, which is a very nauseous occupation, and takes up much labor. It is performed by picking every thing of this kind off the respective leaves with the hand, and destroying it with the foot.' **

No prior experience could prepare prairie settlers for the grasshoppers that descended in Biblical hordes on their crops. As the land came under cultivation, the insects found the settlers' crops more appetizing than wild grasses and ate every morsel, including still-buried onions and turnips. The approaching grasshoppers looked like storm clouds as they rode the wind. When they descended they remained for a few days or a week until another wind carried them away. During 1874, an especially bad year, they coated the ground several inches

moving westward until, by 1860, farmers throughout the nation used them.[4] Early threshing machines were powered by a team of horses on a treadmill. Thresher-separators, which spewed out the grain and straw from two separate portals, appeared later. These huge machines were run by five-horse teams hitched to long sweeps and driven in a circle. The owner of the machine and his hired crew of operators traveled from farm to farm, with each farmer in turn providing the necessary horses. A straw-burning engine replaced the horse teams by 1880. A traction engine for the thresher, introduced five years later, eliminated the need for horses to haul the machinery from field to field.[5] Both of these inventions were part of a trend that saw machines replace horses, as farming entered

An entire family of prairie farmers pitches in to kill grasshoppers in 1875. They raked the still wingless young hoppers into piles and burned them. (Library of Congress)

deep, eating cloth and lumber as well as vegetation. Although chickens ate them voraciously, it made not a dent in their numbers, and the grasshopper diet gave the poultry a strange flavor. Grasshopper excrement polluted surface water to the point where livestock refused to drink it. Settlers tried shoveling the wingless young insects into piles and setting them afire, a desperate move in such a wildfire-prone region. Eventually, they adapted their farming to the life cycle of the insects, planting wheat earlier and diversifying to crops that the hoppers found less appealing.

The farmers of this grasshopper-ravaged country required aid to avoid starvation. Food, clothing, cash, and seeds were sent by relatives and private charities or funded by state and federal government. As still occurs in famine areas today, corrupt individuals helped themselves to many of the goods before they reached the needy.

By the 1880s a variety of agricultural insecticides had come into use, among them pyrethrum, Bordeaux mixture, kerosene, and carbolic acid. Bordeaux mixture originated in the vineyards of France and consisted of copper sulphate and lime diluted in water. An 1890 report from a US Agricultural Experiment Station assured the public:

'It has been shown, both by experiment and by practice, that there is no danger to be apprehended from eating fruit sprayed either with the compounds of arsenic, or with Bordeaux mixture.

a new era where the ability to fix machinery became more important than animal husbandry skills.

Threshing was a group activity, with neighbor helping neighbor, and the women cooking huge meals to feed the crew. Workers always knew who made the best meals. The process of machine threshing required a person to cut the twine from the sheaves and another to feed each bundle into the machine. At the other end, a man packed the grain that came out of the spout into barrels or bags for transport to the mill. A couple of unfortunate boys performed the hated task of stacking the straw that came out on a conveyor belt. This chore caused itching all over the body and irritated the eyes. However, in spewing out the grain and straw through separate apertures,

'A more serious objection to the use of Bordeaux mixture on such fruit as grapes, is the fact that it adheres, if applied late, so as to affect the market value of the fruit.' ***

Thus, with the 'expert' encouragement of the government, the unwitting consumer ate highly toxic foods.

HOUSE PESTS

Travelers observed mosquitos along the Ohio Valley, but not in huge swarms. Farther south, down the Mississippi, they could drive folk to distraction. Nevertheless, people remained unaware of their ability to cause disease. Mosquitos were also plentiful in Oregon. As farmers cleared forests and introduced domestic animals, mosquito populations rose to feed on them. Thus they followed the advancing line of westward settlement, and people could do little to prevent the scourge.

Fleas infested private houses and beds in taverns. From her mission house in Oregon, Narcissa Whitman wrote home asking for a fine-toothed comb to combat the fleas and lice she believed she had caught from the Indians. Many houses also suffered bed-bug infestations. One woman in New Mexico finally eliminated them by pouring boiling water on the wooden bedsteads twice a week, as well as painting the crevices with kerosene. An Oregon household used a mixture of soap, potassium, and water to destroy the eggs. House flies arrived on the frontier somewhat behind the first wave of settlement. So novel were they in early Oregon that young children in one cabin fed sugar to two pet house flies on the windowsill in stormy weather. Stock flies, however, always existed in abundance. The ubiquitous flies were brushed away from the table with anything from peacock feathers to small tree branches.

A wounded sandhill crane in prairie country provided a unique solution to the mouse problem. Luther North, a military man turned rancher, tamed the bird and brought him into the house at night. He soon observed the crane stalking and eating mice, but the bird became satiated after only two or three. North started taking the dead mice away from the crane so that it would continue hunting. After killing a couple of dozen, the crane would receive a few as a reward.

Snakes, had they been left unmolested, might have been an effective check on the rodent population, but they were feared and killed. People particularly dreaded the avoidable bite of the rattlesnake and killed hundreds at a time in organized 'snake drives.' By so doing they eliminated one environmental check on rodents. Meanwhile, they resigned themselves to living amid exploding populations of rats and mice that accompanied all human settlement.

* Peter G. Boag, *Environment and Experience: Settlement Culture in Nineteenth-Century Oregon* (Los Angeles, 1992), p. 61.

** Wayne D. Rasmussen, ed., *Agriculture in the United States: A Documentary History* (New York, 1975), vol. 1, p. 366.

*** Rasmussen, vol. 2, pp. 1249–50.

the threshing machine also automated the job of winnowing, separating the wheat from the chaff. In earlier times, the job of winnowing involved tossing the wheat from one basket or sieve to another while a natural breeze or hand-held fans blew the chaff away.

Another group activity, the sociable husking bee where everyone pitched in to shuck and shell the corn by hand, gave way in the 1840s to husking and shelling machines. These machines did not require the group labor that threshing machines did. Here was another way that machinery changed the nature of farming by allowing individuals to accomplish tasks that heretofore had required communal activity.

The 1870s saw the beginning of riding machinery, although older farmers considered riding a sissified affectation. Corn cultivators, check rowers, gang plows, and disc plows – still in use today and called disc harrows – all spread during the 1870s. The flat prairie landscape, unbroken by stumps and hills, particularly invited the use of machinery.

Another great change in the character of western farming that took place at this time, and something that contributed to the trend away from the pioneering practice of neighbors exchanging work, was increasing dependence on the migrant harvest worker. This was due in part to the spread of large-scale wheat farming: when wheat ripens, it has to be harvested within a few days. Migrant harvest labor developed gradually, beginning in the 1860s, and increasing through the twentieth century. Some early harvest hands were lumberjacks earning money during their off season. Many others came from the ranks of the chronically unemployed. Men traveled from south to north each season, and the railroads charged them no fares. Newspapers coined the word 'tramp' to describe their way of life. Some may have chosen and loved the nomadic life; others had run out of choices. The harvest cost the farmer money, whether in wages for the hired hands or the purchase price of machinery, and then as now money was something the farmer always had in short supply.

As farm machines grew in expense and complexity, fewer could afford to buy them, though many coveted them. Farmers with larger holdings could better justify the investment. Owners of the latest equipment tried to offset the purchase price by hiring the equipment out to do work for other farmers. It became customary for prairie farmers to mortgage their farms to buy machinery. New inventions outdated existing machines before they were paid for. Thus farmers came to walk a treadmill of their own making; debt incurred by too many equipment purchases.

* * *

In Kentucky and in Oregon, the new settler faced yet another task for the first year. Added to that long list – build a home, clear land or break sod, plant crops, build fences – was the necessity of starting an orchard. Fruit trees took years to start bearing the much coveted additions to the diet. Although slow to get started, orchards were not nearly so labor-intensive as field crops. Pioneers did not prune and train fruit trees like they do today. Peach trees bore fruit about four years after planting, apple trees in about seven years. The farmers took most of their peaches to the nearest neighbor who owned a copper still and turned them into peach brandy. Home distillers also produced apple brandy and rye or corn whiskey. The produce of most early apple orchards went into apple cider. This favored drink, delicious when fresh, fermented in a few days into an equally tasty intoxicating beverage.

Oregon pioneers in the Willamette valley found the sparse woodlands easier to clear than the ones in the east, because there was little underbrush. The tangled thorn-covered canes that had ensnared Kentucky settlers did not grab at the clothing of the Oregon settler. Oregon's grasslands were also easier to clear than the prairie sod of the Great Plains, because the wet Pacific climate caused the roots to decompose rapidly, making the sod yield to a wooden plow drawn by just one team of oxen.

The oxen, unfortunately, were usually the same overworked animals that had drawn the covered wagon across the continent. One Oregon booster, in a letter published in eastern newspapers, sang the praises of the ox: 'The ox is a most noble animal, patient, thrifty, durable, gentle, and easily driven, and does not run off. Those who come to this country will be in love with their oxen by the time they reach here.'[6] Apparently the writer, Peter Burnett, was unfamiliar with the expression 'stubborn as an ox.' Many emigrants who arrived in Oregon and encountered Burnett told him that they cursed his name frequently on the trail because of his overly sanguine advice.

In reality, with both man and beast depleted by the journey, the first year's crop was bound to be small. Once fully recovered, a man and his team could break two acres of sod a day, about double what a single team could accomplish on the Great Plains. Unlike Kentucky farmers, the Oregon farmer could do no plowing during autumn or winter. He had to wait until the rains subsided and the soil drained, some time late in March.

The Oregon settlers grew wheat, oats, barley, tree fruits, and garden vegetables. They could not raise that pioneer staple, corn, because summer temperatures did not get hot enough. Oregonians grew wheat as the essential crop, both for household use and for trade, and oats for the livestock. They grew barley primarily for use in brewing.

The early Oregon missionaries and the first emigrants of the 1840s carried some seeds with them from the east, but borrowed most of their seed stock from the Hudson's Bay Company, which also provided fruit tree shoots. In 1847, two Americans hauled 700 fruit trees and grape vines over the Oregon trail. This marked the beginning of commercial growth of tree fruits in Oregon. A proud settler wrote home in 1856 that he had 2,000 apple trees set in his orchard, at 80 trees to the acre, and that he had 20,000 young trees to sell! At first, Oregon pioneers grew all apple, pear, and peach trees from seed. They did not begin to graft shoots onto root stock until after the great importation of 1847.

The climates of New Mexico and South Dakota could not sustain apple orchards, so settlers had to purchase imported apples. A family in Dakota relied upon imported fruit from Michigan or New York:

> 'Whenever we could we bought a barrel of apples for winter use.... It was a family affair to open the barrel and peek inside. On the top were nice, large beautiful fruit that got smaller and poorer as we worked downward.'[7]

In New Mexico, the Mexicans grew corn, cabbage, onions, and a wide variety of peppers on their land. Americans who had prospered in the Santa Fe trade operated extensive ranches where they raised sheep and cattle and grew forage, grains, and vegetables, much of which they sold to the army and the Indian agencies. Lucien Maxwell and Kit Carson jointly operated one such ranch, Rayado, for the Mexican owner, Maxwell's father-in-law. The ranch was established in 1848 in the fertile valley of Rayado Creek, in northeastern New Mexico. The ranch made its first money by selling hay to the U.S. Army and provisions to passing travelers. For about a year, the army used Rayado as an outpost and stationed several dozen soldiers there. In subsequent years, the ranchers continued to cut grass from the land and sell it for fodder, and set livestock to grazing. They made sharecropping arrangements with four farmers who dug irrigation ditches and began tilling the soil to grow wheat.

The main compound, walled against Indian attack, held the big ranch house, a two-story log structure, and small adobe houses for American, Mexican, and Indian employees and their families. The number of employees and dependents grew from a few dozen to several hundred in less than a decade. Outside the walls were corrals, stables, and slaughterhouses. Eventually, Rayado had 200 acres under cultivation, and 15,000 head of livestock grazing on the surrounding pastures.

* * *

To settle and farm the virgin prairie of the Great Plains required a greater cash investment than settling upon wooded land. Not only did the farmer have to acquire and keep more draft animals for breaking, he had to bring in wood from afar and carry in a greater food supply for both his family and his animals. Although advances in farm machinery, well-drilling, transport, and household goods were available to those who could pay for them, most prairie pioneers still lived in isolated and straitened circumstances much as their forebears had a hundred years earlier.

Sod breaking on the prairies required four or five ox teams and two people; one to guide the heavy plow – weighing 125 pounds or more – and the other to drive the oxen. With a heavy plow drawn by six ox teams, a farmer could break three acres of sod a day. A lighter plow that cut narrower furrows could, with one horse team, still break sod, but only at a rate of an acre a day. Not all new settlers could afford to maintain a good team: for them it made economic sense to hire a man and team to break sod. One Dakota homesteader shipped his team out by rail, only to have

A crude prairie sod shack and a nice team of horses. (National Archives)

trouble maintaining their strength and health: 'They are too old a team to go without grain. Tried to get grain and give the team as security but failed.'[8]

The struggling newcomer had somehow to survive on a scanty first crop, because the sod had not yet broken down sufficiently to yield up its wealth. Prairie pioneers planted 'sod corn' as the first crop in newly broken sod, making a cut in the ground with an axe for each seed. The roots of the growing corn helped to break up the sod so it could be plowed more easily the next year. While the prairie farmer grew corn for subsistence, it was spring wheat that would eventually bring in the all-important cash. The cold winters of the Dakotas made survival as a farmer all the more challenging: early fall frosts frequently threatened the corn crop; winter kill menaced fall-planted winter wheat.

The relative rapidity with which established farmers could clear prairie tempted them to plant vast acreages. Advances in farm machinery, most notably the steel plow and the reaper, encouraged them to extend their reach. So thoroughly did the farmers of the Great Plains plow the native sod that today the very few remaining acres of original prairie grasses are a cherished resource. For the pioneers, large-scale cash crop farming proved necessary if the prairie farmer was to make enough money to meet his needs. Not only did the settler have to buy wood for building houses and furniture, but the economy of the late nineteenth century removed production of many items from the home. The pioneer who once made such items now preferred to buy them. Many chose to spend their efforts making money to buy things, where once they had spent time and effort to make things.

The lack of wood for fencing presented yet another challenge to prairie farmers. They resorted to fences of sod or hedgerows of osage orange, whose long thorns kept livestock at bay. The first wire fencing appeared around 1850, and barbed wire in the 1870s. Smooth wire fencing failed to deter animals from climbing through, but barbed wire came to revolutionize fence building. As more manufacturers churned out barbed wire, the price fell and more farmers adopted it. Although osage orange had served admirably in the days before wire fencing, farmers came to curse it for shading their fields. They laboriously grubbed it out by hand so they could put wire fencing in its place.

45

CROP YIELDS AND SOIL FERTILITY: THEN AND NOW

CORN
The Colonies: 20–50 bushels per acre
Kentucky in the 1790s: 50–100 bushels/acre
Kentucky in 1855: 40 bushels/acre
Kentucky in the 1990s: 90–130 bushels/acre

WHEAT
The Colonies: 10–15 bushels/acre
Oregon in the 1850s: 15–20 bushels/acre, without manure: 30-40 bushels/acre, with manure
Oregon in the 1990s: 50–70 bushels/acre
South Dakota in the 1870s: 25 bushels/acre
South Dakota in the 1920s: 16 bushels/acre
South Dakota in the 1930s: 1–2 bushels/acre (drought years)
South Dakota in the 1990s: 32 bushels/acre

COTTON
Georgia in the Colonial period: 275 pounds/acre
Mississippi in the early 1800s: 500 pounds/acre
Mississippi in 1867: 195 pounds/acre
Mississippi in the 1990s: 570–890 pounds/acre

These numbers support the accounts of worn-out soil in the colonies and the fertility of virgin soil on the frontier. Observe that even in its early days, South Dakota's wheat production was lower than that of fertilized soil in Oregon. This is attributable to South Dakota's relative lack of moisture.

Crop yields after some fifty years of agriculture indicate a drop in soil fertility. Particularly in the mid-1800s, soil management techniques were not widely practiced, so continuous cropping had an adverse efect on fertility. The much higher yields of the present day reflect a host of innovations, including widespread use of fertilizers and pesticides, and development of more productive plant varieties.

Prairie farmers, seeking to transplant a familiar sight of home, planted trees on their homesteads, bringing saplings from the east or gathering seeds of native trees. They planted trees around their houses for shade and as windbreaks, and along the edges of fields to help form hedgerows. Some planted woodlots for their future lumber needs. Cottonwood, ash, and box elder did best in the region. Encouraged by state governments, prairie tree-planting burgeoned in Kansas and Nebraska in the 1850s. In the 1870s, settlers in the Dakota Territory continued the practice, aided by territorial tax relief laws for timber culture, and federal legislation that provided a free quarter section of land to a settler who planted a fourth of the acreage to trees. Few were able to plant successfully the number of trees required by the law, but enough trees survived to alter slightly the landscape, mostly in the eastern part of the territory where rainfall was greater.

Terror of prairie fires caused settlers to plow firebreaks around their farms. Such fires, most common in the autumn, driven by the constant winds, could race across the landscape at 30 miles an hour, jumping rivers, destroying crops and killing livestock. A spark from a chimney landing on a haystack was all that it took to lay waste a huge area. On the one hand, burning off the grass in a controlled manner offered the advantage of removing older and less nutritious grass from the prairie so that fresh grass could grow in its place. On the other hand, burned-over ground was harder to plow, because the destroyed grass had served the function of retaining moisture in the ground. In the days before settlers began trying to put out all fires, prairie fires set by lightning occurred in regular cycles and served the purpose of clearing off old vegetation. Today, the wisdom

SOIL CONSERVATION AND MANAGEMENT

The general practice of the colonial farmer with regard to the soil was to farm it to exhaustion, then either move on to new land or accept lower yields. He knew soil as a limited resource, about which he could do little or nothing. The beckoning presence of fresh land just to the west discouraged the farmer from putting great effort into conserving soil. In 1777, North Carolina, displaying some early consciousness of the idea that soil could or should be protected, passed a law that prohibited farmers from burning the woods to clear land, believing that this would be harmful.

In the 1700s, most farmers did not fertilize their fields with manure, although a few used lime or fish. Soil management, such as it was, consisted of planting one crop until it exhausted the soil, then letting the field lie fallow. By the early nineteenth century, farmers manured their fields every few years, but the manure itself had been mismanaged, losing much of its nutrient value sitting out in the barnyard exposed to the elements. They also fertilized with lime, gypsum, fish, seaweed, offal, or human waste. However, the practice of soil fertilization was far from widespread.

Early settlers, including the French in eighteenth-century Missouri, turned livestock out into fields to eat stubble, which had the additional benefit of manuring the soil. The French also farmed the river bottoms, relying on the annual Mississippi floods to renew their soil. In a practice known as 'hogging down,' farmers turned their swine out into a mature cornfield and let them do both the clearing and fertilizing. Fertilizer use increased in the second half of the nineteenth century. In the east, manure spreaders appeared in response to this wider use. Buffalo bones, gathered in the west and pulverized and bagged in the east, became another source of fertilizer.

As the frontier receded farther to the west and it became more difficult simply to abandon a tapped-out farm and relocate, soil management received more attention. For the first half of the nineteenth century, single-crop agriculture, over-cultivation, and plowing furrows up and down hills instead of across them depleted the soil and promoted erosion. Rich black loam gave way to gullies of red clay. On the arid prairies, overgrazing caused wind erosion.

By mid-century, farmers began to raise an outcry against soil neglect and propose ways of conserving the most basic element of their livelihood. Crop rotation, sparing and careful cultivation, and plowing across the hillsides formed the bedrock of a new understanding of soil. Farmers also began to recognize that well-drained soil improved growing conditions.

Writings from the 1860s show that farmers knew certain practices were beneficial without fully comprehending why. They appreciated, for example, that winter was the best time to turn over the soil, without seeming to realize that the practice killed off buried insect larvae by freezing. Farmers had also learned that straw could be composted instead of burned, and then spread on the fields; that a crop of clover restored the soil for corn; that the roots of clover interplanted with other crops helped to break up the sod and aerate the soil; and that manuring grain crops caused them to mature faster, thus beating late insect outbreaks.

of a return to this natural cycle, called the 'let burn' policy, is debated by environmentalists and bureaucrats.

The prairie fires did not take a great many human lives because people could find safety in several ways. They could set backfires, or burn off a small area where they could stand while the fire passed around them. Standing on plowed ground or sheltering in a dugout also afforded protection.

Failure seemed to stalk the hard-working Dakota farmer. Drought, fires, swarming grasshoppers, and extreme winters all took their toll. While Kentuckians saw occasional droughts and dealt with insect pests, it was on a scale not nearly so devastating. New Mexico settlers who grew crops planned for aridity from the outset, and most turned to ranching as the most profitable use of the land. American writers who visited New Mexico frankly described it as poorly suited to agriculture; not so the boosters of Dakota territory. A broadside from the early 1880s boasted of South Dakota:

'She has EVERY RESOURCE necessary to make ALL HER PEOPLE RICH.... She has the unrivaled agricultural resources east of the Missouri River and NO POOR SOIL!... THERE ARE NO POOR LANDS! IT IS WELL WATERED! It is suitable either for AGRICULTURE or STOCK RAISING! It is covered over its entire area with the richest grass in great variety.... Western South Dakota is the best watered country in the west. The water is pure and sweet.'[9]

Modern-day debate has focused on whether cropping the prairie is an inappropriate use of land best suited for ranching, whether, indeed, farmers are forcing the land to fit the agrarian mold. Proponents of prairie farming point to their vast fields of waving grain, grown when rainfall fails with water pulled from deep in the earth. Opponents argue that the underground aquifers are going to run out of water. The failures of the nineteenth century, when nature itself seemed to conspire against the homesteader, were perhaps the opening argument in this debate.

LIVESTOCK: MILK, MEAT, AND MOTIVE POWER

A farmer might survive without keeping livestock for meat, and make up the shortfall by hunting, but he could not do without animals for field work, transportation, and motive power for machinery. Their condition dictated the amount of work a farmer accomplished: 'broke only four houres a day haven't enough grain to work the team all day,' complained a Dakota homesteader.[10]

Oxen and horses each offered a different set of advantages as draft animals. Oxen were stronger and required less grain, and farmers could recoup their feeding costs by slaughtering or selling them for meat when they grew too old to work. Oxen better withstood the hardships of the overland trails and were less prone to stray or be stolen than horses. Their main disadvantage was their low tolerance for the intense heat of prairie summers. Horses were more high strung but more intelligent and biddable. They could cover more ground than oxen when hitched to the lighter machinery of the mid-nineteenth century. Horses gradually replaced oxen as draft animals late in the nineteenth century. During the colonial period, German farmers in Pennsylvania began developing the strong Conestoga horses from English stock. Although never an official breed, these sturdy animals served eastern and midwestern freighters and farmers well. The type no longer exists.[11] In Oregon, settlers instead made use of the small but well-built Cayuse ponies that were so readily available from skilled Indian breeders. American farmers began importing European draft horses, such as the Clydesdale, in the 1850s. Only gradually did they become available in the West.

An Oregon settler spoke for all pioneer farmers when he observed, 'The horse, the ox and cow, the sheep and pig ... were to constitute the basis of pioneer life, from the Atlantic to the Pacific. On the domestic animals we depended absolutely.... We could do nothing without them.'[12] Farmers kept horses or oxen as draft animals, and sheep provided wool. Since mutton neither smoked nor salted well, people preferred to raise cattle and hogs for meat. Hogs cost little to raise, of all animals they provided the most edible meat, and their meat preserved well with salt. Consequently, pork quickly became the staple of the pioneer diet.

To say that frontier farmers 'kept' livestock is not altogether accurate. Most animals were left to wander at will. In summer, farmers led the livestock to available land and placed some salt on the ground. The animals usually remained near the salt. Salt was known to be appealing to animals and widely used as a means of rounding them up. Despite the judicious use of salt and feed to win the animals' loyalty and keep them nearby, feral herds developed.

Early pioneers first concentrated on the critical task of getting crops established before turning their attention to building barns and fences. Any efforts at fence-building aimed to keep livestock out of fields, not in a pasture. When brush or snake-rail fences finally appeared, the livestock

A snake-rail fence, also called a worm fence. The frontier practice was to fence in the house and garden and permit the animals to free range. (Author photo, taken at the Museum of American Frontier Culture, Staunton, Virginia)

could easily knock them down or jump over them to get into the corn fields. Then as now, hogs were particularly adept at outwitting fence-builders.

The zig-zag patterned snake-rail fence, a New World innovation, was usually made of split oak or chestnut rails, but ash or locust also served. A man could produce split rails at rates ranging from 40 to more than 100 a day, depending on his strength and proficiency. The ability to split logs efficiently hour after hour was a prized frontier skill. Recall that in the 1820s, the young Abraham Lincoln worked at this task and earned the moniker 'the rail splitter.' Because the rails of the snake-rail fence were simply laid out on the ground in interlocking tiers, one did not have to dig post holes to build the fence. The snake-rail fence was quick and easy to put up or move, but it consumed more wood in the making and occupied a wide band of arable land.

In Oregon country, home to a thriving cattle trade that led to overgrazing of the grasslands, settlers grew tired of finding cattle and hogs in their crops. They petitioned the territorial government to require livestock to be fenced in, but true to frontier tradition, the resulting law required the settlers to fence their crops in. By the mid-1850s, the Willamette Valley was divided everywhere by snake-rail fences, hedgerows, stone walls, or sod fences backed by ditches.[13]

Dairy cows also ranged freely, returning home each day only because their owners kept their calves penned up. In the Drake family, the son brought the dairy cow back from her wanderings each day so she could be fed at the doorstep while being milked. Son Daniel's job included wrestling the calf off the cow so the family could get enough of the milk. Milking was strictly a woman's chore in the early days, but it could still be rough work. A daughter of Oregon pioneers recalled:

'The summer I was fourteen we were milking 24 cows. We didn't have the money to buy American cows, so we broke the half-wild Spanish cows to milk. Many and many is the time they would tree me....'[14]

A homestead featuring a small clearing, crude rail fencing to keep the animals out, and one-room cabin with wood shake roof. (National Archives)

A century later in Dakota, the taboo against men doing the milking had all but vanished. One typical boy who wished to attend school beyond the eighth grade worked for room and board on a family friend's dairy farm just outside of Huron, South Dakota. His job was to milk some particularly difficult cows that the farmer intended to sell. One of these cows had to be tied to keep her from kicking.

> 'When I tried to put on the belt, she kicked me hard. It came so suddenly and with such force that my temper flared; I got hold of a milking stool and was giving her a good going over when Mr Clark appeared.'

Clark reprimanded the boy and set about demonstrating the proper way to treat a dairy cow. As the owner approached the creature with gentle words, she kicked him twice, knocking him to the muck-laden floor. Clark

> 'forgot how a milking cow should be treated, grabbed a large club, and went after her far harder than I had done.'[15]

In Kentucky, cattle and hogs fattened on the rich forage of the virgin woods. Many early families owned 50 to 100 head that browsed year-round on the cane brakes, but the numerous animals depleted the brakes as the human population grew. As the cane brakes diminished, farmers supplemented their cattle's winter forage with corn stalks, leaves, and husks, along with the pumpkins grown among the corn. When the corn matured, the tops and leaves were cut off for fodder, although this practice reduced the size of the ears. When the fodder ran out in late winter, the animals went foraging once again, wandering far afield.

'The common hog was of an ungainly type, with long legs and snout, a sharp back, of a roaming disposition, slow and expensive to fatten.' Known variously as the Razorback, Alligator, Landpike, Prairie Rooter, Seven-mile, and Hazelnut splitter, early American swine were well-suited to their semi-wild life but produced small hams and little lard. Only in the 1840s did Americans start breeding hogs to put on more meat, although they tried to retain the razorback's legendary thriftiness and endurance. (National Archives)

Hogs roamed the woods at will, thriving on acorns and other nuts, and growing quite wild with the passage of time. When their owners required meat, they hunted down the hogs like any other wild animal. Hungry farmers hauled barrels out into the woods, shot the animals, and salted them into barrels on site. They kept track of hog ownership by marking their ears with cuts, hence the expression 'earmark'. Owners registered brands and earmarks at the county courthouse. The mark had to be unique and difficult for a dishonest man to alter. Bells also identified livestock ownership. Sheep and cows each wore bells of different pitches.

* * *

In both Oregon and New Mexico, livestock survived year-round on native grasses. Cattle and swine were largely self-sufficient in the mild climate. The swine lived on the edges of oak groves, eating acorns and the bulbs of camas, a blue lily that grew abundantly in Oregon's wetland meadows. So avidly did the settlers' swine feast on the camas that the Indians who relied on the bulbs for food felt the loss. The swine population ran rampant in Oregon. They were very competent foragers and produced large litters. The presence of large numbers of predators depleted the herds slightly, but swine fought together to defend herd members with some success.

The difficulty of bringing cattle on the overland trails kept their numbers down in the early days of American settlement. Most Oregon settlers owned fewer than ten head of cattle. In an unusual cooperative venture, the Hudson's Bay Company, the Methodist missions, and unaffiliated settlers drove some 600 Spanish longhorns overland from California to Oregon in 1837. Long-

WATER POLITICS

The Spanish colonists of New Mexico built their settlements along the rivers, particularly the Rio Grande, and tapped them for irrigation water. Both Spaniards and pueblo Indians maintained reservoirs and irrigation ditches, called acequias. They enacted controls on water use based on irrigation techniques derived from pueblo Indian, Spanish, and Moorish methods. Elected officials in pueblo and village supervised acequia construction and maintenance, and regulated water distribution. Each farmer or landowner had to provide labor, namely backbreaking ditch-digging. The main canal, about 15 feet wide and 2 to 6 feet deep, ran from the water source through the acreage to be watered. From the main canals ran networks of smaller ditches, controlled by floodgates. Each system contained miles of ditches that could water up to several thousand acres of field. In the off season the system was shut down.

The Americans continued the acequia system, running it as a public utility. Before and after the American conquest of the Spanish Southwest, water use led to armed confrontations and became a focal point of government activity – in the governor's office, the legislature, and the courtroom. A steady parade of individuals petitioned the government for intervention when upstream construction threatened their water supplies. A Santa Fe trader's comments presaged what was soon to become the American pioneer attitude toward irrigation:

'...art has so far superseded the offices of nature in watering the farms, that it is almost a question whether the interference of nature in the matter would not be a disadvantage. On the one hand the husbandman need not have his grounds overflowed if he administers the water himself, much less need he permit them to suffer from drought. He is therefore more sure of his crop than if it were subject to the caprices of the weather in more favored agricultural regions.' *

In 1847 the Mormons became the first American farmers to practice widespread irrigation in arid, western lands. In Utah, they dammed creeks with rocks, dirt, and brush, and dug diversion ditches using crude wooden wedges. Lacking levels, they placed pans of water in the new ditches to judge whether the water would run downhill at the proper rate. ** Each spring the dams washed out and had to be rebuilt.

The success of the Mormon irrigation venture, as well as that of the Spaniards and pueblo Indians of New Mexico, depended on cooperation and obedience to a central authority. This ran counter to American democratic principles. Boosters of settlement in the dry lands of the West argued that irrigation would actually cause democracy to flower and small independent farms to proliferate. In fact, large land holdings became the norm in irrigated regions. Many nineteenth-century Americans also believed that man was meant to dominate nature, and that irrigation represented a proper approach to asserting dominion.

In areas of plentiful rainfall, Americans had been willing to let the rivers flow largely unimpeded. However, U.S. law began allowing such users as mills, and then larger industries, to use riverine water for anything deemed to serve a higher economic purpose. Thus the principle of exploiting rivers for personal gain was well established as settlers pushed across

Southwestern farmers in the 1870s operating an irrigation system. The inset shows a raised wooden aqueduct, in contrast to the ditches of earlier days. (Library of Congress)

Begin with a river, add back-breaking labor. An acequia (irrigation ditch) to draw water from the Rio Grande takes shape in New Mexico. (Photo by Philip E. Harroun, courtesy of the Museum of New Mexico)

the continent. Crop agriculture, even in arid regions, was commonly viewed as a better use of land than ranching, one which justified tapping a river to extinction.

Settlers who assumed that, as the earliest arrivals, they could stake a perpetual claim to water from a river, found that later immigrants upstream could deplete the river before it reached them. The first decade of agricultural settlement in Colorado set off a chaotic series of claims to water rights, counterclaims, lawsuits won by the wealthy, and ruined farms. By 1879, the new state had cautiously embraced the principle of public ownership and allocation of water. Despite the objections of lawyers who had prospered from water litigation, and the fears of government repression incited by central control, other arid western states eventually followed suit.

While government control helped to equalize the allocation of water rights, few questioned the notion that rivers should be exploited for agriculture and other economic uses. In its 1871 Annual Report, the U.S. Department of Agriculture declared:

'our people, with scarce an exception, would not prefer the rain, as it comes in the States, to irrigation in Colorado. There is no uncertainty in raising a crop with irrigation, properly conducted, with even a very ordinary amount of hard, common sense, and without any scientific or engineering ability whatever.' ***

Lone voices warned of environmental problems posed by irrigation. They feared that the water-filled ditches would bring malaria. Perhaps some even suspected that irrigation would leach out the soil's nutrients and leave salt in their place, eventually destroying the land's fertility. ****

Congress encouraged irrigation with the Desert Land Act of 1877, which allowed anyone wishing to irrigate arid land in several western states to claim and purchase 640 acres for $1.25 an acre. As they had with other land laws seeming to favor homesteaders, speculators found a way to turn this law to their goal of accumulating large holdings without farming the land.

A completed acequia in New Mexico, late 1800s. A smaller ditch runs off the 'mother-ditch (acequia madre). (Courtesy of the Museum of New Mexico)

DRY FARMING

The drought years of the 1890s ruined thousands of farmers on the Great Plains and turned the survivors' attention to irrigation, drought-resistant crops, and finally, dry farming. Dry farming refers to practices that allow agriculture without irrigation in areas of low rainfall. The semi-arid Great Plains averages about 20 inches of rainfall a year, in contrast to 36 to 48 inches farther east. In some years, those 20 inches fall when they can most benefit growing crops, in other years they do not. Additional factors such as rate of evaporation and the ability of soil to hold moisture also influence the line between crop failure and success.

The backbone of dry farming is to leave some portion of the acreage fallow for a summer and keep it clear of weeds, in order to build up a reserve of moisture in the subsoil for the next growing season. Summer fallowing first came into use in the late 1880s. However, farmers preferred to plant a field to a crop with low moisture demand rather than leave it fallow. Corn, potatoes, turnips, sorghum, and sunflowers provided an alternative cash crop, allowed tilling between rows, and did not use all the summer's rainfall.

Tilling, however, had its downside. In dry regions, smooth-tilled land turned to blowing dust. Plains farmers adopted a form of tilling that left ridges to hold moisture and to shelter young crops from wind. In 1890 a South Dakota farmer developed a system of subsoil packing so that the soil could better retain moisture, but later research proved it futile.

* Josiah Gregg, *Commerce of the Prairies* (New York, 1970), p. 49.
** Donald Worster, *Rivers of Empire: Water, Aridity, and the Growth of the American West* (New York, 1985), pp. 76–7.
*** Wayne D. Rasmussen, ed., *Agriculture in the United States: A Documentary History* (New York, 1975), vol. 2, p. 1424.
**** For more detail, see chapter 3, *Rivers of Empire*.

horns were poor milk producers but efficient at fending for themselves and driving off predators. Farmers made some attempts to crossbreed with eastern animals to improve milk production.

Mutton was not a popular meat among Americans, so farmers kept sheep chiefly for their wool. Sheep had to be maintained closer to home because they were less hardy than other livestock, defenseless against wild predators and dogs, and needed shelter from the elements. If a lamb became chilled, the family took it in and taught it to lap cows' milk from a bowl. Oregon's wet climate was hostile to sheep, which drowned in high numbers during the annual spring floods. Not surprisingly, wool-making got off to a slow start in Oregon, so wool became yet another item to be purchased at the store.

While the prairies across the Mississippi offered year-round grazing, provident farmers cut prairie grass and stored it for the winter. For those regions lacking year-round forage, the practice of providing winter shelter to cattle spread, as farmers realized that sheltered animals required less feed. The first pioneers to provide winter shelter for livestock were German colonists: they built fine stone barns on the Pennsylvania frontier. Confining cattle to one site also allowed farmers more easily to collect and use the manure as fertilizer. When western farmers began to plant pastures, they planted clover, a practice they copied from eastern farmers who had been planting clover to rest the soil between grain crops since pre-Revolution days. By about 1820, orchard grass came into use. Those farmers who raised hay or cut prairie grass for their livestock erected haystacks, tightly built to shed rain, out in the fields. Although hay balers began to appear in the 1850s, haystacks predominated until the twentieth century.

During some winters, Dakota did provide year-round forage, since the native grasses retained their nutrients when allowed to dry on the stalk. But when blizzards raged, cattle perished. Farmers who kept their livestock in a barn risked getting lost as they went out to feed during a blizzard; a rope strung from house to barn was a common precaution. A tale is told of a constantly quarreling farmer and his wife. During a fierce blizzard the wife cut her husband's guideline. Somehow he found his way back to the house and survived to make a joke of the tale.[16]

Nevertheless, prairie blizzards were so blinding and the winds so cold that many people froze to death within hailing distance of their homes, others died trapped in buried houses, and animals starved or suffocated as their barns and sheds were cut off by snow. Some people saw the necessity of bringing their livestock, perhaps the all-important team of horses or the milk cow, into the house during blizzards. Cramped and odiferous though it must have been, the animals and their owners survived. In the winter of 1880–81, 11 feet of snow fell on the Dakotas. Hired shoveling crews could not keep the railroad tracks open, and the population went without all imported merchandise. The heavy blizzards of the 1880s convinced farmers and ranchers that they should start raising hay and corn to feed their cattle in winter.

Most farmers kept chickens for eggs and meat, and some kept domestic geese for their feathers and the occasional peacock for his plumage. The picket fence that decorates so many dooryards today originated as a means to keep chickens out of the garden. The sharpened pickets placed close together kept poultry from squeezing through or roosting on top.[17] Women and children tended the chickens and sold the eggs, which were an important source of barter or cash income on the frontier. A Dakota farmer trying to get his chickens through a hard winter fed them oats and baked potatoes. His brother had already lost most of his to starvation, so he killed the rest for food rather than lose them too.

Pioneer families frequently kept dogs, as many as a dozen at a time, who served a real purpose on the farm. Like farm dogs today, they gave the alarm when strangers called, helped round up livestock, assisted at the hunt, finished off wounded squirrels, and even grabbed and held chickens for slaughter. During the Indian wars they loyally fought off intruders. One new but prospering Dakota farm boasted a horse, four oxen, two milk cows, two heifers, three calves, three piglets, a dozen roosters and hens, a dog and two cats. The family expected to eat the meat from one heifer and one pig over the course of the winter.

To the pioneer husbandman, quantity outranked quality. Pioneers paid little attention to selective cattle breeding until the 1830s, nor did they try to improve on the nearly wild 'razorback' hog until the 1840s. The time came when hogs were more highly domesticated and kept closer to home, and the farmer no longer had to hunt them down. After a month or two of fattening the hogs with corn, the farmer called the family and neighbors together for the slaughter on a favorable day when the weather was not too warm, but not cold enough to freeze the meat. The hog was hit on the head, its throat cut, and the body raised by pulley so the blood could all run out. The carcass was scalded in a large kettle or trough, then gutted, skinned, and cooled. The various cuts of meat were either smoked, or cured in a trough with salt and sugar. Little went to waste. Scraps were

RANCHING

The prairie lent itself to ranching with greater ease than it did to agriculture. Cattle or sheep could exist year-round on the native grass, which throve on the minimal rainfall of the region. Ranching attracted wealthy investors who bought or claimed huge spreads. All one needed to make a start was range land with a water source and the cattle themselves. Many extended their range by illegally fencing in government land and combining it with whatever land their employees had previously, and fraudulently, claimed.

Overgrazing, a series of killing winters, and conflicts with farmers and smaller ranches eroded the profitability of open-range ranching. Ranchers and 'nesters' – as ranchers contemptuously labeled farmers – each battled for their way of life. In this battle the two sides deployed threats, theft, and destruction of property, including fences, houses, and livestock. The cutting of barbed wire fences alone is said to have done millions of dollars of damage – at a time when the dollar was worth a lot more than today.

For a while, successive years of drought drove homesteaders back. It appeared that the only result of ranchers winning the battle against the nesters was to set sheep and cattle ranchers at one another's throats. Cattle ranchers believed that sheep destroyed the range and attempted to drive off sheep ranchers by threats and escalating violence. Ultimately, however, farmers trying to survive and profit on the semi-arid prairie learned that they had either to diversify and plant crops that required less moisture, or take up raising livestock. Only by adapting to prairie conditions could they create a viable farm or ranch.

Shearing sheep on a New Mexico ranch. (Photo by Strohmeyer & Wyman, courtesy of the Museum of New Mexico)

The life of the cowboy on the open range has been well documented, but that of the sheep-herder is little known. The Spaniards had introduced sheep ranching into New Mexico in the sixteenth century, and it remained the region's principal enterprise. By the time the United States had annexed the territory, wealthy Mexicans owned enormous spreads and hundreds of thousands of sheep. They contracted the care of the animals out to shepherds, near-penniless men who received a number of sheep in payment for their labor. Each shepherd tended a flock of about 2,000 animals, traveling and living with them from pasture to pasture, often assisted by a dog. On the larger ranches, the shepherd reported up to a multi-layered chain of command, consisting of vaqueros, caporals, the mayordomo, and the superintendent. Both the larger and smaller operations employed seasonal help at lambing time and shearing time. *

* Rupert Norval Richardson and Carl Coke Rister, *The Greater Southwest* (Glendale, CA, 1935), p. 374.

chopped up with a hatchet and stuffed into the intestines for sausage. Even the head and feet were boiled to extract bits of meat for sausage. Some saved the blood to make a blood pudding. The lard found numerous uses in frontier cookery. Doughnuts and crullers fried merrily in the freshest lard on hog-killing day to feed the helpers.

From the daily grind of establishing a frontier farm, multiplied many times, rose a patchwork of farmsteads and fields, crossed and re-crossed by roads, fences, and hedgerows. After only fifteen years of settlement, Mason County, Kentucky, on the bank of the Ohio River, contained some 1,200 farmsteads, each with about 10 acres cleared.[18] One inhabitant observed that he could no longer go a mile in any direction without coming upon a clearing of several acres, with a brush fence surrounding a one-story cabin. Every year, more land came under the plow. Frame, stone, or brick houses rose to replace log cabins, and log cabins were turned over to the livestock. The necessities of daily life – food, dishes, clothing – grew more varied and plentiful.

[1] Peter H. Burnett, 'Recollections and opinions of an old pioneer,' *Quarterly of the Oregon Historical Society*, V:2 (June 1904), pp. 151–2.

[2] John T. Schlebecker, *Whereby We Thrive: A History of American Farming, 1607–1972* (Ames, Iowa, 1975), p. 113.

[3] Fred Lockley, 'Reminiscences of Martha E. Gilliam Collins,' *Quarterly of the Oregon Historical Society*, XVII:4 (December 1916), p. 366.

[4] Percy W. Bidwell and John I. Falconer, *History of Agriculture in the Northern United States, 1620–1860* (Washington, 1925), pp. 215–16.

[5] Everett Dick, *The Sod-House Frontier, 1854–1890* (New York, 1937), pp. 293–4.

[6] 'Documents,' *Quarterly of the Oregon Historical Society*, III:4 (December 1902), p. 418.

[7] Ruth Cook Frajola, ed., 'They went west,' *South Dakota History*, VI:3 (Summer 1976), p. 294.

[8] Ruth Seymour Burmeister, ed., 'Jeffries letters,' *South Dakota History*, VI:3 (Summer 1976), p. 318.

[9] Robert F. Karolevitz, *Newspapering in the Old West*, (Seattle, 1965), p. 72.

[10] 'Jeffries letters,' p. 319.

[11] Bidwell, p. 113.

[12] Scott, Harvey W., 'Pioneer character of Oregon progress,' *Quarterly of the Oregon Historical Society*, XVIII:4 (December 1917), p. 248.

[13] Peter G. Boag, *Environment and Experience: Settlement Culture in Nineteenth-Century Oregon* (Los Angeles, 1992), pp. 110–11.

[14] Lockley, p. 367.

[15] Frajola, p. 300–1.

[16] Frajola, p. 295.

[17] William A. Bowen, *The Willamette Valley: Migration and Settlement on the Oregon Frontier* (Seattle, 1978), p. 74.

[18] Marion Tinling and Godfrey Davies, eds., *The Western Country in 1793: Reports on Kentucky and Virginia by Harry Toulmin* (San Marino, 1948), p. 76.

III

'FIXED UP VERY NICE'

Easterners and Europeans were accustomed to living in wood frame, brick, stucco, or stone homes. On the frontier these materials were either hard to come by or completely unavailable. They aspired to duplicate such structures as soon as possible. It often proved beyond their reach. In the open lands west of the Mississippi, the newly arrived settler had to go a long way to find timber, if he could find it at all. A Dakota Territory pioneer wrote his wife in 1861, 'I have found a small grove of Oak timber some 15 miles up the Vermillion river and can get plenty of oak from there in the spring and float them down. There is no person here knows of that timber.'[1] Even where wood was scarce, settlers preferred it and went to great effort and expense to build their homes of it. When railroads reached the frontier, those who could afford lumber imported it by rail. Less fortunate settlers, hurrying to put roofs over their heads and start farming, turned to sod houses, adobes, and dugouts as substitutes for log cabins.

Keturah Belknap moved with her husband and in-laws to Iowa in 1839, where they bought a crudely 'improved' 160-acre pre-emption claim from a squatter. This purchase did not give them legal ownership: it gave them only the first right to buy the land when the government eventually put it up for sale. The family worked hard to develop the farm, all the while saving money for the government land auction at some uncertain future date. Such transfers were a common frontier practice.

A sizeable house of roughly hewn logs in New Mexico. (National Archives)

58

The open land of the claim lay two miles from woodland, and the husband spent his days cutting and hauling trees for fence rails. They broke and fenced 20 acres of prairie the first year, and produced enough to make their living plus 20 dollars of profit. They grew corn and wheat, raised chickens, pigs, and sheep, and sold butter, eggs, meat, corn, flour, linen, and wool.

The younger Belknaps shared a two-room house with their elders for two years until they were able to build a 16 by 24-foot frame house with a stone chimney. The two men and a hired carpenter traveled four miles to a stand of oak from which they hewed lumber with a broadaxe. The husband made the shingles by hand over the course of many winter evenings. Finally, Mrs. Belknap could report, 'We have got fixed up very nice in our new home; have a good well close to the door; a nice little natural grove on the west...'[2] As prairie farmers, the Belknaps were fortunate in their relative proximity to woodland.

Adobe, or mud brick, construction predominated in the Spanish southwest. The craft of adobe-making, passed down over the centuries, was described by an army wife:

> 'They had wooden moulds just like a box with the top and bottom out. These they would lay on the ground, scoop up two or three double handfuls of the mud, and throw it in the mould, smooth it with their hands, then pull up the mould and put it in a new place, leaving the brick standing. The sun dried these adobes in a few days, and then they are ready for use. All the houses in this country are built of them, and when they have a roof that does not leak they will last for years and years. But usually the little one-story houses here have a flat roof made of logs filled in with mud, and this affords but a poor protection against the rain.'[3]

The adobe bricks received a finishing coat of earth-colored plaster, giving the houses a smooth appearance. Both Mexicans and Americans applied whitewash on the interior walls and hung cloth along the lower 6 feet of wall to protect their clothing from the whitewash. Planks finished the ceilings, and carpets covered the bare earth floors. For added insulation, a householder put down a layer of straw or sawdust under the carpet. Finally, a small fireplace built into a corner kept the house warm.

The first American families to settle New Mexico were town-dwelling traders or soldiers billeted in forts. Ranchers, eager to graze livestock on the territory's vast rangelands, soon followed. These Americans adopted adobe construction for many of their ranches and forts. Wood was scarce, and the thick adobe walls retained heat in the winter and coolness in the summer. However, by all accounts, the mud-chinked log roofs of these typically one-story structures leaked copiously whenever it rained, and plaster or mud fell from the ceilings. Too often, people awoke after a storm to find their beds surrounded by water. Over the course of years, the occupants added more dirt to the leaky roof, until it weighed tons and had to be supported by stout pillars. Wooden spouts placed at intervals around the roof were designed to carry off rainwater, but they were ineffective in heavy rain.

In regions with more plentiful trees, settlers in the southwest combined building techniques. A family of pioneers to southeastern Colorado in 1871 built a log house with a hand-hewn wooden door, and windows covered with flour sacks soaked in deer tallow. They plastered the entire interior, a practice they had picked up from their earlier life in New Mexico.

Families everywhere learned the same lesson that today's would-be renovators of old structures have learned: nothing substitutes for good construction practice in the original building. An army family in Texas received a two-room log house for their quarters, complete with a stone chimney, porch, and a detached kitchen. To outward appearances it seemed to promise a fine billet. However, the logs had been set vertically while still green. Over time they twisted and bent as they dried, making windows and doors impossible to hang properly, and opening the interior to the characteristically wretched, west-Texas weather. The gaps that developed also admitted the ubiquitous rodents and serpents. The splendid billet became a most disagreeable, unpleasant place to live and raise a family.

* * *

Like settlers in wooded areas across the continent, Oregon settlers built their cabins of round logs or logs hewed square. They took timber from the river bottoms, sawed the logs into boards, and built frame houses. The settlers whitewashed their houses, and the early missionaries made their own whitewash by burning clamshells to produce lime. Some purchased contrasting paint for the trim wood from the Hudson's Bay Company. Soon, white frame houses with picket fences were a common sight. Oregon settlers tried to reproduce the houses they had known back East: southern dogtrots rose alongside colonial two-story houses and New England saltboxes.

The first American family to erect a house in Oregon country, the Methodist missionaries Marcus and Narcissa Whitman, built a 30 by 36-foot mission house, one and a half stories tall, that imitated the New England saltbox. It was partitioned into several rooms, with a two-room lean-to attached, and was floored with wood. Split logs were fitted into grooved corner posts and chinked with mud. The roof of poles was covered with several inches of straw and sod, but it still leaked. Rock being hard to get in Oregon, the chimney was built of poles and mud like the 'cats and clay' chimneys of the older frontiers. The builders made adobe bricks for the foundation in order to economize on wood. Although the mud for making adobes was plentiful, it was no small feat to make sun-dried bricks in a rainy climate. Such a task doubtless had to wait for favorable weather.

Until they received their windows, sent from Fort Vancouver, the Whitmans hung blankets over the door and window openings. Mrs. Whitman herself installed the newly arrived panes of glass in their frames. Wooden shutters completed the house. In contrast, the Spaldings, another

A commodious sod house. Perhaps the small outbuilding was the original house. Notice how four garments came from a single bolt of cloth. (National Archives)

family of missionaries who had come west with the Whitmans, built their mission house in an area of more plentiful wood. Their 32 by 22-foot cabin was entirely of wood, and boasted a much more watertight roof of cedar shingles. The Whitmans, intending to establish a major mission, dug a millrace, built a gristmill, and added a full complement of farmstead dependencies, including a smokehouse, barns, corrals, workshops, and storehouses. They also built a church and a school-house where they ministered to the Indians' spiritual development.

Not every home builder possessed talent equal to his ambition:

> Father built his first cabin on the point of a ridge a hundred and fifty feet above the valley. He said that in the river bottom where we lived in Missouri we had chills and fever. He wanted to build where we could get plenty of fresh air. In this he was not disappointed, for the sea breeze kept the boards on the roof rattling all through the autumn season, and the first storm of winter blew the roof off.'[4]

The family had to camp out for some weeks while a new and sounder roof was put on.

The passage of time did not bring improvement in housing conditions for everyone. A new-lywed Oregon couple in 1854 started out on a purchased homestead. It consisted of 12 fenced acres and a 12 by 14-foot unchinked and windowless log cabin with a dirt floor. Poles secured the hand-made shakes in place on the roof. Their homestead also boasted one shed, a calf pen, and a corral.

Although timber was plentiful in the Oregon country during the first decade of settlement, sawn lumber was not. Accordingly, most settlers built one-room cabins of unhewed fir logs, just as their Kentucky forebears had done. The cabins had puncheon floors and cedar shake roofs. The land of Oregon yielded up its abundance willingly, but its pioneers had to make do without many of the manufactured goods of the east. Like many other construction needs, nails were very hard to come by in early Oregon. By necessity, the first settlers became adept at mortise and tenon joints.

* * *

New arrivals in Dakota Territory in the 1870s lived in tents or in their wagons until they could build a sod house or a wood shanty of pine and tar paper. The only lumber required for a sod house was for window and door frames and the roof. So alien was the sod house to most settlers that they hoped to acquire the lumber to build a frame house as soon as possible and relegate their living quarters to the livestock. Indeed, from the beginning, sod served for barns, outbuildings, and walls around fields. Like adobe, the thick sod walls retained heat or coolness, providing a comfortable interior temperature, but they were always damp and often downright wet. Sod houses had other disadvantages as well. Their roofs leaked, the occupants were plagued by loose dirt falling into the interior, and the ubiquitous insects and rodents burrowed through the walls at will to take up residence with their new neighbors.

A builder of a sod house first hitched up the team to the breaking plow to turn up strips of sod about 3 inches thick and a foot wide. He then cut the strips into 3-foot sections and laid out the walls a row at a time, with staggered joints packed with loose dirt. Forked willow poles held up the ridge pole for the roof. Anything from brush and sod to lumber and tar paper was laid over the rafters. Sod roofs, when rain-soaked, became extremely heavy and sometimes collapsed. Provident builders erected interior pillars to support the roof, but such pillars took up valuable living space. Aside from interior temperature moderation, sod had the major advantage of being wind- and fire-proof, no small thing on the prairie. After six or seven years, however, some houses subsided back into the ground from which they had sprung.

Far easier than cutting and stacking sod, one could take up a shovel and dig a room into the side of a hill. This enterprise yielded a dugout, with three earth walls and a wood or sod front wall. Dugouts admitted water through the three earth walls during rains. The occupants countered this

An entire farmstead built of sod in Dakota territory, 1885. (US Library of Congress)

by digging drainage ditches around their floors. Like sod houses, dugouts had few windows, which made for a dark and gloomy interior. Starting one's new life in a dark, damp, cavelike hole in the ground, with a leaky roof, must have been discouraging indeed.

Like householders everywhere, settlers tried to brighten up their earthen houses with decorative touches or furnishings brought from their former homes. Sod house and dugout interior walls sported whitewash, and often a cloth covering to try to keep loose dirt at bay. Other householders used wallpaper made of newspapers, or plaster made of clay and ashes. Some people hung sheets across the ceiling to catch falling dirt; these had to be taken down and shaken regularly. By 1882, one family of Norwegian immigrants was well on its way to success, as the mother reported:

'Oh, well! if one isn't too spoiled perhaps it can pass, although without a doubt the interior is much more inviting than the exterior. The house...is built of sod and for safety as well as warmth, it is dug quite deep so the floor lies...below the ground level and the windows are at ground level.

'As a result the roof begins not far above the ground, so we must go down 4 steps to enter into our palace. The interior is like a fairy palace. We have first a kitchen, which is also Christian's bedroom, our dining room and usually our sitting room.'[5]

This underground 'palace' also featured draperies, wallpaper, afghans, books, and embroidery.

The fortunate few prairie dwellers who lived near river bottoms hauled cottonwood and willow to their claims to build log houses. Cottonwood, however, tended to warp, which opened up great gaps in the walls. The occupants deployed tar paper, wallpaper, and blankets in the attempt to keep out the constant wind. A wood and tar paper shanty did not have to be as flimsy as it sounds:

'Have a good warm Shanty...my floor is double thickness the sides are double also with a thickness of tar paper between the boards. The roof is one thickness of lumber,

sheets of tar paper and one thickness of Sod on over the paper...I do not suffer with the cold while indoores.'[6]

FURNISHING THE PIONEER HOME

Wood suitable for making fine furniture – cherry, maple, walnut, and poplar – abounded in the forests east of the Mississippi, but for most early pioneers, anything would do. A simple platform attached to the wall and supported by wooden props fastened to the floor served as a bed. Bedding consisted of bear or buffalo skins, or feather beds brought from home or made on site. People filled their feather beds by plucking the household geese every couple of months, or by killing a wild goose. They considered chicken feathers to be inferior. Corn shucks and prairie grass also found their way into mattress stuffings. An especially creative – and desperate – pioneer in 1856, 'went down to the marshy land and gathered a load of cattails, which I stripped and made me a good bed and pillows. They were as soft as feathers.'[7]

Most households owned bed sheets, blankets, and handmade quilts, but not everybody saw sheets as necessary. A traveler in New Mexico in the 1850s reported that his innkeeper made the tablecloth do double duty as the bed sheet for his guest. Each morning the sheet was taken off the bed and put directly on the table, and then moved from table to bed at night, without a break for washing.

A large split log with four legs served as a long and narrow table; the benches were just smaller versions of the table. People sat on three-legged stools or hickory-framed chairs with deerskin seats. The table, made as it was from a single piece of wood, was called a 'board,' so that board became another word for meals, as in 'room and board.'

A spacious log ranch house in southern Dakota Territory, 1888. Even today, such a house would attract buyers. At center is a days-old colt. (Library of Congress)

*Inside an early pioneer cabin. Sparse furn-
ishings, a few possessions hanging from
walls and ceiling, and the lady of the house
smoking a pipe were all common sights on
the frontier's leading edge. (In Reverend
Hamilton W. Pierson,* **In the Brush: Old Time
Social, Political, and Religious Life in the
Southwest,** *New York, 1881)*

As the household grew more affluent, the farmer turned his hand to making the home more comfortable by building dressers, chests, and cupboards. Until then, people stored their belongings on the pegs and shelves that lined the walls. They drove wooden pegs into the gaps between the logs, or hung up antlers to hold clothing, drying meat, or rifles. Even the most solitude-loving hunter was likely to have a fiddle hanging on his cabin wall. Fiddle strings were commonly made of catgut, a term that referred to dried and twisted pieces of intestine, usually from sheep, but sometimes from other animals. One pioneer made his fiddle strings from raccoon gut.

The missionary families who settled Oregon in 1836 relied on handmade furniture just like the early Kentucky pioneers did. As new arrivals, they sawed green cottonwood by hand for their furniture. Their beds consisted of platforms attached to the wall and propped by two legs, their bedding of corn shucks or dried grass covered by blankets. They made chairs with woven deerskin seats. During ten years at the mission, they accumulated – by handicraft or purchase – settees, rockers, tables, washstands, clothes presses, bookcases, looking glasses, spinning wheels, and feather beds. For many years, they did all cooking over the open fire, until long-awaited cookstoves arrived from the east. Many emigrants to Oregon attempted to bring furniture with them overland, but they either lost it in river crossings or abandoned it on the trail when forced to lighten their wagon loads.

Families of soldiers stationed at the remote forts of the southwest resorted to makeshift constructions for the goods they could not bring with them. The wife of the commanding officer at Fort Union asked the quartermaster to build her some pine shelves for her adobe quarters. She used crates for furniture and blankets for curtains, yet she was able to have a melodeon shipped to her at Fort Seldon two years later in 1869. Before her family headed back east, she sold it to a Protestant church. Army households returning east commonly auctioned off their large furnishings, including such items as cookstoves and sewing machines. They commanded high prices because goods were so scarce at the frontier forts.

Dakota settlers relied on the railways to bring some pieces of furniture to their homesteads, and used handmade and makeshift to fill in the gaps. One family sat on packing crates or benches to eat. Another household assembled a pair of cane-seated chairs, one rocker, and the bed to sit on at meal times. A piano or melodeon, a decorative hanging lamp, a handmade table, a cupboard, and an alcove with built-in shelves complemented the more fortunate homes. Wallpaper, braided rag rugs, curtains, potted geraniums, and decorative touches such as cushions or pictures adorned

FOUR FRONTIER HOUSEHOLDS

William Clinkenbeard and his wife arrived in Kentucky in 1782 possessing little more than a knife and a cooking pot. They felt wealthy when they could afford to purchase some wooden trenchers to grace their table.

Bethenia Owens, an Oregon bride of fourteen, wed in 1854. Her hard-working parents had started out in the territory with little to their names, but they prospered, and gave her a dowry of goods and livestock. The prospective bride herself sewed quilts, muslin sheets and pillowcases, tablecloths and towels, and calico dresses in preparation for her married life. Her dowry included two cows, a calf, wagon and harness, and mare and saddle. These she took to her husband's newly purchased homestead, where stood a 12 by 14 foot cabin with a dirt floor. The bed platform in the corner, fastened to the walls and supported by one leg, waited to receive her new feather bed. Three shelves accommodated the tin dishes, two-tined forks, German silver spoons, pot, tea kettle, coffee pot, frying pan, and iron bake oven. A butter churn, milk pans, wash tub and board, and water bucket and dipper completed the bride's housekeeping supplies. From these beginnings, Owens went on to become a pioneer in medicine. She trained and practiced as a doctor and put her son through medical school as well.

Only three years later, an American widow established a boarding house from a rented adobe in Albuquerque. Mrs. Sloan fed her boarders at a long homemade table covered with oilcloth. She set the table with a tin set of salt and pepper shakers, heavy crockery plates and cups, and bone-handled steel utensils. The dirt floors sported mats or rugs, in contrast to the skins of the backwoods. Had the widow been more affluent, she could have owned waffle irons and bed curtains, all brought in by the Santa Fe trade. More than a decade later, after the Civil War, the struggling widow's daughter possessed an impeccably curtained four-poster bed her husband had made on a turning lathe, as well as velvet settees, a claw-footed table, a cookstove, and fancy shaded oil lamps imported from Kansas. But like pioneers of the backwoods, the members of her family kept their rifles on a deer-antler rack over the door.

In 1884, Wilburn Wallace Jeffries left his family behind in the relative ease of Wisconsin to get established on a South Dakota homestead. He began his new household in a tar paper shack with almost as little as a Kentucky pioneer of a hundred years earlier. He possessed a bed and a stove, but his cookware was limited to a frying pan, a tea kettle, and a coffee pot. He owned, in addition three plates, a cup and saucer, an eight-quart tin pail, and a few knives and forks.

even the more modest sod houses.

All frontier householders faced the Herculean labor of keeping their homes clean. Dust blowing through chinks between logs, or dirt falling from sod house walls rendered this challenge nearly insurmountable. The sole weapon in the war on dirt was a rough homemade broom. One made a broom by peeling the last few inches at the end of a hickory sapling – or hazel in Oregon – into thin strips. Since the strips tended to curl, they were bound straight with a strip of buckskin. A broom made from home-grown broom corn was a luxurious alternative, much more flexible than a sapling broom. The homemaker made scrub brushes in a similar manner by peeling back strips from a smaller piece of wood.

HOME FIRES

The constant use of wood fires for a host of household activities – laundry, cooking, maple sugaring, soap making, whiskey distilling – soon turned the forests of the frontier into a patchwork of open fields. A single household used 15 to 20 cords of wood every year – the timber from about three-quarters of an acre. A cord of wood consists of a pile 8 feet wide, 4 feet deep, and 4 feet tall. Today, as wood-burning stoves for home heating grow in popularity, a household in frigid Maine uses at least three cords of wood per heating season. A mid-Atlantic household, one in Virginia for example, uses half that much. Bear in mind that today's houses are larger but more airtight than pioneers' cabins.

Settlers' fires burned year-round for cooking: therefore, the chimney required regular cleaning. A homemade brush was the usual cleaning implement, but an extra-tall chimney was sometimes cleaned by dropping a live chicken down it. The bird's fluttering wings knocked down the soot deposits. Another effect of the need for a year-round cooking fire was that the house grew too hot in the summer. As a result, a detached 'summer kitchen' became a popular addition to the farmstead.

Kentucky pioneers cut 4- or 5-foot logs as needed to fit the wide fireplaces. Children were often put in charge of gathering and cutting kindling. As the Indian threat subsided, some settlers built labor-saving horse doors for their cabins. Located at either end of the cabin, the doors allowed a horse to drag in a long log for the wall-width fireplace. The horse marched in, the people rolled the log into the fire, and the horse continued out the opposite door.

Because wood remained plentiful even twenty years after initial settlement, coal did not find favor except among tradesmen, such as blacksmiths, who needed to generate high temperatures. Early map makers made note of coal deposits in trans-Appalachia, but these deposits were not widely mined commercially until the early 1800s. Coal, mined in Kansas, was burned on the prairie frontier only by the few who could afford it.

The prairie country and the arid southwest were not so generous with firewood. New Mexico settlers burned mesquite, cedar, and piñon in their fireplaces. Such softwoods are inferior to hardwoods as fuel, but at least they were wood. Buffalo chips or cow chips – the popular description of dried manure – were a primary fuel source on the prairies. Pioneers remembered gathering them as children each autumn and storing them in a shed. One recalled, 'I would stand back and kick them, then reach down and gather them carefully, for under them lived big spiders and centipedes.'[8] A Dakota woman supplemented her farm's income by making and selling gunny-sack aprons for gathering buffalo chips. Dried manure, sometimes called 'Dakota soft coal,' inspired a song among the settlers who 'mined' it:

> 'Our fuel is of the cheapest kind,   With bag in hand and upturned nose,
> Our women are all of one mind,   They gather chips of the buffaloes.'[9]

Prairie dwellers also burned twists of grass and straw for heat. The twists were known as 'cats,' and families spent long hours making them. As they became accustomed to these fuels, they spoke highly of their efficiency. Burning hay provided a hot and steady fire, but one that required constant feeding and attention. Because it was so highly flammable, stacks of hay waiting for the fire could ignite from a spark whenever anyone opened the stove to tend the fire. Inventors developed a variety of hay-burning stoves for use on the prairie. These stoves employed metal drums or tubes that the user stuffed with hay and positioned atop the coals like a chimney. One Dakota homesteader had burned so much of his hay to keep warm that, by March, he began to fear having to 'either freeze or let the horses starve.' He decided instead to knock down a precious wooden outbuilding to heat his house.[10] Corn stalks or corncobs, with or without the corn, provided an alternative fuel for the settler who had managed to raise a first crop. Some prairie dwellers tried raising fields of sunflowers so they could burn the stalks.

The pioneer home was typically a dark place. Few people were as fortunate as one Oregon woman who traded with some Indians who had found a whale washed up on shore. She received enough whale oil to illuminate her cabin for the entire winter. In addition to heat, cooking, and home manufactures, the hearth fire served as the main source of evening light in the frontier cabin. Additional light came from oil lamps, tallow candles set in tin saucers, or torches. Hickory or pitch-pine torches were often necessary for finding one's way outdoors at night. Prairie pioneers set out lanterns on tall posts to guide people home in the dark.

When a pioneer killed a deer, his wife brought out the candle molds to make candles of the tallow. On candle-making day, an industrious woman made perhaps twenty dozen candles at a time. Those who did not own molds made candles by dipping the wicks and allowing each layer to harden between dippings. In the absence of buffalo or deer, cattle provided the tallow. When pioneers were so poor that they owned neither lamp nor candle, they resorted to a twisted rag set in a puddle of grease on a tin dish. 'When we could get grease for a light, we put a button in a rag and braided the top, setting the button in the grease, after dipping the braided part in the grease.'[11]

Kerosene lanterns came into use by 1870. They gave better-quality light than candles, but required constant cleaning. Kerosene was yet another item that late nineteenth-century pioneers had to purchase rather than make for themselves. It was first distilled from coal tar in the 1850s, and later was made from petroleum.

Pioneers living in narrow circumstances economized on everything, even matches, which seem like such a basic necessity today. Matches began to see general use in the 1830s, but few could afford them. In a world without matches, one kept a fire alive at all times, banking it back overnight, so that there would be coals to restart the fire in the morning. Lacking live coals, one set out for the neighbor's, metal pot in hand, to 'borrow fire.'

WATER BY THE BUCKET

The value of a farmstead rose with its proximity to water. The earliest arrivals in every frontier territory took up the land nearest water. Not every farmstead boasted year-round supply: many sources ran dry each summer. More typically, a family started out with only a wet weather surface spring or a hand-dug shallow well – 20 to 30 feet deep – that dried up for the summer, and sometimes for good. Abandoned open wells dotted the countryside. Come summer, the family went a half-mile or more to a year-round spring, pond, or stream. They hauled water in a bucket balanced on the head or in whiskey barrels carried on a wagon or logging sled. Watering the livestock grew difficult in late summer.

People visited ponds in warm weather to bathe, and gathered there for outdoor wash days. They usually hauled their clothes to the water rather than the reverse. Those who carried wash water home re-used it to clean their floors or water their gardens, getting the maximum return possible for their labor. Every cabin had barrels to collect rain from the roof. When the homesteader found time to make improvements, he dug a cistern to store the roof runoff.

Across the Mississippi, settlers often found river water muddy and well water brackish. Geology rendered even deep wells brackish in some locales. Most settlers preferred rain water for their drinking water supply, although even that gave out in dry climates. If they had to resort to river water, they waited for the mud to settle out. Many farmers dug a small pond to catch springtime runoff, but pond water tended to be silt-laden and to teem with mosquito larvae. It had to be boiled or strained before use.

The only reliable, year-round water supply lay deep beneath the ground, and its pursuit remained a struggle throughout the frontier years. One homesteader counted himself fortunate because his 'water stick' had told him of a vein of water only 50 feet from his house. Whether he actually found water here is lost to history.

Mechanical methods existed for drilling wells, but few could pay for them. Therefore, settlers dug wells of 100, 200, or even 300 feet by hand, using pick and shovel. An assistant pulled up the loads of loose dirt and rock with a bucket on a rope. Only one person could fit into the well shaft to work on it. Some perished from heavier-than-air gases, known as the 'damp,' as they worked their way deeper. From these fatalities, people learned to start each work session by lowering a bundle of hay into the hole and churning the air to dissipate the gas. Well-diggers also secured a rope around the worker's waist, kept watch over him, and pulled him up if he lost consciousness. Cave-ins presented yet another danger.

The father of young John Muir, future naturalist, set him to work on the Wisconsin frontier hand-chiseling a deep well. The boy's smaller size was enough to qualify him for the job in his

In the arid southwest farmers and ranchers relied on windmills to bring up water from deep wells. A windmill-powered pump raised a few gallons a minute, enough for household use and watering the livestock, but not enough for crop irrigation. (Arizona Historical Society)

father's eyes. Tethered to the surface with a rope around his waist, John spent every day for several months chipping away at sandstone, which was hauled up in a bucket, until the well reached 90 feet deep. One day, he nearly passed out from trapped carbonic acid gases deep in the shaft and was pulled out just in time. Only then did his father learn from neighbors how to combat the 'deadly choke-damp.' Young Muir continued the daily grind from dawn to dusk, hauled up from the shaft only at lunchtime. Years later, his resentment found expression: 'Father never spent an hour in that well. He trusted me to sink it straight and plumb, and I did.'[12]

The earliest mechanical drill used on the frontier, a hand- or horse-powered sweep drill, featured a long pole to turn the bit. Another early drill possessed a long flexible wooden pole fixed to the ground at one end, with a drill bit on the free end. The pole rested on a fulcrum, a forked stake pounded into the ground. One or two men forced the free end of the pole up into the air and then let it snap back down. Other methods included pointed pipes driven into the ground, with lengths of pipe added until they struck water, or a post-hole auger with shaft extenders. Such drills, with bits at the end of long shafts, could not penetrate the earth more than about 50 feet before the shaft grew liable to bend or break. Heavy pieces of lumber or hollow logs, preferably from gum trees, served as early well casings to prevent the walls from collapsing. The worker used clay to chink the joints between the pieces of casing.

Most households drew up the water with a hand-cranked windlass and a wooden bucket, the sole means of doing so until hand pumps became available. Settlers of more arid regions such as the Great Plains and the southwest needed very deep wells to reach water. They still had to dig by hand. However, finding that the prairie's constant winds offered an ideal power source, by the mid-nineteenth century settlers erected windmills to pump the water to the surface. At first only cattle barons could afford them, but mass production brought down the price, and they became widespread by the 1880s.

AT THE FRONTIER TABLE

Until the first crop came in, emigrants either ate the supplies they had carried west, purchased food from neighbors and merchants, or hunted wild game. Pioneers wise in woodland lore had greater success at finding wild nuts and fruits or tracking animals. Walnuts, pecans, hickory nuts, berries, plums, persimmons, crabapples, and grapes all awaited gathering from the woods, and pioneers considered them a treat. They also knew the uses of edible wild greens such as pokeweed. Cooks boiled the greens and then fried them with bacon. A 1782 group of Kentucky women, lacking knowledge about wild greens, followed the cows to see which ones they ate. At best, the gathering of wild edibles could supplement the pioneer diet. To live, the first settlers had to hunt.

During Kentucky's early years, wild game was plentiful. A pioneer arriving in 1785 reported, 'We had then a house to build & ground to clear to raise corn, & all the meat we used to procure by hunting as there was none to purchase. From the first of April to the end of the year I had killed sixty Buffaloe beside deer, bear, elk & turkees.'[13] This tally, which should have yielded a prodigious amount of meat, indicates that the hunter was extremely wasteful.

As late as 1765, hunters from North Carolina and Virginia who had trekked to Kentucky reported seeing great herds of buffalo. Yet everywhere east of the Mississippi white men exterminated them rapidly. Often they merely took the buffalo tongue and left the rest to rot. William Clinkenbeard arrived in Kentucky in 1782 when buffalo were still somewhat plentiful. Having shot a buffalo cow, he kept the calf and tried to raise it. It soon grew ornery, and the women of the station became afraid to go out and milk their cows because they feared the beast. Likewise, attempts to breed domestic cows to buffalo failed because the cows could not deliver the large-humped offspring. The last reported buffalo sightings in Kentucky occurred in the early 1800s. Elk and bear had also been common in Kentucky and frequented the salt springs in the area. Only a few years of settlement served to kill most of them off and drive the survivors westward. Hunters reported seeing the last elk in the region during the 1820s.

Buffalo disappeared from the eastern portion of South Dakota by the 1850s. The 1870s saw the last of them in the western part of the territory. Americans had deliberately hunted them to extinction, taking only their skins and leaving the carcasses to rot, in order to demoralize and control the Indians whose way of life depended on buffalo. In addition, ranching interests on the plains did not want the buffalo to compete with their cattle for forage.

Hunting secured survival when all else failed, until an area became too settled and the game got hunted out. Survival then might depend on knowing such lore as how to shoot several roosting grouse before the flock took off. One aimed first for the bird on the lowest branch, so that it would drop without startling the others perched higher up; then a skilled shot could bag another. In open country, prairie chickens abounded and graced many a table. These birds actually seemed to profit

Buffalo saved early pioneers from starvation and supported the Plains Indian way of life. When pioneers no longer needed the buffalo, white men deliberately hunted them to near extinction to make way for cattle and to demoralize the tribes. (Arizona Historical Society)

THREE GUNS THAT OPENED THE AMERICAN WEST

Few pioneers could expect to survive in their new lives without a firearm. They required a rifle that was both easy to carry and fire and accurate enough to drop animal or human targets at ranges of 200 yards or closer. The rifle needed an uncomplicated mechanism so it could be repaired by the owner in the wilderness. Since the frontiersman had to carry his powder and lead a considerable distance, the rifle had to fire economically. German and Swiss gunsmiths in Lancaster, Pennsylvania designed a weapon to meet these requirements, a weapon that became known as the Kentucky rifle. These were hand-crafted weapons, no two rifles exactly alike. Firearms of this era utilized a flintlock mechanism. Squeezing the trigger caused a lump of flint, held securely in a metal jaw, to contact a steel plate. This produced a spark that ignited a propellent charge, sending the bullet on its way.

A long-barreled Kentucky rifle hangs over the cabin door, so it would be quick at hand whenever the frontiersman went out. (Author photo, reconstructed nineteenth-century frontier home, Museum of American Frontier Culture, Staunton, Virginia)

The rifle had a smaller bore than a musket and thus its bullet used less lead. Its 36 to 42-inch-long rifled barrel, with caliber ranging from .32 to .6 of an inch, imparted a spin to the projectile, making it fly truer than a smoothbore projectile. Weighing only about 10 pounds, it was not too heavy a burden to carry. The weapon's drawback was its relatively slow rate of fire. As was the case with all the era's flintlock weapons, the rifle had to be reloaded after each discharge by ramming a new round down the muzzle. A frontiersman had to make his shot count because in most situations he would not get a second chance. Until about 1830, the Kentucky rifle was the weapon of choice on the frontier for both hunting and defense.

People made their own bullets with lead and bullet molds, and they could not fire indiscriminately. One of the earliest Kentucky settlers of 1779 recalled, 'We were saving of lead. I shot a buffalo, got the bullet and then shot a deer, after chewing the bullet round.' * Shot bag, powder horn, and wiping tow completed the outfit required by the rifleman. Often settlers purchased a rifle's components – the barrel, lock, and stock – for home assembly. The modern expression, 'lock, stock, and barrel', derives from the time the pioneer assembled his own rifle.

from settlement. Their population grew as they gleaned grain from farmers' fields. Squirrels and rabbits, too, remained abundant despite farmers' efforts to eradicate them.

Deer, turkey, wild geese, pigeons, and ducks also provided a good deal of food for frontiersmen. But sometimes it was impossible to find game. An Oregon pioneer relates, 'For the first two years after our arrival in Oregon we were frequently without meat for weeks at a time, and sometimes without bread, and occasionally without bread and meat at the same time. On these occasions if we had milk, butter, and potatoes, we were well content.'[14] The fact that even bread was unavailable in a territory where wheat grew abundantly gives insight into early pioneer condi-

In the early 1830s, a New England Yankee named Samuel Colt patented an invention that was to revolution-ize frontier warfare. He made the first practical revolving gun, featuring automatic revolution and locking cylinder, with the entire mechanism operated by cocking the hammer. News of Colt's six-shot, 'patent revolv-ing pistol' spread across the land. Immediately orders to Colt's factory came from Texas, where American set-tlers appreciated that a repeating hand gun could make an individual the equal of a squad of Mexican soldiers armed with single-shot muskets. The success and fame enjoyed by the Texas Rangers led to the widespread dispersion of the Colt revolver throughout the western frontier. A young doctor in the 1870s reported that he was never without his Colt revolver. In the towns of New Mexico he needed it for defense, not against Indi-ans, but in public places where lawless, belligerent white men challenged one another on thin pretext. Over time, Colt improved his design, first with percussion caps and then cartridge pistols. His 1872 model, the so-called Peacemaker, was the king of its class, the best-known revolver on the western frontier.

Just as the name Colt became synonymous with revolver, so the name Winchester became a generic term for car-tridge rifles. The Civil War had proven the utility of breech-loading, repeating rifles. Throughout the Old West hunters, trappers, miners, cowboys, outlaws and sheriffs alike coveted these weapons. Oliver Winchester and his associates created the New Haven Arms Company to meet the demand. Like the Colt, the Winchester changed the nature of Indian warfare. Until its introduction, the typical Indian tactic was to draw the fire of the white man's single-shot rifles and then charge before the rifles could be reloaded. These tactics failed against the Winchester repeating rifles. The Winchester Model 73 was said to have killed more Indians, and more U.S. regulars once the Indians got hold of them, than any other weapon. Buffalo Bill Cody proclaimed it the best gun he ever used.

* John D. Shane, 'Interview with pioneer William Clinkenbeard,' *Filson Club History Quarterly*, II:3 (April 1928), p. 104.

tions. Turkey breast slices substituted for bread in some homes. When all else failed, Oregon pio-neers ate horses, and southern pioneers ate alligators.

Hungry for sweets and lacking an easy or cheap source of sugar, pioneers again turned to the wild. They searched for bee colonies from which they took wild honey. The bee-hunter waited by a patch of flowers or devised a lure by burning a bit of honeycomb. He then followed the bees as they made a 'beeline' to their colony, chopped down the tree, and helped himself to the coveted honey. Europeans had imported honeybees to the New World, and the first settlers carried the bees to Ken-tucky during the 1780s. The bees escaped, multiplied, and spread westward just ahead of white set-tlement. In the late 1830s, a Santa Fe trader observed them as far west as western Kansas. Settlers coming to Oregon in the 1840s found they had arrived ahead of the bees, so had to do without honey.

* * *

Settlers spent the first planting season clearing land and sowing Indian corn and a few garden veg-etables. The earliest Kentucky settlers lived in forted stations and grew corn in common fields. Each station family had a garden allotment outside the walls, which they worked at peril of Indian attack. Nevertheless, everything the pioneers knew about growing and using corn, they had learned from the Indians.

Indian corn, also known as field corn, stored well and was fed to livestock or ground into meal for bread. Settlers roasted and ate the first ears of summer on the cob, and ground the more mature corn after the kernels hardened. Cornmeal went into the making of bread and cakes. Peo-ple ate cornmeal mush with milk for breakfast. Hominy, kernels with the hulls removed, provided food in a more solid form. Children carried cornbread and molasses to school for lunch. Cooks served all of these corn dishes in many variations, with bacon drippings, meat, milk, syrup, or eggs. Pioneers gave them such names as 'hasty pudding' and 'johnny cake.' Cornmeal, water, and salt made up hoe cake or cornpone. For more complex baked goods, one substituted a pinch of lye for baking soda. The unrelieved diet of corn caused people to crave seasoning. Since typically there were few herbs or spices, they turned to whiskey to flavor many meals, including breakfast! The whiskey, in turn, was distilled from the ubiquitous corn.

Farmers either milled their corn at home or hauled it to a commercial mill. Some carried small millstones through the Wilderness to Kentucky. These stones, used in hand-cranked mills, weighed about 30 pounds and were hewn from limestone. At many homes, a child did the hand-grinding with a 'hominy block.' A wood block, approximately 3 feet high, with a hollow burnt into it, formed the mortar, and an iron log-splitting wedge set in a wooden handle served as the pestle. One then separated the hulls from the meal with a sieve. A typical frontier sieve consisted of a perforated piece of deerskin stretched over a hoop. So highly did frontier cooks value them that some paid to have them repaired. A Kentucky woman who skillfully repaired her neighbors' sieves with horsehair earned enough in hemp seed to grow 200 pounds of this most useful crop.

Horse- or water-powered mills, few and far between, were always busy. Furthermore, the mill streams tended to dry up in late summer. The pioneer farmer expected to haul corn and wheat at least ten miles to the nearest mill and return for it hours or days later. The miller kept a portion of the grain as payment. Milled wheat produced several grades of flour: only the whitest and finest was actually called flour. 'Middlings' and 'shorts' were lower grades, suitable for livestock. As with corn, if the gristmill was too far away, settlers found a means of milling wheat at home. The job of running the wheat through a coffee mill provided a hard-working child with many hours of tedium.

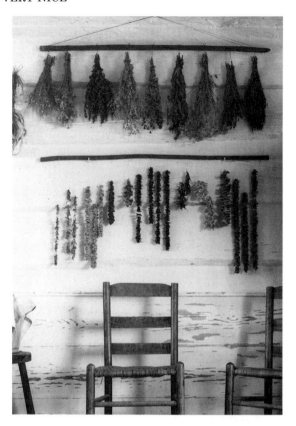

Strings of dried fruits, vegetables, and herbs hang in a reconstructed nineteenth-century farm home at the Museum of American Frontier Culture, Staunton, Virginia. Drying was the principal way of preserving fresh produce. Rehydrated fruits and vegetables kept scurvy at bay and provided badly needed meal-time variety.
(Author photo)

The pioneer vegetable patch yielded a full complement of garden vegetables: potatoes, cabbages, beets, beans, peas, tomatoes, cucumbers, and especially melons and turnips, which grew extremely well in the newly cleared soil. Sweet potatoes, easy to grow, became another staple of the pioneer diet. The cook preserved the summer's vegetables for winter consumption by air-drying them. The new process of canning in glass or ceramic jars, an early nineteenth-century French invention, had not yet made its way to the American frontier. Strings of cut and dried vegetables, as well as peaches and apples, festooned the cabin walls. The cook soaked them in water when the time came to eat them. Cooks preserved some vegetables by pickling them in brine. They then rinsed off the salt to make the food palatable.

Pioneers salted down the year's meat supply in barrels. Salt was essential to food preservation because it prevented mold and other organisms from developing. Another common method of preserving meat was to dry it slowly on a rack over a fire. The resulting product was known as 'jerk' or 'jerky.' Lacking refrigeration, one even salted butter.

Cabbage and potatoes could keep in a cellar for several months. During a frigid Dakota winter, one homesteader who lacked a cellar protected the potatoes from freezing by wrapping them in a horse blanket and storing them inside a haystack. As of late April, he was still unable to plant the early crops – onions and turnips – in his vegetable garden because it was too cold. In contrast, those living in a milder climate, like that of the mid-Atlantic region, planted the first vegetable seeds by late February or early March.

Emigrant women did most trailside cooking over an open fire, but some people hauled small sheet-metal stoves in their wagons. Frequently unscrupulous outfitters sold shoddy merchandise to ignorant emigrants. These unfortunate people found out too late that most stoves were flimsy and often fell apart. Abandoned cooking equipment littered the overland trails. Even with adequate equipment, outdoor cooking imposed severe limitations, as poor fuel and high winds sometimes made it impossible to generate enough heat.

Once they reached their new homes, women did all cooking over the open hearth, in a kettle hung over the flames, a frying pan, or a Dutch oven set on the coals. The pioneer baked pies, bread, or hard biscuit in the Dutch oven, a three-legged covered pot. She first warmed the lid of the oven in the coals to distribute the heat more evenly. The small size of the baking kettle and the difficulty of getting the coals hot enough made baking a particularly slow process. A cheerful pioneer woman recalls, 'A Dutch oven, a three legged skillet, a crane and kettle over good oak coals could broil grouse or venison, roast potatoes, boil wheat, brown hominy, bake salt rising and gin-

RECIPES

WHISKEY: Makes five gallons of 110-proof *
Add two bushels of coarsely ground corn to a fifty-gallon barrel of water, stir out the lumps, and allow the mash to ferment. The water must not have a trace of iron or sulphur; iron turns the brew black. Boil the mash in the still, stirring to avoid scorching the mash, until the water and alcohol boil off and condense in another container. A second distilling yields higher alcohol content. Test the alcohol content by dropping tallow into it; if the tallow sinks, the whiskey is strong enough. Feed the cooked mash to the hogs.

The home still consisted of a copper pot with a rounded covering, or bonnet. From the center of the bonnet rose the 'worm,' at first a pipe made of tin or wood leading to a cooling tub. Later, a coil of copper tubing linked the two parts.

PEACH BRANDY: One gallon
Place seven bushels of whole peaches in a large vat. Allow to rot. Press out juice and distill.

VINEGAR
Add three gallons molasses and a small amount of yeast to a barrel of rainwater. **

* Harriette Simpson Arnow, *Flowering of the Cumberland* (Lexington, KY, 1984), pp. 272–6.
** Everett Dick, *The Sod-House Frontier, 1854–1890* (New York, 1937), p. 87.

Open hearth cooking. On the left is a baking kettle set in hot coals. The cook also placed hot coals on the kettle's lid, which has a raised edge to hold them. (Author photo, reconstructed mid-nineteenth-century farm kitchen, Museum of American Frontier Culture, Staunton, Virginia)

Left: Early cookware. The legs held the vessels above the coals of an open fire. On the left is the Dutch oven, or baking kettle. (National Archives)

Right: The cookstove, coveted by pioneer women, represented a great advance over the baking kettle. This one graces a southwestern home in the late 1800s. (Arizona Historical Society)

gerbread, what more could one desire?'[15] Apparently vegetables and fruits had a very limited dietary role! Eastern cooks began acquiring cookstoves in the 1830s, but decades passed before westerners could afford to import them. The pioneer cook countered the lack of kitchen implements by creating her own out of the available materials. If she needed a grater, she punched holes in an old tin pan. In a pinch, an empty medicine bottle did quite nicely as a rolling pin. Mechanical aptitude and imagination dictated what the frontier woman could accomplish with limited kitchen equipment.

When the pioneer family sat down to eat, women set their tables with hand-carved wood or metal ware. Only in the well-equipped household did a basin and a spoon or fork grace each place setting. Otherwise, two or more people shared, passing the utensils back and forth, while some just ate with their fingers. The wife and daughters placed all the food on the table at once, and everybody ate rapidly without stopping to converse. If one's attention wandered for a moment, the food disappeared. To the fastidious it must not have been a pretty sight. When the small supply of pewter or tin wore out, a traveling tinker, equipped with molds and a soldering iron, patched basins, cups, and kitchen ware.

Frontier food showed little variety from meal to meal. Salt pork and cornbread often appeared on the table three times a day. The midday meal was traditionally the largest. An early missionary to Oregon periodically killed game, but his family had neither flour, milk, butter, nor eggs. During his family's first winter, they relied entirely on boiled wheat and potatoes. Another family considered it a blessing when, after all other supplies had run out during a hard winter, they managed to find some old, tough potatoes that they had missed during the first harvest. The ensuing meal tasted poorly, but they were thankful for food of any sort.

The diet in established frontier communities soon expanded to include all of the staples of American country cooking. Farmers worked hard and consumed huge portions of food without growing obese. Today Americans eat as much as their pioneer ancestors, but do not perform daily physical labor to burn off the calories. Families of modest means made their tables groan with bountiful meals. One holiday meal on a prairie farm featured spare ribs, sausage, chicken, and potatoes, all smothered with lard and flour-based gravy; bread and butter; pickles, plum preserves, and apple sauce on the side; and for dessert, doughnuts, pumpkin pie, and pudding.

For many Americans, dessert was, and is, the highlight of the meal. When they could not find wild honey or afford refined sugar from the store, rural people made maple syrup from the sap of sugar maples, or grew sorghum to make molasses in the unforested regions. Boiled watermelon juice served as a substitute sweetener, and the pumpkin patch provided molasses, sugar, and a wonderful ingredient for pies.

At sugar maple groves, the site of 'sugar camps,' people tapped the trees in late winter and boiled the sap down in iron kettles over log fires. Once the sap thickened, they cooled and stirred it until sugar formed. The Drakes of Kentucky rented a sugar camp, which held a rough shed to shelter the fire from rain. People used axes to cut a gash in each 'sugar tree' and let the sap run out through a hollow stick into a wooden trough. Nearly everybody in the area made maple sugar, and some people sold it.

To the bountiful country meal, an Oregon settler might have added salmon, trout, and freshwater clams. American settlers in New Mexico sometimes adopted aspects of Mexican cookery

Maple sugaring at the sugar 'camp,' an open-fronted shed. Despite the hard work involved, days at the sugar camp offered a welcome break from farm and household drudgery.
(Library of Congress)

while retaining their traditional reliance on bread and meat. They learned to relish mutton and goat meat, beans, and tortillas. The more venturesome used blue Indian corn to make cornmeal mush for breakfast and made liberal use of the many peppers that grow so well there. Scandinavian immigrants in Dakota adopted American foods while retaining some of their native dishes, like smorrebrod – open-faced sandwiches.

The diners needed something to wash down all of this food. Early settlers drank both water and milk, but neither was popular. In the pre-refrigeration era, milk quickly soured, and people drank it beyond the point considered safe and palatable today. They placed fresh milk in cold water, perhaps in a springhouse, to cool it quickly, but such practices were barely adequate. The springhouse or cellar, further cooled by a block of pond or river ice, remained the only place to cool and store milk and food until well past the mid-1800s. In the forested country east of the Mississippi, the stone springhouse built over a hillside spring cooled milk and food in the summer; in winter, the constantly flowing water prevented foods from freezing.

With milk often gone sour, and water often murky and suspected – with good reason – of causing illness, it is not hard to fathom why pioneers preferred to drink corn whiskey, home-brewed berry wine, potato beer, peach brandy, apple cider, tea, or coffee. Small vineyards existed in Kentucky and other states as early as 1780, but they relied on European grape varieties and had little success. American-made wine did not become popular until the Catawba grape became established after 1820.

For those who could not afford to buy tea, the sassafras tree offered a wild alternative, free for the gathering. Coffee gradually replaced tea and became popular as an accompaniment to all three meals. It was sometimes hard to buy on the frontier, and always expensive. Coffee substitutes, such as chicory root, parched grains, burnt pumpkin, or charred cornmeal and molasses boiled in water, made a pale imitation of the real bean, but the resulting beverage was drunk with gusto because it was all that was available.

HOMESPUN, HANDMADE, AND STORE-BOUGHT

Farm households kept sheep for their wool, grew flax for linen, tanned the skins of the wild game they shot, and grew a small patch of cotton if the climate permitted. Once the farmer sheared, harvested, or tanned the raw material, his wife and daughters took over production of cloth and gar-

At the loom. A spinning wheel stands in the background. The glimpse of high-quality furniture gives evidence that the weaver lives in settled country. (National Archives)

THE WELL-OUTFITTED TRAVELER

An 1856 inventory of an American bound from St. Louis to Santa Fe shows that some basic possessions had changed little from the turn of the century. In addition to clothing, horse and mule tack, food, and bedding he carried: *

for firepower, a rifle, pistols (including a Colt revolver), shotgun, bullet and shot pouches, lead, bullet molds, shot, powder horn and powder, gun wads, and percussion caps;

for cooking and eating, matches, kettle, skillet, tin coffee pot, tin cups and plates, covered stew pan, frying pan, coffee mill, and knives, forks, and spoons;

for general use; knife, 2 hatchets, whetstone, ropes, lantern, candles, cedar bucket, 5-gallon keg, and a waterproof tarp.

* Barton H. Barbour, ed., *Reluctant Frontiersman: James Ross Larkin on the Santa Fe Trail, 1856–57* (Albuquerque, 1990), pp. 123–6.

ments. Most produced their own thread and then sent it out to be woven into cloth: more women could spin than could weave. Two households sometimes traded work, with one woman spinning the thread and the other weaving the cloth. Some sent their raw wool or cotton to commercial establishments for carding on water-powered carding machines. The business produced the thread and wove the cloth, taking part of the cloth in payment. Women used the remaining cloth to make the family's clothing at home.

Householders tanned animal skins in several ways. In one approach, they soaked the skins in water with lime, scraped the hair off, steeped the skin in a solution made by boiling the animal's brains, and then smoked it over a fire. A second method involved soaking the skin in water and ashes to remove the hair, then leaving it for weeks or months in a solution of water and pounded black oak bark (from which tannin is derived), and greasing the skin to soften it. Wooden troughs served as the soaking vessels.

At shearing time, farmers drove the sheep to a stream and washed their wool. By the 1850s this practice began to fall into disfavor because people realized the sheep became chilled. After shearing came the laborious work of hand-picking burrs out of the fleece. The farmer's wife spun

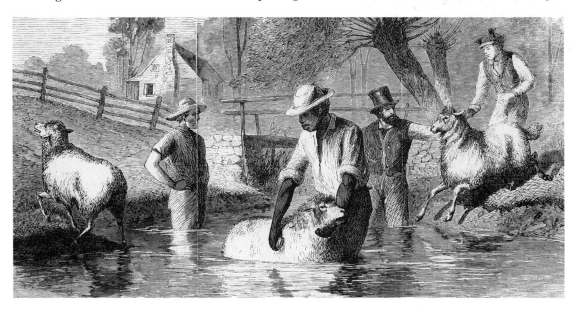

Wool-washing time, in the 1860s. The tricky part was to keep the sheep clean until they were sheared. Some farmers built temporary holding pens at the washing site. (Library of Congress)

the carded wool into thread, which she either wove into cloth or sent to a weaver. A weaver usually took as payment either corn or a portion of the cloth.

Farmers planted flax, first brought to the colonies by the Scotch and Irish, by broadcasting it in a plowed field. They permitted the flax to go to seed, from which they derived linseed oil. After soaking the flax stalks in water to soften the bark for easier removal, farmers dried the stalks and broke them to remove bark from fiber. The women combed the fiber with a tool called a hackle – a paddle with iron teeth set in it. They loomed the resulting tow (fiber) into linen cloth or used it to clean out gun barrels. Most farmers sent their flax fiber away to be loomed, then left the fabric out in the sun to bleach. Their wives made the linen into shirts. The wealthy, on the other hand, imported European linen.

In the early days of Kentucky settlement, people resorted to spinning thread from nettle fibers. They gathered the nettles in spring when the stalks had begun to rot and soften. Then they combined the nettle fiber with long, springtime buffalo fur to make a softer material. Early Kentuckians who grew hemp for the rope-making business also made from hemp a sturdy cloth that was useful for work clothes. One pioneer noticed that when he rotted the hemp in a pond, it killed all the fish. In the Mississippi Valley, hemp burgeoned into an 11-foot weed that could not be eradicated.

A family who grew cotton for home use often owned a hand-cranked roller gin, with grooved rollers for removing cotton seeds from the fiber. However, gin owners still needed to hand-pick a few remaining seeds. Households also required cotton cards, wool cards, and dye pots to produce the raw materials for clothing. A settler who arrived in Kentucky in 1780 brought along 4 pounds of unpicked cotton. Picking the seeds out of this small parcel, she was able to give some of the seed away to neighbors, raise 14 pounds of cotton for her own family, and trade the resulting cloth for a sow, salt, and money.

Across the continent, the emigrants' wagon covers found new use as garments. Unable to grow cotton, and lacking sufficient sheep for producing wool, some settlers tried making yarn out of wolf fur. This proved unsatisfactory: the resulting yarn was coarse and broke easily, and one had to kill dozens of wolves to make a garment of any size. Old grain and flour sacks contributed their fabric to a variety of garments, from trousers to underclothes, as did old army blankets. One wife cut up one of the household's two bed sheets to make some more urgently needed shirts. Eventually, the stores imported a heavy muslin known as factory cloth. The unbleached cloth ended up in the pioneers' dye vats.

Butternut, a yellowish color, came from the bark of the white walnut. Widely used imported indigo served for blue dye, madder root for a dirty red, and the hulls of black walnuts for black. Alder bark boiled in water produced a light brown. Whether homespun or factory, cloth was a monochrome creation. The rare printed calico was an object to be coveted when the peddler visited or the family went to the village store. Beginning in the east around 1840, cloth production moved out of the home and into the factory. The household spinning wheel and loom gave way, ultimately, to the sewing machine of the 1880s.

Because most pioneers were living a struggling, subsistence life, they wore their clothes until they completely wore out. Settled Oregonians who were desperate for material virtually stripped new, and hungry, recent arrivals who staggered in from the Oregon Trail. They drove hard bargains that saw clothes bartered for food. Pioneer Peter Burnett had advanced his lot to the point where he was a judge of Oregon's supreme court. Still, when he and his son were in the fields wearing their last, tattered work shirts, he wondered where and how he could procure new material. Like all Oregon settlers, the Burnetts had perfected the art of patchwork, but there was only so much that could be done with threadbare material. A few days later a young neighbor asked him to perform a marriage ceremony and paid him with an order on a store for five dollars. The judge purchased the best blue-twilled cotton available, out of which his wife made shirts. The material wore well, with the minor inconvenience that until its color faded it left the wearer's skin stained blue.

Eli Whitney invented a type of cotton gin called a saw gin in 1795. It could remove the seed from more than 500 pounds a day. Large plantations had their own horse-powered cotton gins and rented their services out to small farmers. This gin, however, is operated by a slave turning a hand crank. (National Archives)

The single outfit of clothing owned by the Oregon pioneer sometimes met a fate worse than excessive wear and tear – skunks. Two brothers foolish enough to stalk a skunk (armed with the miniature cast-lead cannon they had ingeniously built) had to bury their clothes in the garden overnight. They therefore appeared naked at breakfast. They later unearthed and donned their clothes, only to be denied admission to the cabin and have their lunch pushed out onto the porch with a long pole. For five days, the boys buried their clothes by night and lived as pariahs by day, until their suffering family deemed them acceptable once again.

In winter, men and boys wore outfits made either of buckskin or of 'butternut' colored linsey (linen and wool blend), gaiters made out of old stocking legs, hats, and mittens. Some possessed knitted stockings, or socks made of buffalo yarn, while the less fortunate lined their shoes with leaves or wrapped their feet in rags. For summer clothing, linen replaced leather and wool.

Early hunter-farmers wore long 'hunting shirts' – essentially a belted tunic of buckskin or linsey-woolsey – over long buckskin trousers or knee-length breeches. Buckskin hunter's dress persisted among men on the frontier even late in the nineteenth century. Judge Burnett encountered a recent emigrant on the streets of Oregon City in 1847. The young man wore a new dressed buckskin hunting shirt purchased from the Indians. Burnett recognized quality and asked, 'What will you take for your leather hunting shirt?'[16] Seven bushels of wheat, came the answer, and Burnett immediately agreed. In dry weather, dust did not adhere to the shirt and it stood up to rough work. He wore it through a fall and winter in the California gold mines. Upon his return to Oregon he lent it, still in quite serviceable condition, to a nephew who traveled once more in 1849 to prospect in California.

Buckskin, however, had one major disadvantage. In wet weather, it took on the shape of the wearer, and when dried, shrunk into that shape permanently. Pants became particularly stiff,

DIRTY LAUNDRY

Families set out rain barrels, or troughs made from dugout logs, under the eaves of their cabins to collect rainwater for the washing. Sometimes neighbors met at a stream or pond to do laundry together, making a fire to heat the water. Laundering was an outdoor task, one that occupied the better part of a day.

Clothing was placed in hot soapy water, removed for scrubbing and pounding, boiled, and finally rinsed and wrung. A broom handle served to lift clothing out of boiling water. One had to take care not to break the buttons while pounding. Fences and tree branches served as clothes lines. Women subtracted or added steps according to their habits and the color of the fabric. Some women added ashes to the wash water to soften it and promote sudsing.

Blueing involved rinsing white items in an indigo-tinted solution in order to counteract the tendency of white fabrics to yellow. The blueing solution usually derived from a piece of blue clothing dipped into the rinse water to tint it blue. Those who starched their clothing made starch out of a mixture of flour and water, or from water that had been used to boil potatoes. Finally, the hot coals went into the box iron, or the flatiron was pulled out of the fire.

Wash day in the southwest, late nineteenth century. Like frontier dwellers of a century earlier, westerners still hauled their washing to a stream and made the laundry a social occasion. However, earlier wash days featured cedar washtubs instead of metal. (Arizona Historical Society)

The washing was invariably a woman's job. Apparently, the skills involved in washing clothes were far from universal among married women. A New Mexico army wife in 1858 wrote:

'Unfortunately for us, the day...was Sunday, and not a camp-woman at the post would do anything for us....Here was an unlooked-for dilemma; we were obliged to leave next day, and we must find a laundress somewhere.

'After a consultation it became very evident that if there was to be any washing done that Sunday morning, the ladies must do it themselves; and we went to work, borrowed tubs and boards, rolled up our sleeves in true laundress style, and did our best.

'The results were far from satisfactory; though we used all our energy and strength, the articles looked rather worse than before they had passed through our unskillful hands.' *

The Civil War-era invention of the wringer washer helped mainly with the wringing. The water still had to be hauled and heated.

* Lydia Spencer Lane, *I Married a Soldier* (Albuquerque, 1964), p. 75.

causing the unfortunate wearer no end of discomfort: 'Trousers, after frequent wettings and dryings would assume a fixed shape that admitted of no reformation.'[17] The Oregon climate was hard on all leather goods.

Breeches ended at the knee in garters or buckles. The buckle material – ranging from hand-carved wood to silver – indicated the man's wealth. Long trousers became popular because they permitted laborers to save on stockings. Soon overalls became the common garb of the laboring farmer. Overalls were made of a heavy blue cotton, which today we call denim. In the 1800s, people called this fabric 'jeans.' It had served as a fabric for work trousers for at least a hundred years. In the mid-nineteenth century, Levi Strauss introduced blue denim work pants for miners, and these pants themselves came to be known as jeans. Men readily accepted jeans, because they had been wearing some items of store-bought clothing since the early 1800s.

More formal dress for men featured shirts of linen, topped by waistcoats, coats, and finally caped greatcoats in cold weather. In the frigid Dakotas, buffalo skins became men's overcoats or fur robes for winter driving. Men wore coonskin caps or felt hats during the cold season, and a handkerchief knotted around the head or a straw hat in warmer weather. Straw, of course, was plentiful on most farms. Underclothes, in the form of flannel drawers, were the exclusive province of affluent men.

Women wore long skirts of linsey-woolsey, and blouses – called waists – of linen, wool, or cotton. Calico and other cottons cost more to purchase than linen. Over the skirts and waists, women wore aprons at work and indoors, and jackets while outdoors. Cloaks provided coverage for inclement weather. Cotton stockings and cotton gauze slips served as undergarments. Cuffs, handkerchiefs, gloves, and straw or calico sunbonnets all embellished a woman's outfit. Frontier women continued to make rather than buy their dresses for most of the nineteenth century. A woman running a trading post in New Mexico after the Civil War traded three head of cattle for enough silk to make herself two dresses.

Buttons could be purchased where peddlers or stores did business, but many pioneers made their own. They carved buttons of wood or cast them out of pewter. To make cast pewter buttons, one melted down old dishes or spoons and poured the molten metal into molds carved of soapstone.

Pioneers of all ages often went barefoot in warm weather, even to church. During the critical plowing and planting time, one farmer's boots wore out. But he 'was determined to save my wheat at any sacrifice, and I therefore went barefoot. During the first week my feet were very sore; but after that there came a shield over them, so that I could work with great ease, and go almost anywhere except among the thorns.'[18]

SOAP

A woman made soap for her household by straining water through fireplace ashes to make lye water, and boiling the lye water down until an egg could float on it. She then added grease to the lye water, and boiled it for several hours until it achieved the right consistency. Boiling soap smelled so strongly that it was usually boiled outdoors. When cool, the soap formed into a soft mass. Dried gourds provided storage containers for the soft soap. To make hard cakes of soap, one added salt and boiled the mixture longer, finally pouring it into molds.

When the weather demanded it, people wore moccasins or rough homemade leather shoes with wooden soles. In early Oregon, before there were tanyards, pioneer men made their family's shoes. As Peter Burnett's entire family was nearly shoeless, he set about 'to take the measure of the foot, make the last [a wooden mold of the foot], fit the patterns to the last, cut out the leathers, and make the shoes. I had no last to copy from, never made one before, and had no one to show me how.'[19] The resultant footwear was ugly, uncomfortable, and ill-fitting. Not until an experienced shoemaker showed Burnett how to make a pair of right and left form-fitting lasts did he realize how poor was his work. He tossed his lasts in the fire and set about making new boots. Even so, he had to soak the shoes each night to make them soft enough to wear.

Pioneers blackened their shoes with a mixture of soot and fat, and applied tallow in an attempt at waterproofing. Those who could afford to purchase boots bought them a couple of sizes large because they became misshapen when wet, and shrank when dry. Only affluent townspeople wore dress shoes of fine leather.

A looking glass, hairbrush, and razor were the basic grooming items of the household. The entire household and any guests used the single hairbrush or comb, and shared the washbasin and towel.

Pioneers striking out for the far west from St. Louis frequented the city's bountiful stores to the extent of their solvency. A well-to-do St. Louis man's traveling clothes in 1856 included a buffalo robe, waterproof cape, overcoat, 2 heavy jackets, waterproof boots, shoes, 2 pantaloons, 4 red flannel shirts, 3 calico shirts, 4 red flannel drawers, 6 pair socks.[20]

The hoop skirts or bustles so fashionable for women in the East were adopted primarily in the towns of the West: few farm women wore other than a simple calico dress, with high neck and long sleeves, perhaps embellished with a ruffle. Eastern women traveling the overland trails, if sensible, abandoned the stylish hoop skirts of mid-century; the hoops made it exceedingly awkward to climb in and out of wagons. A soldier's wife who had traversed the Santa Fe Trail several times decided to abandon another ladylike convention, the one that called for pale skin:

> 'Those hot prairie winds were very trying to a woman's complexion, and husband often compared the color of mine to a new saddle. I never tried but once to take care of my skin.... Some one made me a chamois-skin mask, which I put on one day and frightened the baby so badly that...I never made an effort again to preserve my complexion.'[21]

[1] Isreal Trumbo, 'A pioneer's letter home,' *South Dakota Historical Collections*, VI (1912), p. 201.

[2] Kenneth L. Holmes, ed., *Covered Wagon Women: Diaries & Letters from the Western Trails, 1840–1890* (Glendale, CA, 1983), vol. 1, p. 206.

[3] Sandra L. Myres, ed., *Cavalry Wife: The Diary of Eveline M. Alexander, 1866–1867* (College Station, TX, 1977), p. 77.

[4] Maude A. Rucker, *The Oregon Trail and Some of its Blazers* (New York, 1930), p. 189.

[5] Lorna B. Herseth, ed., 'A pioneer's letter,' *South Dakota History*, VI:3 (Summer 1976), p. 309.

[6] Ruth Seymour Burmeister, ed., 'Jeffries letters,' *South Dakota History*, VI:3 (Summer 1976), p. 317.

[7] Cathy Luchetti, *Women of the West* (St. George, Utah, 1982), p. 167.

[8] Marian Sloan Russell, *Land of Enchantment: Memoirs of Marian Russell along the Santa Fe Trail* (Evanston, 1954), p. 25.

[9] Ruth Cook Frajola, ed., 'They went west,' *South Dakota History*, VI:3 (Summer 1976), p. 290.

[10] 'Jeffries letters,' p. 317.

[11] Luchetti, p. 167.

[12] John Muir, *The Story of My Boyhood and Youth* (New York, 1913), p. 234.

[13] 'A Sketch of early adventures of William Sudduth in Kentucky,' *Filson Club History Quarterly*, II:2 (January 1928), p. 47.

[14] Peter H. Burnett, 'Recollections and opinions of an old pioneer,' *Quarterly of the Oregon Historical Society*, V:2 (June 1904), p. 179.

[15] Julia Veazie Glen, 'John Lyle and Lyle Farm,' *Quarterly of the Oregon Historical Society*, XXVI:2 (June 1925), p. 140.

[16] Burnett, p. 178.

[17] Rucker, p. 194.

[18] Burnett, p. 175.

[19] Burnett, p. 174.

[20] Barton H. Barbour, ed., *Reluctant Frontiersman: James Ross Larkin on the Santa Fe Trail, 1856–57* (Albuquerque, 1990), pp. 123–4.

[21] Lydia Spencer Lane, *I Married a Soldier* (Albuquerque, 1964), p. 86.

IV

'WE NEED PROTECTION AND WE NEED IT NOW'

To be a man in Kentucky during the 1770s and 1780s was also to be a member of the militia. Virginia's militia laws applied to Kentucky and they specified that all free men above the age of eighteen and under fifty had to serve. Those who failed to heed the militia muster received fines, but the real motivation for militia service was manifest need. The ever-present peril of Indian raids impelled the male settler to comply with the militia laws. Peer pressure also played a part. Men who risked their lives to help protect their neighbors did not take kindly to excuses from those neighbors for shirking militia duty. Survival depended upon neighborly cooperation. Those who failed to respond to a militia call were 'drummed out' of a fort or station. This was tantamount to a sentence of exile. The outcast and his family had no choice but to return east.

There were legitimate exemptions, but in the breach they were often ignored. As one militia muster prepared to mount and pursue some Indian raiders, a man stepped forward and asked for an exemption on the grounds that he had sight in only one eye. His officer responded that the best man who had ever served him happened to have only one eye. That settled it. Fully sighted or not, every rifle was needed; the one-eyed militia man accompanied the column. Like the reluctant one-eyed man, some tried a variety of ruses to shirk their duty. One man swallowed a chaw of tobacco to make himself ill. Another hid his horse in the cane brake to prevent its being requisitioned for a campaign. In the early years such people were the exceptions. Armed with a rifle or flintlock musket, tomahawk, scalping knife, powder and ball, most of Kentucky's menfolk struggled for survival against some of the continent's most warlike Indians.

Kentucky's fighters did not carry the scalping knife for decoration: white men, even army regulars, readily took up the practice of scalping in their warfare with Indians. In fact, a few decades onward, the Mexican government would try to confront the Apache threat by offering bounties for Apache scalps. In the soon-to-be American southwest, there existed an open market on scalps: American pioneers availed themselves of this money-making opportunity.

Kentucky's first white settlers lived in forted stations made from palisaded logs. They worked the nearby fields and gardens in order to provide a subsistence living and kept alert for signs of Indian attack. But it is the nature of farming to demand attention to the work at hand. Someone hoeing potatoes or scything corn seldom could hear the stealthy footsteps of another human being bent on his destruction. So it was with hunting. A successful hunt required solitary trekking into the tall trees of Kentucky's wilderness. The moment the hunter fired his weapon he broadcast his position to anyone within hearing range. It took great skill to stalk prey, make the kill, dress the carcass, and carry it back to one's family without oneself becoming the prey of Indians.

'We started home with one load of powder, that in my gun. When we got to Mudlick there was a buffaloe in the lick. I shot & wounded it & persued in hopes it would fall. I saw an Indian shift his position behind a tree; I continued to run, took a circuit & came back to the men. We immediately moved off slowly untill we were out of sight of the lick; we then ran the greater part of the way.... The next day...Dickerson & Isaac Baker went to a deer lick. Dickerson was killed and Baker severely wounded.'[1]

83

Defense of Boonesborough, at this time still a forted station. Note the wood chimneys. Women frequently took an active role in defense, tending the wounded and 'running bullets,' or loading rifles. One young woman at a Kentucky station under attack ran out of the fort and dragged in a log to bar the gate. (National Archives)

While the menfolk were by necessity absent in the fields or at the hunt, they left behind near-defenseless women and children. A resourceful handful could defend themselves. One Kentucky woman:

> '...was in her cabin, boiling soap. Had her gourd, and was standing by to keep it from boiling over. The first that she knew there was any one about, an Indian took her by the arm. She dipped up a gourd full of the hot soap and dashed it in his face. The violent screaming of the Indian frightened the others, some one-half dozen, at the door, and they run. She then took up the axe, and despatched him, and then took off for the fort.'[2]

Too often a hunter returned to find his cabin a smoking ruin, his family either kidnapped or slain. The Indians welcomed captives because after 1776 the British paid twice the bounty for a live captive as for a scalp. But the war parties needed to travel fast to avoid vengeful pursuers and this often meant killing those captives who could not keep up. Among numerous accounts there is the story of a woman captured in 1789. She saw three of her children killed during the attack on her home. On the subsequent forced march toward Indian territory, the pregnant woman's captors tired of her youngest son's crying and dashed his brains out against a tree. After she gave birth, they drowned her infant. Such brutality was all too common.

A cabin under attack. Many first-hand accounts tell of women and children huddling on or under beds during the fighting, like the ones shown here in the background. (National Archives)

Existence in Kentucky was literally a life and death struggle for Indians and whites alike. The Indians correctly understood that the influx of whites represented a mortal challenge to their way of life. For the whites, the choice was a vigilant defense or a surrender that typically meant either immediate death or torture at the stake for the men, and death or captivity for the women and children. The Indians welcomed a select handful of captives into their tribes to replace fallen warriors. Over time, some grew to become among Kentucky's most ferocious enemies. Marmaduke Van Swearingen, adopted into a Shawnee tribe following his abduction at age seventeen, received the Indian name Weh-yah-pih-ehr-sehn-wah because of the blue shirt he wore when abducted. He grew to be entirely loyal to his Indian brothers. Among many exploits, he once managed to infiltrate a Kentucky militia camp, read a camp bulletin announcing the column's objective, and escape to warn his brothers of the pending invasion. As Chief Blue Jacket, Van Swearingen became feared and hated by all Kentucky settlers.

From the time of first settlement to the mid-1790s, thoughts of safety and survival from Indian attack played a huge role in day-to-day life. During the typical summer of 1782, one-fourth of Kentucky's men between the ages of eighteen and forty-five remained on active duty to defend against the Indians. The remaining men were on alert to respond to emergencies.

The settlers brought a great deal of the trouble onto themselves. In 1774 a criminal band of white trappers wiped out a small camp of Mingo Indians. Among the slain was the sister of Chief Logan. Heretofore Logan had been a great friend to whites. This atrocity set Logan and his followers on the warpath. Later in the year, Cornstalk, a prominent Shawnee Chief, received a summons to attend peace talks at Fort Pitt. He arrived with two others and while under military escort was attacked by a mob. The mob badly wounded one Indian before guards could intercede. Profuse apologies meant little, the attack shattered all hope of peace.

Most whites made no distinction among Indians. So it was in 1782 when some militia, bent on retaliation for a recent Indian raid, approached a village of Delaware Indians living in eastern Ohio. These people had adopted Christianity and lived in peace with the whites. The Indians welcomed the militia with open arms. The next day, in cold blood, the militia used a wooden mallet to execute methodically thirty-five men, twenty-seven women, and thirty-four boys. The cycle of atrocity and revenge inflamed the Ohio River Valley throughout the early days of Kentucky settlement. Settlers would repeat this cycle again and again as the frontier advanced westward, attacking friendly tribes and turning them into enemies.

Simon Kenton was about to make a name for himself on the frontier as a famous Indian fighter. It would be said that only a few white men were ever as good as the Indians at the Indian game. Kenton and Daniel Boone were. As young Kenton prepared to depart western Virginia for the dangerous voyage down the Ohio River to Kentucky in 1771, he found the following sign scrawled in a cabin. It gave some sense of what the frontier was about:

> WARNING
> THER HAS 20 PERSONS BEN ROBBED BY INJENS
> ALSO 19 HORSES STOLE
> AT EAST FORK M RIVER AND TYGERTS VALEY
> 2 INJENS WAS KILED

Such warnings deterred a few. Kenton, like most others, carried on. At the hands of experienced trappers and traders he learned how to stalk noiselessly through the wilderness, after animals and humans alike. He perfected the amazing feat, mastered by few others, of running while loading his rifle. A born loner, Kenton displayed an uncanny ability to arrive on the scene just in time to rescue hapless emigrants from capture or massacre by the Indians.

The onset of the War for Independence imposed tremendous hardships on Kentucky. Suddenly large numbers of frontiersmen loyal to King George, men who possessed the same skills as Kentucky's militia, joined the raiding Indians. Their common goal was to annihilate Kentucky's settlers. Initially the onset of war also meant a large influx of new settlers when people fled the war-torn east for the prospect of a new start. They came down the Ohio River in every conceivable craft. The rich brought slaves, horses, wagons, herds of livestock. The poor came with little more than an ax and knife. What united the emigrants of all classes was a near total ignorance of frontier survival skills.

Kentucky relied upon certain key goods and supplies from across the mountains to the east. War reduced this necessary flow to a trickle. Consider the matter of salt, iron kettles, and powder. Salt was absolutely necessary to preserve food. Kentucky's own salt resources were limited to some salt licks where much labor was required to obtain minimal supplies. During the most dangerous years, 1775-85, treks to the salt licks faced almost certain ambush by Indians. Actual salt-making could not be performed without substantial militia guards. With the men absent at the salt licks, women and children back in the cabins and stations were hugely vulnerable.

Salt-making, in turn, required large iron kettles to evaporate the water. With Indian warriors and Tory raiders interdicting the two routes east, the Ohio River and the Wilderness Road, kettles became impossible to obtain. In consequence, Kentucky suffered a salt famine. By December 1777, Harrod's Fort, among many, had exhausted its salt supply. Settlers sickened after eating inadequately preserved food. They petitioned Virginia for help. The members of Virginia's General Assembly had to consider petitions from the frontier as matters of decidedly secondary importance. The presence of the Royal Navy off the coast and the ability of redcoated regulars to march at will through the colonies commanded their attention. Still, Virginia managed to send several large iron kettles that arrived late in 1777.

The next February, Daniel Boone took a thirty-man militia company to Blue Licks to make salt. Normally, Indian attacks abated during the winter months. Nonetheless, a war party of some 200 Shawnees surrounded the salt-makers and compelled their surrender. Boone's prestige among the Indians was so high that he and his party avoided the usual death by torture inflicted upon white prisoners. Instead the Indians handed them over to the British in Detroit. But the fact that a frontiersman of the highest skill could be captured along with his company of vigilant, rifle-toting militia, hints at the daily peril endured by those who tried to scrape out a life in Kentucky's 'dark and bloody ground.'

As much as they needed salt, the Kentucky settlers also needed gunpowder. Meat on the table – the deer, buffalo, and bear that provided most of the settler's protein – came from hunters' rifles. Powder was equally indispensable to keep the Indians at bay and it was terribly scarce. Cut off from regular supply from the east, a handful of intrepid men traveled to Spanish territory on the Mississippi River to buy or barter for powder. So critical was the shortage that in 1777 some unknown heroes canoed all the way to New Orleans and back to bring gunpowder to the desperate colonists.

The final years of the American Revolution were the most harrowing for the Kentucky settlers. Small Indian war parties kept every section of Kentucky in continual alarm. Settlers fled to their palisaded stations and forts and watched helplessly as the raiders burned their homesteads and slaughtered their livestock.

> '...the Indians had been at the Station and killed all the sheep; cattle, drove them in groups at some distance out of shot from the fort into the field where they in the fort could see them kill them; and then called to the men in the Station to come and get their cattle. The Indians would kill them all. And when they shot one that kicked up, or cut any capers, they would ha! ha! ha! as loud as to be heard all through the fort.'[3]

At least they had the sanctuary provided by their fortifications. At least, that is, until the summer of 1780 when a British officer named Henry Byrd decided to invade Kentucky with a 600-man force consisting of a handful of British regulars, French-Canadian trappers, and Indians. His avowed purpose was to 'run the settlers' out of Kentucky. To accomplish this, he brought along a six-pounder cannon.

The 400 some people who lived around Ruddell's Station responded to their scout's reports about the approaching enemy by flocking to the safety of the station. Heretofore in Kentucky's history, determined defenders sheltered by wood stockade walls could defy vastly superior numbers of Indian raiders. As the men peered through the loopholes at the enemy hordes, they had no reason to think that it would be any different this time. Captain Byrd ordered his cannon loaded and aimed. The gun boomed and there was a great crash when its ball struck Ruddell's northern blockhouse. It smashed apart an entire section of the fortification. Near panic ensued inside the station. Here was a weapon for which the defenders had no answer. John Ruddell raised a white flag. Byrd cantered up on his horse and demanded unconditional surrender in the name of King George III. He promised that the settlers could travel in safety to the nearest settlement. It was not to be. Once the settlers opened the gate, the Indians rushed inside and began to slaughter. They tore Ruddell's infant son from his wife's arms and threw him into a fire. She ran into the flames to save him and fell with a tomahawk wound. Ruddell tried to save them both and likewise received a skull-crushing tomahawk wound. By the time Byrd could stop the massacre, some twenty people lay dead and scalped.

Byrd took his fort-crushing cannon five miles to Martin's Station. This time it did not even require a shot to force the station's surrender. Burdened by hundreds of prisoners and laden with plunder, sickened by his inability to control the Indians, Captain Byrd called off his campaign and retired north across the Ohio River. Had he continued he could have wiped out virtually every Kentucky settlement.

In retaliation, militia colonel George Rogers Clark mobilized all members of the Kentucky militia. He adopted draconian measures, commandeering guns, powder, lead, horses, and supplies 'without compunction of conscience.' Clark drafted every male, even transient visitors, into the militia. In August 1780, he led over 1,000 vengeful riders across the Ohio to invade the Shawnee capital of Chillicothe. This time it was the Indians who had no answer to the attackers' strength. They did not try to defend their towns. At a cost of fourteen killed and thirteen wounded, Clark's column marched 480 miles, burning buildings and destroying crops as they went. Clark's expedition initiated a strategy that eventually would prevail: rather than exclusively defend settlements in Kentucky, the fight would be taken directly to the Indians in their own homes.

This then was the military cycle in Kentucky during its years of worst conflict. Raid and counter-raid, periodic invasion north and south across the Ohio River, unspeakable atrocities committed by whites and Indians alike, truces and treaties made and broken by both sides. But in the end, the Indians could not resist the huge white tide that flooded west. Harrodsburg, Kentucky's first permanent settlement, was founded in 1774. By 1777, Indian attacks had forced the settlers to abandon all territory except Harrodsburg and Boonesborough. A mere 103 able-bodied men defended these two settlements. Yet the next year more than 1,000 emigrants arrived and the settlements grew larger and stronger. In the spring of 1781, at least another 3,000 came and that year Harrodsburg grew to a population of 2,500. These were manpower numbers the Indians could not match.

The Indians continued to strike, but the blows lacked power. In August 1782, some 200 Indian warriors attacked a weakly defended settlement six miles north of Lexington. Livestock and dogs were made uneasy by the Indian presence but the settlers paid no heed. In spite of the ensuing surprise, thirteen men, aided by musket-toting women and children, manned the station's loopholes and held the attackers at bay. The attackers could not persist because they knew that by now Kentucky possessed an effective defense network that would send a mounted militia column to relieve any settlement under attack. Sure enough, the arrival of forty-five mounted riflemen from nearby Harrod's Fort sent the warriors fleeing.

The early 1780s saw the scene of conflict shift from Kentucky to Ohio. No longer was the issue whether white settlements in Kentucky would endure. No longer did massed war parties strike throughout the territory. Small Indian bands still preyed upon isolated cabins or the solitary hunter or farmer. Among the obscure killings in 1786 was the grandfather of Abraham Lincoln. Most attacks now came at night with the raiders most interested in stealing horses, rifles, powder, and slaves. The days when anxious settlers fled to their fortified stations and prepared for siege and assault had passed. Still, prudent settlers kept a rifle, scythe, and axe near at hand throughout the night. Come morning, a family did not unbar the door until someone had climbed to the loft and peered out to make sure no Indians were about.

If the Indians lacked the ability to challenge the settlements in Kentucky's interior, they could still attack the stream of emigrants floating down the Ohio River. Quite simply, the new settlers, many of them recent arrivals to North America, had no survival skills. Many could barely con their watercraft. Instead of hugging the relative safety of the Kentucky shore, they drifted with the currents in midstream or, even worse, along the Ohio shore. Spying a white person, particularly a small child, gesturing some way ahead, they approached the Ohio shore. A deadly hail of fire, canoes packed with Indians seemingly materializing from thin air; another perfectly sprung ambush and then the litter of scalped bodies, overturned boats, and plundered rafts floating downstream. Simon Kenton did all he could to help emigrants arrive safely. Time and again he encountered an unwary group camped for the night along the shore of the Ohio River, a blazing fire serving as a beacon, no one on guard. Knowing that this was Indian country, Kenton stamped out their fires, showed them how to build a small, near-smokeless cooking fire using white oak bark, instructed them in the myriad things that they needed to know, and warned them that they must remain vigilant with rifles at the ready.

Slowly through the decade of the 1780s, the white invasion into Ohio, an invasion in violation of numerous treaties signed with the Indians, drove the warriors north from Kentucky. The early days when every musket counted gave way to a new system whereby draftees could honorably hire substitutes. Some of the poor performed militia duty, and in exchange, their richer neighbors cared meanwhile for their farms and families.

By 1793, attacks on Ohio River boats had all but ceased, and parties crossing the Wilderness, now reduced to a mere 100-mile-wide strip, were only in danger of attack if they were few in number. Only those living on the remotest frontier had to worry about Indian attack. One visitor in 1793 deemed it perfectly safe to make the 66-mile, three-day journey from Limestone to Lexington. Slightly more than a decade earlier this would have been a trip full of deadly peril.

Overall, as Indian sightings became far less common, frontier survival skills became less important than the ability to farm intelligently, the wisdom to establish a business at an important crossroads, or the capital to buy up prime land. Many of the early settlers found life crowding in upon them and they did not like it. Men like Daniel Boone headed west for virgin territory, leaving in their wake the rudiments of a new society.

Meanwhile, the final episode in the Kentucky conflict between whites and Indians occurred in the Ohio territory. General Anthony Wayne led a United States regular army supported by a large body of Kentucky Mounted Volunteers from his base in Cincinnati toward the remaining Indian strongholds along the banks of the Maumee River. Opposing him were the Shawnees, Miamis, Weas, Wyandots, and Delawares who had fought for more than twenty years to keep the whites out of their country. Leading the Indians were some of the same chiefs – Little Turtle, Blue

Militia muster, showing the typical lack of uniforms and weapons, and festive ambience. Several of the men drill with brooms. A more rural militia drill would have featured hoes and cornstalks as 'weapons.' **(Harper's Weekly, 24 October 1857)**

Jacket, Tecumseh – who had conducted attacks against Kentucky's farms and stations. At the decisive Battle of Fallen Timbers on August 20, 1794, two Kentucky privates, Sherman Moore and William Steele, volunteered to scout ahead of everyone else. The Kentucky cavalry, acting as Wayne's advance guard, saw the two carefully track through an open wood and enter a belt of fallen timber. An unseen foe shot down the two scouts. A rolling volley struck the cavalry and routed them.[4] But Wayne's regulars stood firm and repulsed the Indian onslaught. They fixed bayonets, advanced into hostile fire, and at pointblank range fired a heavy volley of buckshot. The smoke had not cleared before the regulars closed with the bayonet. The Indians could not withstand the charge.

Wayne's victory at Fallen Timbers sealed the fate of the Northwest Indians. Remembering Little Turtle's prophecy that unless the Indians talked peace with Wayne, the Great Spirit would hide his face in a cloud, an Indian survivor concluded, 'the Great Spirit was in the clouds, and weeping over the folly of his red children.'[5]

In sum, a ten-year span between 1775 and 1785 witnessed an amazing change. The first six years featured a raw struggle for survival. Anxiety about Indian attack was part of the fabric of life. Indian warriors stalked settlers as they worked outdoors and assaulted them at night when they rested in their cabins. The presence of an intelligent, active, and brutal foe whose paramount aim was to eliminate white settlement made early Kentucky life one of surprise and terror. Things gradually changed when the end of the American Revolution brought an unstoppable flow of emigrants. In numbers came safety. After 1789, Kentucky's more settled areas suffered few attacks, and farmers no longer feared to work in fields far from their cabins. Then came the victory at the Battle of Fallen Timbers that opened a vast new territory to settlement. In the wake of the Indian retreat came new hordes of settlers willing to risk all for the prospect of cheap land and the chance to carve out a new life.

* * *

A typical soldier in the 1st Kentucky Volunteer Rifle Regiment wore 'a hunting-shirt made of linsey with a slight fringe border, color either blue, such as is obtained from indigo, a pale yellow made from hickory bark, or a dingy brown obtained from black walnut. His pants were Kentucky jeans, and he walked in shoes or moccasins as was his fancy. Around his waist was a leather belt, on one side of which was a leather pocket fastened by leaden tacks, instead of thread, and in this was placed the indispensable tomahawk. Across his shoulder was the strap that held up his powder horn, in which strap was another leather case containing his formidable butcher knife, and another to hold his bullets. A knapsack of home manufacture contained his clothing, and the outside of it was garnished with a glittering tin cup. His well-tried rifle...was his weapon of war.'[6]

The reduction of the Indian threat as the frontier moved west and north changed the nature of the militia system from an absolute necessity for survival to a social institution. Company, battalion, and regimental militia musters still took place at regular intervals in centrally located villages. In more remote frontier areas, the musters took place at a man's house. Many men showed up to muster bare-footed and without firearms, and had to carry cornstalks in drill. The drills lasted a few hours, and then the men fell out to socialize, trade, and drink. Shooting contests, feats of fancy riding, and the inevitable fighting ensued. The militiamen had always elected their own officers. It was a system that worked against maintaining discipline. Increasingly social status rather than military merit became the basis for becoming a militia officer.

Yet before the Indian threat disappeared, the Kentucky militia proved again its prowess. In 1811 the great Indian chief Tecumseh organized a confederation of tribes to try to oust settlers encroaching on Indian land in Ohio and Indiana. Supported by British-Canadian fur interests, Tecumseh gathered a formidable host. The governor of the Indiana territory, William Henry Harrison, resorted to the tried and true method of dealing with Indian threats by calling out the militia and attacking Tecumseh's capital. Kentucky volunteers joined men from Indiana and a regiment of U.S. regulars to invade Indian territory. Harrison's victory at the Battle of Tippecanoe dealt a severe blow to Tecumseh's prestige. Two years later, during the War of 1812, a well-trained regiment of Kentucky mounted volunteers spearheaded victory with a charge through a line of British regulars and Indians at the Battle of the Thames. Success here, along with the death of Tecumseh, caused the final collapse of the Indian confederacy. Kentucky and the adjacent territory was secure forever.

* * *

Oregon pioneers in the 1840s, living six months and 2,000 miles from the United States, felt keenly their isolation when Indians rode to the attack. The Oregon country did not attain territorial status until 1848. By the time U.S. Army regulars arrived, the settlers had been fighting Indians on their own for more than a decade.

The Indians of Oregon, like Indians across the country, faced obliteration of their way of life. Even before the great influx of Americans in the 1840s, white men's diseases – smallpox, malaria, measles, diphtheria, and others – had reduced their numbers and demoralized them. These diseases started making inroads early in the nineteenth century as traders landed on the coast. Over time, more than half, and perhaps ninety percent, of the Indian population fell to diseases introduced by white settlement. Today, the remnants of the tribes comprise less than one percent of Oregon's population.

The first white families – missionaries – had arrived, so they believed, at the invitation of friendly tribes curious about Christianity. Two of these families, the Whitmans and the Spaldings, maintained widely separated missions, each near a different tribe, east of the Cascades mountain range. They met only mixed success in fulfilling their missions. The Spaldings did better among the Nez Perce, in part because of the genuine affection Eliza Spalding bore for her pupils. Narcissa Whitman, on the other hand, held herself aloof from the Cayuse. Despite her sincere religious devotion, she was temperamentally unsuited to be a missionary among Indians. The difference between the two women and their missions is starkly demonstrated by just one fact: Mrs. Whitman ordered an extra 'Indian room' built onto the mission house and reserved the rest of the house for her family so she could retreat from her ever-curious charges:

> '...We told them our house was to live in and we could not have them worship there
> for they would make it so dirty and fill it so full of fleas that we could not live in it.'[7]

This stance mystified and offended the Indians. Accustomed to living in communal lodges, they resented not having the run of the house. Dr. Marcus Whitman as well had an unyielding temperament that fated him to offend the Cayuse.

From the autumn of 1843, the Whitmans' mission served as a way station for white emigrants en route to the Willamette valley. Many of these, exhausted by the hardships of the overland journey, spent a season living and working at the mission. The Cayuse, who already resented the Whitmans' presence on their land, suspected that the Whitmans were promoting white settlement in order to dispossess them of their land. The new settlers also brought measles to the Cayuse, who saw their families decimated by a disease that appeared to spare all white children. The Indians viewed Dr. Whitman's ineffective medicines as deliberate attempts at poisoning. When the chief's child died of measles in 1847, the Cayuse raided the mission, killing the Whitmans and eleven other residents, setting fires, and taking captives.

Thus began the episode known as the Cayuse War. The American militia failed, due to poor leadership and desertions, in its attempt to free the hostages. The volunteers ranged about killing friend and foe alike, arousing the enmity of at least four other tribes. The provisional government appealed to the Hudson's Bay Company for help, which they rendered freely. The Company paid ransom for the captives and never asked to be reimbursed. By this time, the British had relinquished Oregon by treaty and cooperated with the American settlers as a matter of self-interest.

To the west, settlers on the Willamette took possession of a valley in which fewer than 500 surviving Indians wandered in search of a dwindling subsistence. These remnants of tribes who had once found a plentiful living by hunting and gathering were reduced to begging at settlers' cabins. Some settlers fed the Indians regularly and befriended them; most summarily drove them off.

For their part, the children and grandchildren of Kentucky settlers viewed all Indians with suspicion. They remembered the more warlike tribes of the Ohio valley and were not disposed to coexist. The citizens of Oregon territory wanted to be admitted to statehood as soon as possible, so that the federal government would support a military presence and remove the Indians to reservations.

Unlike their Kentucky ancestors, the Willamette settlers did not at first live under constant threat of ambush, but each household willingly contributed to anti-Indian campaigns. The two Applegate brothers were ten and fourteen years old when the Cayuse war erupted in 1847. They were too young to fight, but a family friend who lived with them went to war. The younger boys gave him their toy lead cannon to melt down for bullets, and their father and uncles provisioned the volunteers. Six years later, at ages seventeen and twenty-one, the brothers went off as volunteers to fight the Rogue River war, on the Oregon-California border. By that time, whites and Indians were embarked on a lethal cycle of raids and counter-raids that would not end until Oregon's Indians were confined to reservations. Settlers now went about their work under the same sense of imminent danger that had once afflicted their Kentucky ancestors:

> 'He left here four week before with a load of aples going South. They killed the whole company up set wagons took the horses & strewed the aples in every direction.
>
> 'O what horrible crimes they have committed it would chill your blood to hear...they have to keep rangers out all the time...The Indian Agent has brought seven or eight hundred Indians in to this Valey & boucht a tract of land [Grand Ronde reservation] & placed them on it & there is already doubts as to there friendly disposition there is no trusting them. Those you think to be the most friendly are the first to murder the whites.'[8]

The U.S. Army arrived in Oregon by the mid-1850s. The settlers, now thirsting for Indian blood, deemed the army regulars insufficiently zealous. Many settlers, up to and including the territorial governors, wanted the army to hound all Indians to extinction or place them in captivity. The Indians in turn stepped up the hostilities with each new influx of white emigrants. The settlers ardently desired an army presence, but were dissatisfied with the commander's restraint. The army commander decried the genocidal sentiments of the volunteer companies and the persistence of 'private war.' Nevertheless, the army regulars decisively defeated the tribes by the end of 1858. As a final humiliation, the victorious colonel summarily hung a number of warriors, one of them in the presence of his father. Killing children in front of their parents had long been a favored practice of Indians in their struggle with whites. White men, as they had with the practice of scalping, embraced the enemy's savagery and made it their own.

On other frontiers as well, tension simmered between the U.S. Army, under orders to pacify the Indians by the least violent means possible, and an armed, pugnacious civilian population who wanted to annihilate them. These civilians had lived under daily fear of Indian attack and grown to distrust all Indians. No longer willing to distinguish among Indians, they raided indiscriminately. Too often, hot-headed civilian volunteers on campaign with army regulars started battles

Fort Union, New Mexico. As the last stopping place before Santa Fe, it drew words of praise from weary travelers who knew that they were close to journey's end. It was a safe haven from bandits and Indians, who came to trade by day and raided the surrounding area after dark. (National Archives)

with noncombatant Indians. Not subject to military discipline, they ignored truces and fired their weapons prematurely, drawing into battle both soldiers and Indians who had not intended to fight. Then they fled, leaving the soldiers to finish what civilians had started. Unwilling to back down, both sides fought on, upping the ante until the Indians surrendered.

The practice of relocating Indians to reservations had begun with the removal of eastern tribes to the vast territory west of the Mississippi. By the time the United States defeated the Indians of the Pacific Northwest, the nation was running out of places to send them. The victors first considered sending the Indians of the humid Willamette Valley eastward to the unclaimed arid lands across the Cascades range. Realizing that the Indians would perish in such an unfamiliar environment, the US Indian agent instead granted them reservations near the coast. So began the confinement of Indians to small reservations. Beginning in 1855, treaties consigned Oregon tribes to reservations at Umatilla, Warm Springs, Grand Ronde, and Siletz.

* * *

The war with Mexico brought the U.S. Army in force to the trans-Mississippi West. By 1851, the army had established a chain of forts in New Mexico. Soldiers provided escorts for the mail, the army paymaster, and selected citizens. Isolated travelers and settlers still died at the hands of hostile Indians, and it remained wise to travel in large parties between settlements. Indians took captives and melted away into the desert. Some captives disappeared into thin air and were never seen again: even army rescue efforts failed to turn up any sign of them. Still, the presence of well over 1,000 troops made an enormous difference. Individuals continued to carry firearms for personal defense, but no organized militia system required their participation. On occasion, volunteers took up arms and fought side by side with army regulars, and when raiding parties evaded the army to attack settlers, the settlers remained armed and ready to defend themselves.

The Indian threat they faced was different as well. The arid West supported a less numerous Indian population, and most hostile tribes living in the West followed a more nomadic existence. Consequently, the pioneers did not confront periodic invasions by hundreds of hostile people,

Officers' quarters at Fort Union, New Mexico, built of unfaced adobe bricks with American-style wood window frames. (National Archives)

nor was there a British presence to arm and support such invasions. Instead came hit-and-run raids, equally deadly for individual victims but not of sufficient scale to threaten the very existence of white settlement. The Indians' tactical arsenal utilized speed, stealth, and ambush. Their motivation to fight was the same as that of the eastern Indians: anger at white encroachment.

From the earliest days of Spanish settlement, New Mexicans had coexisted with the agrarian pueblo Indians but suffered raids by hostile nomadic tribes. Indians killed and kidnapped unprotected travelers and stole all kinds of livestock; cattle, sheep, mules, and horses. Josiah Gregg, an American Santa Fe trader of the 1830s, summed up the prevailing view of Mexican defense efforts against Indian raids:

> 'The haciendas and ranchos have been mostly abandoned, and the people chiefly confined to towns and cities.... Occasionally a detachment of troops is sent in pursuit of the marauders, but for no other purpose, it would seem, than to illustrate the imbecility of the former...'[9]

Like other frontier tribes, in the intervals between livestock stealing forays, the southwestern Indians traded with whites for liquor and other goods, to their own detriment. As Gregg also noted, 'the Apaches are passionately fond of spirituous liquors, and may frequently be seen, during times of peace, lounging about the Mexican villages, in a state of helpless inebriety.'[10]

At Fort Union, New Mexico in 1852, a band of Indians, having peaceably played marbles with white children by day, that night attacked a stage coach station two miles from the fort. Soldiers rode out to the rescue too late to prevent the torching of the station, the scalping of a stable-hand, and theft of the horses. The same year, a young father had quarreled with the other men in a traveling party, and turned his family back from a wagon train. Indians soon overtook this defenseless group and killed the husband and two sons. They took the pregnant wife captive and argued about killing her for her red-haired scalp. She escaped by stealing a knife, cutting off her braids, and giving them to the Indians. They struck her for her impertinence but allowed her to flee. Mexican travelers picked her up, half-starved, some days later. She survived to have her baby but took little joy in it.

The army conducted a series of anti-Indian campaigns. Like the settlers, they failed to make distinctions between hostile and friendly Indians. If a drunk and incoherent settler accused a friendly band of stealing his livestock, no one tried to obtain confirmation of his garbled account before the army rode out to chastise the alleged offenders. In just this way, groups of peaceable Indians became implacable enemies. In a few years' time, however, army campaigns so reduced the threat of Indian attack that settlers had more to fear from American and Mexican criminals. The outlaws stole from wagons and houses, and were quite willing to kill for plunder. One family suffered a theft, an attempted break-in, and an attempted robbery in the space of just two years.

Navajos persisted in their raids until 1864, when the army finally crushed them after years of unrelenting campaigning. The army forcibly relocated the Navajos to the squalid Bosque Redondo, at Fort Sumner, New Mexico. There the Indians had a miserable existence. Typically, the federal government failed to provide sufficient food rations for reservation Indians, and corrupt bureaucrats withheld a share, so Indians starved. Unclean water caused dysentery that claimed scores of victims. En route to Bosque Redondo, it is said, soldiers shot those Indians unable to walk. In 1868, once conditions at Bosque Redondo became generally known, the demoralized Navajos received part of their homeland as a reservation, which they retain today.

Only those settlers who chose to live in Apache territory continued to face a formidable risk. In the decade beginning in 1860, the Apaches killed some 1,000 miners and settlers in Arizona. A partial list of Apache depredations around Fort Bayard, high in New Mexico's northern mountains, gives some idea of the extent of the Indian risk for the New Mexican settler: January 1870, one woman killed; April, mules stolen from two ranches; May, two men dead of thirst after unsuccessfully chasing Apache rustlers; February 1871, mules stolen; March, six killed while bringing supplies to fort; April, one man killed, stripped, and mutilated outside of fort followed by killing of a soldier, teamster, and sheep herder. The Apaches' tremendous mobility – individual warriors took several horses along on raids and shifted from one to another in order to keep the mounts fresh – and their knowledge of local terrain posed an enormous problem for the army. The commander of the Department of Arizona complained that only two officers in his entire command 'really grasped

'Apache Raid,' a painting by Edward Zinn. (Arizona Historical Society)

the situation,' six others 'could carry out orders understandingly,' while the balance, although brave and hard working, were useless. Worse, officials in Washington were 'hopelessly at sea...in [their] knowledge of these people, their mode of warfare, or the problems of catching them.'[11]

Even ostensibly friendly relations did not guarantee security from Indian attack. At one northern New Mexico ranch in the 1870s, a band of Utes always arrived at milking time expecting free milk. One day the rancher turned them away because too many had come and he didn't have enough milk. That night the tribesmen burned the haystacks, the settlers' entire winter feed supply. On another occasion, the same band pursued the rancher's son in an effort to seize his horse, but the boy outrode them. In yet another incident, a lone Ute tried to climb in the cabin window, but the family dog, who – like some Americans – had a bad habit of attacking friend and foe alike, saw him off.

Outlaw, outcast, renegade American and Mexican men known as the 'Comancheros' joined the Comanche and Kiowa Indians in preying upon New Mexico settlers. The Comancheros provided the Indians with weapons, ammunition, and whiskey in exchange for rustled livestock, stolen property, and human captives. The army tried to put a stop to this trade but it proved impossible, particularly given the willing participation of many New Mexico settlers as well as the soldiers themselves. In a typical exchange, one army wife at Fort Bascom, New Mexico traded a copper kettle and a blanket for twelve cattle, undoubtedly the rustled property of some other hapless New Mexican or Texas pioneer. Soon such incidents persuaded many that Fort Bascom's commanding officer and his subordinates were in league with the Comancheros.

In spite of such scandals, it was better to have the army present than absent. Time and again, when an army garrison abandoned a post, bandits moved in to fill the void. As late as 1891, one general conducting an inspection of frontier forts reported 'we find that the very presence of

Fort Sumner, New Mexico. Except for the course of the Pecos River, the landscape is dry and dusty. (National Archives)

Navajo Indians assembled for 'counting' at Bosque Redondo, following their final defeat by the U.S. Army. (National Archives)

troops is a restraining influence.'[12] Geronimo's surrender in 1886 marked the end of the Indian wars in the southwest. By that time, Indians nationwide had been confined to 187 reservations.

* * *

As long as most people viewed the plains west of the Mississippi River as the Great American Desert, the Dakotas were not subjected to overwhelming white encroachment. However, as accurate knowledge of this region became available, attitudes changed, and people began to view the region as a potential Garden of Eden full of rich farmlands and valuable mineral deposits. The majority of whites believed the Indians who lived there were not realizing the land's bounty in an appropriate manner. Thus came pressure to evict them. A thousand white settlers crowded the border of present-day South Dakota in 1859, waiting for the dubious Yankton Treaty to be ratified. Others had already slipped in ahead of the official opening. To the U.S. troops, present in the territory since 1855, fell the thankless task of enforcing law: they had to run off premature settlers, and keep traders from selling liquor to the Indians who were so fatally fond of it.

The Sioux uprising of 1862–68 occurred because of objections to land cession treaties that had been hastily concluded without agreement of all the tribesmen. This volatile situation was made worse by the 1863 ejection of the Sioux from Minnesota into Dakota. The warfare, coinciding with crop failures, caused close to half the settlers to abandon their farms and return east. The US Army wanted to evacuate the remaining settlers, but were instead ordered to establish a chain of forts to defend the territory and its inhabitants. Troops went out on patrols in the effort to minimize the impact of Indian raids.

Peace came in 1868, when the federal government established in the Treaty of Fort Laramie a Sioux reservation on 60 million acres of land in western South Dakota. It promised that the Sioux could retain their sacred Black Hills forever. Then in 1874 came the rumors followed by thrilling confirmation: gold was in those hills!

Initially the army tried to prevent white intrusion into the Black Hills. This proved impossible. While some military men made sincere efforts to force settlers to obey treaty lines, many others, including Lieutenant Colonel George Custer, were sure that giving the Sioux 'a sound

Officers' quarters at Fort Dakota in 1866. Officers had to look out on the same treeless and wind-lashed prairie landscape as the enlisted men. (National Archives)

drubbing' was the best policy. But the frantic search for gold superseded all else. As President Grant told the nation in 1876, 'an effort to remove the miners would only result in the desertion of the bulk of the troops that might be sent there to remove them.'[13] So the scene was set again: white encroachment and treaty violation; Indian resistance.

The army did not eject the treaty violators, but neither did they protect them. Miners organized for their own defense, and set bounties on dead Indians. Loopholes in the walls of miners' cabins bore witness to their precarious position. Food and supplies sold for exorbitant prices, calculated in gold dust, because Indians raided the supply wagons as they wound their way to the Black Hills.

First the federal government tried to purchase or lease the gold-laden Black Hills, which the Sioux held sacred. Failing in that plan, the United States decided to take the land by force. Although the Sioux and their allies – most notably the Cheyennes and Blackfeet – enjoyed famous successes in 1876 at the Battle of the Rosebud and on the Little Bighorn River, they could not withstand the aroused might of the US Army. The plains Indians always had lived a near-subsistence life. Relentless winter campaigns drove them from their villages and destroyed their carefully husbanded food stores. Worse from the Indian perspective, the wanton slaughter of the American bison – the animals were nearly exterminated in the 1870s – eliminated the Indians' chief food supply and greatly reduced their capacity to fight.

Sioux Indians at Rosebud Agency, Dakota Territory. White children in foreground signal the existence of friendly relations. (National Archives)

Except for the miners who operated in advance of the army, most Dakota settlers now had little to fear from the Indians. These pioneers moved into areas already secured by the military. Settlers seldom had contact with the Indians once the army herded them into reservations.

Throughout history civilians have profitably exploited the presence of military garrisons. In Dakota, communities sprang up around the forts for economic reasons as much as for security. Farmers and ranchers living near forts received contracts to provide the garrison with food and firewood. Just as it is in the 1990s, when rumors of a military base closure arouse the local citizenry, so it was in the 1870s. A Dakota newspaper reported that 'the monthly pay of these troops let loose such a dazzling deluge of money' that the settlers 'couldn't let them go.'[14] So the locals exaggerated the Indian menace in order to retain the garrisons. Around Camp Cheyenne, 'Every man, woman and child...who had anything to sell, or who could make moccasins or anything else liable to be needed, united in a petition setting forth the dangers from Indians if the troops should leave.'[15]

By the 1880s, the rising generation of pioneer children thought of Indians as 'friendly' and 'colorful.' Bands of Sioux provided, for a fee, entertainment at Independence Day picnics. They moved at will between reservations, the dust clouds of their passage visible to homesteads for miles around. When the opportunity presented, they stopped at farmhouses in hope of a free meal:

'We had no screens on our doors and they would come in quietly in their moccasins without any thought of knocking. Mother would hear a grunt, look up, and there would be an Indian waiting and smiling. Doubtless it was Mother's liberality with her bread that caused them never to pass us by.'[16]

The Indian Agencies at such reservations as Pine Ridge and Rosebud distributed food and clothing to their wards. As surely as the buffalo herds were cut down, so was the land area of the reservations. Through every means possible, including forgery of Indian signatures, land sale agreements went to Congress. Just as Congress ratified a major land cession in 1889, the Indian Agencies reduced the size of the Indians' meat rations, rewarding them with starvation for ceding their land. Thus rose the Ghost Dance movement, which led to the final chapter of US–Indian warfare at Wounded Knee.

With the unrest of 1890, the Indians once again became fearsome, to settlers and officials alike. In November, the US agent at Pine Ridge Reservation cabled Washington: 'Indians are dancing in the snow and are wild and crazy. We need protection and we need it now.'[17] Even those settlers whose farms lay far from Pine Ridge, the center of the unrest, were little reassured by the presence of army troops. Neighbors met to decide what action to take if the Indians started raiding again, and daily scanned the horizon for the dust of their travel. While the starving Sioux performed the Ghost Dance rituals, in which they placed their last hope of eliminating the white man, settlers took fright at rumors, that spread like prairie fire, of rampaging Indians. The fright was short-lived. The arrest and slaying of Chief Sitting Bull, and the shooting of some 200 of his unarmed followers by army troops, brought an end to war on American soil. Henceforth, the homesteader could turn his attention to other enemies.

[1] 'A Sketch of early adventures of William Sudduth in Kentucky,' *Filson Club History Quarterly*, II:2 (January 1928), p. 56.
[2] Otto A. Rothbert, 'John D. Shane's interview with Colonel John Graves of Fayette County,' *Filson Club History Quarterly*, XV:4 (October 1941), p. 241.
[3] John D. Shane, 'Interview with pioneer William Clinkenbeard,' *Filson Club History Quarterly*, II:3 (April 1928), pp. 100–1.
[4] A good eyewitness description of the confused initial encounter is in 'Daily Journal of Wayne's Campaign,' *American Pioneer*, I (September 1842), p. 318.

WHAT REALLY HAPPENED AT WOUNDED KNEE?

Americans in South Dakota a century ago took a different view from what history books say today about the infamous 1890 massacre at Wounded Knee. The modern consensus holds that, as the Indians reluctantly surrendered to U.S. troops, a shot fired into the air from an Indian's rifle triggered the fighting, and that some of the Indians had not yet surrendered their firearms. Contrast the words of Annie Tallent, a Dakota settler writing in 1899, with those of the Encyclopaedia Britannica in 1990.

Encyclopaedia: 'The Indians were surrounded and nearly disarmed when a scuffle broke out over a young brave's new rifle. A shot was fired from within the group of struggling men, and a trooper fell. From close range the soldiers, supported by machine guns, fired into the Indians, whose only arms were the clubs and knives that they had hidden in blankets.' (vol. 12, p. 763)

Tallent: 'Like a flash they drew their concealed guns from beneath their blankets, and fired a deadly volley into the closed ranks of the soldiers.'*

Encyclopaedia: 'Fleeing Indians were pursued, and some were killed miles from the camp.'
Tallent: 'The women and children fled to the hills when the firing first began and many were unfortunately killed while on their flight and in their hiding places, which in the confusion was, no doubt, unavoidable.'

*Annie Tallent, *The Black Hills* (St Louis, 1899), pp. 710-11.

Chief Sitting Bull's encampment on a Sioux reservation in Dakota Territory. Soldiers and ladies look on. The picture was probably taken after his 1881 surrender and return from Canada. He then lived at Standing Rock Reservation until his death in 1890, except for two years touring with Buffalo Bill Cody's Wild West Show. (National Archives)

5   Paul David Nelson, *Anthony Wayne: Soldier of the Early Republic* (Bloomington, IN, 1985), p. 266.

6   Rene Chartrand, *Uniforms and Equipment of the United States Forces in the War of 1812* (Youngstown, NY, 1992), pp. 61–2.

7   Clifford Merrill Drury, ed., *First White Women Over the Rockies* (Glendale, CA, 1963), vol. 1, p. 138.

8   Kenneth L. Holmes, ed., *Covered Wagon Women: Diaries & Letters from the Western Trails, 1840–1890* (Glendale, CA, 1983), vol. 1, p. 94.

9   Josiah Gregg, *Commerce of the Prairies* (New York, 1970), p. 96.

10 Gregg, p. 95.

11 Robert Wooster, *The Military and United States Indian Policy 1865–1903* (New Haven, 1988), p. 38.

12 Herbert M. Hart, *Old Forts of the Far West* (New York, 1965), p. 146.

13 Wooster, p. 52.

14 Robert Lee, *Fort Meade & the Black Hills* (Lincoln, NE, 1991), p. 104.

15 Ibid., p. 104.

16 Ruth Cook Frajola, ed., 'They went west,' *South Dakota History*, VI:3 (Summer 1976), p. 296.

17 Alan Axelrod, *Chronicle of the Indian Wars* (New York, 1993), p. 248.

V

'AMBITION, HOPE, AND PRIDE'

From Subsistence to Surplus

For the pioneer farmer, the first order of business was survival. Some wanted little beyond a modest subsistence and freedom from interference. The vast majority aspired to something more; a farm to call their own, a certain level of comfort, moderate prosperity, and land to leave their children. A Dakota Territory settler summed up what land ownership could offer a person: 'Our riches were good health, ambition, hope, and pride.... We considered ourselves people of importance.'[1] Yet others saw in the unclaimed West the opportunity to amass untold wealth by whatever means possible: 'There seem to be but little thought of in Portland but to get rich nor does there seem to be much else thought of in Oregon...' said a settler in 1847.[2] Where farmers went, soon followed the merchants and tradesmen to provide whatever the farmers could afford to buy.

By the end of 1787, seven sellers of general merchandise – groceries, dry goods, tools and hardware, and medicines – did business in Kentucky, six of them in Lexington. This number grew to thirteen by the following year, and fifteen by 1789. The merchants closed their stores each spring or fall and went east to Philadelphia or Baltimore to restock, bringing back goods by the wagon load. Some brought goods from New England down the Ohio River. Kentucky merchants marked up the goods they imported from the East by 100 percent or more over Philadelphia prices.[3]

The most basic store inventories included coffee, tea, sugar, spirits, spices, paper, dishes, cloth, and nails. Customers purchased the coffee beans still green and roasted them at home. They bought the tea, sugar, flour, salt, spices, soap, and whiskey in small lots from supplies stored in bulk. Brand names were virtually unknown outside the patent medicine field. The same store sold leather goods such as harnesses, a full range of tools and hardware, all manner of dishes and kitchenware, medicines, books, a wide variety of cloth by the yard and items of clothing. Some stores even stocked panes of glass in assorted sizes. General stores in new settlements also sold apples and cider, until the new orchards started producing. Farmers traded their surplus produce – corn, wheat, eggs, butter – for store-bought goods. Some frontier people dug ginseng root, which the merchants accepted for eventual sale to China.

Traveling peddlers circulated door to door on foot, horse and wagon, or boat, selling merchandise brought from New England. They traded in many of the same items carried by general stores and took bartered goods in payment. Frontier people perhaps unjustly disliked 'Yankee peddlers' and accused them of selling phony goods at exorbitant prices. Yet their appearance broke up the monotony on an isolated farmstead and rarely went unrewarded. Traveling salesmen also sold maps, books, and Bibles. In fact, almost any item that could be sold was sold by traveling salesmen: lightning rods, windmills, school books, sewing machines, jewelry, tree seedlings, to name just a few.

Western farmers, once they attained subsistence and paid their accounts at the store, engaged in other enterprises to make money. These included selling their surplus farm production, making and selling clothes or other household necessities, taking in boarders, or finding paying work during the off season. They bartered freely with their neighbors, trading one kind of labor for

CURRENCY

Not until the Civil War was a national currency established. Individual banks, with or without state charters, each issued their own bank notes. These bank notes fluctuated in value and differed in appearance, making counterfeiting easy. Newspapers and dedicated bank note guides published lists of sound and unsound bank issues. One enterprising set of counterfeiters also printed up a fake currency guide that approved their notes.* The currencies of different states or regions were variously expressed in such units as shillings, sixpences, eleven penny bits, thrips, half-dimes and dimes, bits and half bits, and picayunes.

Frontier merchants doing business with eastern concerns had difficulty in safely transmitting negotiable currency to them. Money could be sent with travelers, who might be robbed, or sent through the mail, which could also be stolen. Some actually cut currency in half and mailed it one half at a time, as half a banknote could be recovered for its full value following a lengthy procedure.

Kentucky: Bartering was predominant, with coonskins a common medium. Receipts given for such items as skins and tobacco in turn circulated as a form of currency. Land warrants and promissory notes also served as a form of 'paper' money. Very little actual money circulated in Kentucky until General Wayne's army arrived across the Ohio in 1793 and began purchasing horses from the pioneers. Currency gradually gained in use during the 1790s, but barter, credit, and trust remained commonplace. The frontier ethos expected merchants to extend credit to consumers for a year or more.

Spanish currency in the form of silver dollars came into use once the Mississippi opened to American trade. The Spanish silver dollar, on which the later U.S. silver dollar was modeled, had a different value in each state. Silver was turned into 'cut money' to make change, although the cuts were not always made honestly. Silver dollars were cut into eight wedges called 'sharp shins' or 'bits.' Thus, a quarter was 'two bits'. The sharp edges of the cut money necessitated leather purses to protect pockets from tearing. Farther south in cotton country, cotton and cotton gin receipts served as currency, along with gold specie, U.S. dollars, and Spanish and French coins.

Oregon: The provisional government of Oregon declared wheat to be legal tender, making official the common practice of bartering with wheat. A bushel of wheat equalled one dollar. Another common practice was for settlers to exchange notes drawn on one another's store accounts; thus paid, one could take the note to the store and exchange it for merchandise. Oregon farmers returning from California during the gold rush years brought gold dust with them and used it as currency.

Southwest: At Council Grove, Kansas, along the Santa Fe Trail in 1860: the trading post accepted a pony from an Indian in exchange for a sack of flour. In turn the pony was traded out to another Indian and a buffalo hide filled with corn accepted as payment. ** New Mexicans in the 1850s relied primarily on gold and silver for currency.

* Everett Dick, *The Sod–House Frontier, 1854-1890* (New York, 1937), p. 93.
** Marian Sloan Russell, *Land of Enchantment: Memoirs of Marian Russell along the Santa Fe Trail* (Evanston, 1954), p. 79.

another, cloth for livestock, meat for flour, the use of a horse for half a hunter's kill. In early Oregon, barter took a cruder form: 'It was easy to distinguish the new from the old settlers. They were lank, lean, hungry, and tough; we were ruddy, ragged, and rough.'[4] New arrivals wore fine broadcloth and linen but lacked food and the wherewithal to plant. The older settlers experienced great difficulty in securing any kind of decent clothing but had mature farm plots. The newcomers, seeing their neighbors wearing rags while covetously gazing at their jeans, cottons, and calicos, tried to buy on credit, and were refused. 'We reasoned in this way,' relates an established pioneer, 'that if they wished to place themselves in our ruddy condition, they should incur the risk of passing into our ragged state.'[5] Amid much grumbling, the parties exchanged clothing for food.

In older communities, farmers sold their produce and other locally made items – among them cheese, butter, molasses, and sugar – to new immigrants. Many farmers distilled beverages

At a commercial apple cider maker's. The press is run by a horse-powered sweep. The horse wears blinders to prevent dizziness. (Library of Congress)

for themselves and their neighbors. Such homemade efforts could grow into larger businesses as was the case in 1780 when Evan Williams made Kentucky's first commercial corn whiskey. Kentuckians always took pride in their bourbon. Although they did not openly join in the Whiskey Rebellion they ignored the 1791 federal whiskey tax and continued a tradition of quality bourbon production that persists to this day.

During the years that the Spanish interdicted American Mississippi River traffic to New Orleans, Kentucky had no economical way to export surplus corn. Wagon roads over the Allegheny Mountains did not yet exist. Hauling corn on the backs of pack animals made no sense; the entire cargo would have gone to feed the animal carrying it. Therefore, much surplus corn went to make whiskey. Corn whiskey became a medium of exchange in the barter economy. Farmers also fed surplus corn to livestock, which drovers then took to market. Thus corn was converted to meat and sold. Trans-Allegheny farmers sent livestock east in huge drives, moving hundreds of horses, cattle, or hogs to the seaboard states. They sold the animals to drovers who in turn sold them in the eastern markets. Until railroads took over livestock transport, blacksmithing enterprises and 'drove stands' operated along the established routes. Farmers managed most drove stands, providing pens and feed in order to put up drovers and their charges at night.

After Spain opened the Mississippi River to American trade in 1787, Kentucky producers sent goods by flatboat the 1,500 miles to New Orleans. Flatboat cargos included pork, corn, flour, whiskey, tobacco, hemp, and limestone. So committed were the cotton planters of the lower Mississippi to one-crop agriculture, that they imported their household meat and flour from upriver. Boats originating in the old northwest, or west of the Mississippi River, carried lead, iron, salt, furs and hides, livestock, bacon, flour, and spirits to New Orleans.

Although some farmers grew small patches of tobacco for their own use, tobacco made a difficult cash crop because it required intensive labor. Tobacco growers tended thousands of delicate seedlings for weeks until they could be transplanted, one by one, in the field. Each plant required hand-tending; pruning, weeding, and removal of worms. The leaves, once cut and hung to dry, took six weeks to dry enough for shipping. Hemp, grown for rope and rough cloth, also required much labor and attention to bring it from seed to market. Kentucky and Missouri led the nation in production, but hemp never succeeded as a cash crop on a wide scale.

* * *

The first permanent American settlers in Oregon relied on the trading posts of the Hudson's Bay Company for many of their goods, including cloth, ready-made clothes, shoes, tools, coffee, sugar, and salt. Trade vessels from Russian settlements, the Sandwich Islands (present-day Hawaii), California, England, and the eastern United States called at the Pacific ports. They brought English goods and exchanged them for wheat, fish, furs, and timber. The Company in turn sold the imported goods to American settlers, on credit and at reasonable prices, accepting wheat in payment.

Still, the very breadth of the ocean imposed limits on what the Oregon settler could buy. Easterners knew of Oregon's reputation for shortages of goods. One settler received a gift of spectacles from long-time friend President James K. Polk, with the following advice: 'Take these glasses with you, Neal. You don't need them now, but if the time comes when you do need them and you can't get any out there in Oregon they will come in handy.'[6]

A merchant owed a lawyer forty-nine dollars and asked to pay in goods. The only problem was, the merchant had little in his store just then. He suggested waiting until a new supply arrived from Honolulu. Three months passed and the lawyer and his wife returned to call upon the merchant. They wanted to buy 6 pounds of sugar and many dry goods: 'I asked him if he had any satinets? None. Any jeans? None. Any calico? None. Any brown cotton? None.' Exasperated, the lawyer asked what was available, only to learn that the merchant mostly had tools, and that those were offered at an extravagant price. Having purchased thirteen dollars-worth of tools, the lawyer became disgusted with paying prices more than double those at Vancouver for 'articles I could do without for the time, and inquired if he had any brown sugar and at what price.' Finding the price acceptable, he received his balance due in sugar – some 36 pounds, six times more than he had intended – "knowing that we had sugar enough to last for a long time.'[7]

The discovery of gold in California changed Oregon from a backwater trading outpost to a prosperous commercial center. By 1850 a pioneer recalled, 'We could get the world's commodities here which could not be had, then...in the interior of Illinois or Missouri.'[8] Ships brought goods and produce from across the Pacific and from South America. In this way, access to the sea made pioneer life in Oregon far different than elsewhere.

By sheer weight of numbers, American settlers had convinced the British-run Company that coexistence and cooperation were the prudent course. To Dr. John McLoughlin, the Company's remarkable chief factor, maintaining peace in the valley was the highest priority. When destitute settlers arrived in Oregon in the autumn of 1842, he employed the men for the winter and provided them with goods and seed wheat on credit. He feared that if he failed to help the first wave of emigrants get established, they in turn would be unable to help next year's arrivals, and famine and rioting would result.[9]

So committed was McLoughlin to keeping the peace, that when the American provisional government voted in 1845 to ban alcoholic beverages, he again fell in with American desires, in part because he wished to limit the access of Indians to alcohol:

'In this measure, the gentlemen of the Company perform a very efficient part, and although their own store-houses are full of intoxicating liquors, they sell none to any person. Upon the arrival of a vessel freighted with ardent spirits, the doctor McLoughlin, has been known to purchase the whole cargo, in order to prevent its sale among the settlers, when at the same time, he had hundreds of barrels in his own store-houses.'[10]

Dissenting settlers persisted in setting up stills in remote places and selling their product to the Indians. A local justice of the peace discovered one such man distilling a product called 'blue ruin,' a near-deadly concoction of Hawaiian molasses.[11]

The first settlers traded most of their farm produce to the Company store in exchange for merchandise. The California gold rush of 1849 marked a turning point in the economy, as the call came from the gold fields for ever more beef and grain. Many Oregon farmers left their wives and children in charge of the farms and went to California. When they returned, the successful ones brought gold dust, which circulated along with wheat as a form of currency.

Through the first years of American emigration to the Willamette valley, the crossing of the Oregon trail impoverished each band of settlers. They lost their possessions fording rivers, or found themselves compelled to abandon them at trailside to lighten their loads so they could beat the winter snows. The first year of farming was often one of bare subsistence – on potatoes, swine, and wild game. All they could offer in trade for the things they needed was their labor. The established settlers sold supplies to the newcomers, and took their labor in payment. No frontier farm or home existed that could not benefit from an extra pair of hands.

Tabitha Brown, a sixty-six-year-old widow, traveled to Oregon in 1846 with her children, grandchildren, and eighty-one-year-old brother-in-law. On her arrival in Salem, the enterprising widow earned room and board for herself and the old gentleman by running a minister's household. She possessed only a half-bit in currency, which she found by chance among her baggage, and used it to buy three needles. Trading some of her clothing to Indians for leather, she made several pair of gloves and sold them for a total of $30. After her son got situated on his claim, she lived with his family for a period, but ultimately went out on her own again to found a school for orphans.

Once established on their farms, Oregon settlers produced wheat and raised livestock as their cash crops. By the mid-1850s, they drove cattle by the thousands to California. As the gold rush slackened, wheat became the primary cash crop. Dugouts and flatboats carried it down the Willamette to market. The early 1850s saw the first steamboats carry market cargo on the Willamette.

* * *

Santa Fe long held pride of place as the commercial center of the West. The opening of the Santa Fe trade to Americans in 1821 gave rise to the seven-days-a-week activity in the town's central plaza. As the trade caravans entered Mexican territory, the customs authorities took a casual, purely discretionary approach to the assessment of tariffs.

The American conquest of the Spanish Southwest added 2,000 soldiers and their families to the mix of American traders, nomadic and pueblo Indians, and long-time Mexican residents. The Mexicans continued to trade, farm, and operate sheep ranches, while American officials and traders bought up land and pursued government contracts for provisioning the army and the Indian agencies.

Far from navigable rivers, New Mexico relied on overland freighting from either the Mississippi River or the Gulf of Mexico. A number of large freighting companies dominated the Santa Fe trail. The largest one, Majors and Russell, at its peak owned 3,500 wagons, 40,000 oxen, and 1,000 mules, and employed 4,000 men. Mules went faster, but oxen pulled more weight. Most trains comprised about twenty-five wagons drawn by six oxen apiece, each wagon hauling more than three tons. Wagon-masters and teamsters conducted the wagons over the trail.[12] Today, a 'teamster' drives tractor-trailers; yesterday, he drove ox or mule teams. Trade goods carried over land remained expensive as long as the trail remained perilous. So great was the danger of Indian raids and highway robbery, that traders could not insure their cargos. They bore all the risk and passed on their losses in the form of higher prices.

A wool and peltry dealer receiving the wool from a single New Mexico ranch. The wires are telegraph wires, which first spanned the continent in 1861. In the background, a windmill powers the town's water pump. (Library of Congress)

After the Civil War ended, a former Union soldier and his wife opened a trading post in Tecolote, New Mexico, a place on the Santa Fe Trail where an adobe village had grown up around a watering hole. The couple purchased a lot and built a stone building for their store and house. They stocked tools, animal feed, household goods, clothing, blankets, horse tack, and provisions. The merchants bought food and livestock from Mexicans and Indians. Among the items the people brought in to trade were goats, sheep, chickens, firewood, peppers, onions, blue corn, beans, pumpkins, cheese, pottery, blankets, jewelry, and beadwork. These items, in turn, the merchants traded to the wagon trains. The store, like stores everywhere, became a gathering place. The American traders also collected salt from a salt-sink and traded it to Indians for cattle. They procured feed and sold it to freighters for their draft animals. Later they gave up the store and turned to ranching. From the yield of their dairy cows, they made about 200 pounds of butter each week, which they traded for meat, vegetables, and cash. For transport, they wrapped the butter in cheesecloth and packed it in salt.

* * *

The settlers of Dakota Territory frequently sought off-farm work to help their families survive the early years of sodbusting. They trapped animals for fur, broke sod for neighbors, built railroads, or gathered buffalo bones for sale to the eastern fertilizer market. Some went to town to find jobs, like one farmer who spent a winter tending for a brick mason. His wife and children stayed on the farm and looked after the livestock.

The Montana gold rush brought prospectors through Dakota Territory, and emigrants seeking land farther west passed through. Dakota settlers made some profit by selling supplies to these travelers. The army bases and Indian agencies provided another market for surplus grain and livestock. Like farmers on the earlier frontiers, South Dakota homesteaders settled their store accounts with proceeds from their grain sales each fall. Butter and eggs provided a few pennies toward reducing the balance during the intervening months.

In pursuit of the wheat crop that would finally turn a profit, late nineteenth-century farmers willingly went deep into debt. Many felt they must have the latest in farm machinery to keep up with the competition. Most walked unwarily into this trap, despite ample warning from no less than the U.S. government:

> There is another item in reference to the farming population of this country, which certainly adds to the number of its lunatics; it is that grim specter DEBT, which is voluntarily set up in the households of three farmers out of four...'[13]

Only one constraint kept the level of borrowing down: a homesteader could not use the farm to secure a loan until the claim was proved up. Until that day, he used chattel property to secure small loans. Loans secured by chattels charged high interest, because there was nothing to prevent the borrower from selling or making off with the animal or wagon he had signed over to the lender. Lending and borrowing, however, had come to stay. Banks, lenders, and mortgage companies opened offices in every town. In newly settled areas, they charged from 12 to 36 percent annual interest on loans. When, as in Dakota Territory, the legislature set a legal limit on interest rates, lenders got around it by discounting the amount loaned; that is, making the borrower pay 'points' up front for the privilege of borrowing. In older settlements, the interest rates stabilized around 7 percent.

The ready availability of loans worked two ways, however. Following a series of bad years, so many people mortgaged their farms and abandoned them, that lenders went broke trying to keep up tax payments on all the abandoned properties they suddenly owned. Local feeling invariably ran

Trading post in the southwest, late nineteenth century. Hand-woven woolen rugs were unique to the region. (Photo by Ben Wittick, courtesy School of American Research Collections, Museum of New Mexico, Santa Fe)

Distributing food rations at an Indian agency. Settlers sold their surplus to the federal government, which in turn undertook – usually inadequately – to feed the Indians with the produce of their former lands. (Library of Congress)

against the lender: when a farmer abandoned his mortgaged property, the neighbors with complete impunity carted off the house and outbuildings, piecemeal or in their entirety. Thus the properties securing mortgages lost much of their value shortly after the owner's wagon pulled away.

The early establishment of railroads distinguished the Dakota frontier from those of earlier times. The railroads permitted farmers who lived far from waterways to sell their produce to distant markets. However, the railroads controlled the fees charged for freighting, and these sometimes exceeded the value of the produce. As drought years, low wheat prices, and heavy debt pushed prairie farms over the edge of failure, farmers began organizing to protest railroad pricing policies.

Newly arrived settlers, financially unprepared for the long struggle ahead, learned a harsh lesson:

> 'This is a hard country on a poor man. They all are independent and won't sell anything unless they can get a price for it, and us poor chaps have to stand it. If we ever get fixed we will do just the same.'[14]

VILLAGES AND TOWNS

Frontier communities grew out of forts or formed around a crossroads store. Groups of settlers who migrated en masse founded towns, and speculators purchased and promoted their own town sites, particularly after the War of 1812. Town sites selected for county seats usually throve, but a few exceptions remained merely a crossroads with store, courthouse, jail, and postmaster's house. Pre-planned towns were invariably laid out to a rectangular plan.

The rough cabins housing a store and a tavern often served as the first buildings of a new village. Doctors, lawyers, teachers, and craftsmen, such as the blacksmith, followed hard on the heels of the first merchants. Some doctors operated apothecaries to sell the remedies they prescribed. The first professionals and trades-

A New Mexico town in 1880. A typical raw western town with one dusty street, dominated by saloon, liquor store, and hotel. (National Archives)

men lived at the tavern – or hotel in later years – or boarded with families until they could afford to build houses. More substantial towns boasted a newspaper, regular stagecoach service, larger stores and more numerous tradesmen. By the time towns came to Dakota Territory, saloons offered oysters, ice cream, and soda pop. Few farmers coming to town to do their marketing could afford such treats. They had to be content with a small sack of candy from the general store.

Frontier towns hosted regular markets for farm produce. Four different weekly markets functioned in Cincinnati by 1815. Most towns also had a butcher's shop. The butcher sold wild game and bought cattle from local farmers. Butchers rang bells or blew horns to inform the populace when they were about to slaughter an animal for sale.

The collection of log cabins eventually acquired a covering of board siding, and then paint, as the farmers and villagers prospered. Board sidewalks and hitching racks fronted the commercial establishments, and picket or rail fencing the houses. The streets were dirt roads, by turns dusty or muddy, the buildings no more than two stories, and the water supplied by rainfall and collected in cisterns. A squad of free-ranging dogs and pigs 'collected' the trash. Wherever people gathered in large numbers to live and work, some form of pollution resulted. Horse and cattle droppings swarming with flies, dead animals, rotting cotton seeds, and slaughterhouses all contributed to a frontier town's noisome ambience.

Towns required each man to serve a rotation as town watchman or town crier. The men worked for the constable, patrolling the town at night and calling out the hours. In the absence of street lights, anyone going out at night had to carry a lantern.

Most early towns dug wells from which townspeople carried water. As early as 1804, Frankfort, Kentucky boasted a public waterworks, which featured a gravity-fed pipeline of hollowed cedar logs running from a spring-fed reservoir uphill of the town. During the same period, Natchez, Mississippi held a lottery to fund cisterns and wells. In some towns, an entrepreneur hauled water from the town well in a tank wagon and charged each home for the service of filling its water barrels. Washing clothes, a most water-intensive task, impelled townspeople to find creative solutions. Some frontier towns established an informal 'washing camp' at a pond or stream some distance away. Women congregated on wash days to socialize over the steaming kettles.

Deadwood, South Dakota in 1879 began constructing its public water system, a more extensive enterprise than those of earlier towns. The system began eight miles from town at a mountain spring. Miles of bedrock flumes carried the water to a reservoir 200 feet above the town. From the reservoir, pipes carried the water down to mains, and from there into service pipes running to each home and business.
A multitude of wood houses built close together, each with its fire going full blast day and night, presented

a constant fire hazard. The first volunteer fire departments relied on 'bucket brigades' to put out fires. A line of men passed full buckets from water source to fire, and a line of women passed the empty buckets back. With greater wealth and organization, towns acquired carts equipped with ladders and buckets, and eventually, pumps. The pumps drew water from cisterns placed strategically around town. In contrast, the water system of Deadwood, served by an elevated reservoir, provided such water pressure for the firefighters' hoses that they needed no pumps. They simply opened one of the towns placed hydrants.

MASON COUNTY, KENTUCKY

A group of families that had migrated together from New Jersey pooled their funds in 1788 to purchase 1,400 acres. The families clustered their cabins together for mutual defense, and named their community Mays Lick (after the original owner and the salt lick on the premises), a name which persists today.

Small town in Kentucky. The houses are small, but civic pride shows in the neat rows of trees lining the single street. (In Lewis Collins, History of Kentucky, Covington, KY, 1878)

Mays Lick soon held a store and two taverns, along with such tradesmen as a blacksmith, carpenter, tanner, tailor, weaver, and shoemaker. The village grew over the years to a market center for the settlers living within about ten miles in any direction. Several hundred households from Virginia and Maryland joined the original 52 New Jersey emigrants.

Local citizens earmarked Saturdays, the day the local courts convened at Mays Lick, as the time to come to town for all their purchases. The men lingered in town for horse trading and racing, dog and cock fights, and drinking to intoxication. Mays Lick also served as the site for regimental militia musters, political campaigns and meetings, and 'singing schools' where the inhabitants practiced religious music. After such assemblies, the gathered men stayed on to wager, fight, and drink.

Washington, another Mason County village, covered one square mile divided by three main streets running north–south, with the smaller cross streets running at right angles. The central town lots consisted of one-half acre and the outlying lots were five acres. The town possessed a stone courthouse, a wooden jail surrounded by a high stone wall, a jailer's house built of brick, and handsome stone and brick houses on the main street. The Baptists had their own meeting house, but the handful of Presbyterians held worship in the courthouse. By the 1790s, all the towns of Mason County boasted stone or frame houses. The houses had glass windows, walnut shingles, and floors of blue ash.

NATCHEZ, MISSISSIPPI

Natchez, Mississippi, as a river port town, presented a much rowdier aspect than the common run of frontier towns. Englishman Henry Fearon visited Natchez in 1817. At the boat landing, he saw 'about thirty houses, the greater part of which are whiskey shops, gambling and other houses, in which there is a degree of open profligacy, which I had not before witnessed in the United States.' * By 'other houses,' he surely meant houses of prostitution, which lined the streets leading to the boat landing. Natchez in 1817 mirrored the status of the Ohio River port of Louisville, Kentucky during the 1790s. Such lawless riverboat towns in time grew relatively sedate, their ardors dampened by encroaching, and often disapproving, civilization.

American settlers lived in Natchez alongside the previous Catholic occupants, the Spanish and French Creoles. Balconies and piazzas adorned many of their houses. The entertainments offered by Natchez included card parties for men, and in the early days, dances featuring the handful of bold women from a very scarce female population. Later, as Natchez gained respectability and more women settled there, both sexes attended traveling shows, music societies, and amateur theater groups. Men joined fraternal lodges and volunteer military companies, chiefly for the social advantages they offered. Horse races, bear baiting and gander pulling, fights, and contests in throwing at targets filled out the available amusements. Natchez remained the largest of Mississippi towns in the early 1800s, none of which exceeded 5,000 in population.

* Henry Fearon, *Sketches of America* (London, 1819), p. 267.

PORTLAND, OREGON

With the arrival of the first sizeable emigrant party from the States, small towns sprung up along the Willamette and Columbia rivers and competed to become the primary market center of the region. They built wharves on the banks and roads out into the surrounding farm country in the effort to attract the settlers' produce. First came Oregon City on the Willamette in 1842. John McLoughlin, chief factor of the Hudson's Bay

Portland, Oregon, 1852. (Library of Congress)

Company, established the town and hired destitute emigrants to build a mill and other structures. Portland, 12 miles up the Willamette from its confluence with the Columbia, soon outstripped the others.

The first streets of Portland were laid out in 1845. The town site was heavily timbered, but its location at the falls of the Willamette outweighed this disadvantage. Large vessels from the Columbia could not ascend the

Willamette any farther than Portland: in 1847, about twenty ships called there. Each autumn, exhausted emigrants, impoverished by their overland journey, poured into town to work and stay for the winter. Springtime sent them out into the Willamette Valley to find land. The small permanent population began to expand by 1849. Most families headed out into the valley to begin farming; single men stayed in the towns to try their hands at business.

Within a decade, people saw through Portland's modest façade to its future as 'a great commercial city.'

'Now it has a very poor wharf, a few small wooden business houses along the water front, a row of residences and shops with a little wooden hotel on first street....It was with some difficulty that we found a smooth place among the stumps and fallen trees to drive our wagon and pitch our tent beyond the limits of front and first streets.' *

* Kenneth L. Holmes, ed., *Covered Wagon Women: Diaries & Letters from the Western Trails, 1840-1890* (Glendale, CA, 1983), vol. 8, p. 161.

SANTA FE, NEW MEXICO

During the Mexican era, Santa Fe held about 3,000 people. The population grew by a couple of thousand shortly after the Americans won it. By 1854, the town had gained a Baptist church, an American cemetery, a new state house, and a new penitentiary. It also held a hotel, a printer, about two dozen stores, two tailors, two cobblers, two blacksmiths, an apothecary, a bakery, and a number of grog shops.

The adobe houses of New Mexican towns faced away from the streets, showing no windows to outsiders. Dogs, chickens, goats, and burros had the run of the dusty streets. In fact, 'goats and small burros lay unmolested on the narrow board walks.' *

A dusty and treeless Santa Fe, New Mexico. Founded by the Spanish in 1610, Santa Fe de San Francisco had no doctors, lawyers, or newspapers until Americans began arriving in the 1830s. (National Archives)

Santa Fe served as the trading center for an area extending from California to Texas and Kansas. Wagon trains arrived daily to fill the central plaza. The Mexicans sold food, rugs, jewelry, clothing, and household goods in the open-air marketplace. Among the produce they offered were wild grapes, plums, and berries, milk, bread, and cheese, bundles of hay, and venison, turkey, pork, and mutton, all hauled into town on the backs of donkeys.

The plaza was not shaded by trees as it is today. The draft and pack animals left their droppings everywhere. American newcomers often described the town as filthy and lacking in amenities. They had not yet seen Albuquerque to the south, population 1,500, reputed to be plagued by sand storms and supplied with unusually muddy water.

* Marian Sloan Russell, *Land of Enchantment: Memoirs of Marian Russell along the Santa Fe Trail* (Evanston, 1954), p. 53.

TOWNS OF SOUTH DAKOTA

In 1861, Yankton held 300 inhabitants in a motley collection of sod huts and log cabins. The population consisted mostly of young single men. A hotel and a law office were among the few amenities. Nearby Vermillion boasted a general store and a sawmill.

The town of Deadwood rose rapidly and illegally from the gold-laden Black Hills. Established in 1876 in blatant contravention of the U.S. treaty with the Sioux, it soon held 7,000 people living in tents, wagons, wood shanties, and log buildings. Deadwood's hotels, eating places, theaters, dance halls, saloons, and gambling establishments also catered to 20,000 miners in the environs. Gold dust served as the primary medium of exchange. Basic supplies were often scarce and expensive, because Indians raided the freight wagons.

Boom towns also sprung up in areas that lacked the inducement of gold. In anticipation of a railroad station and a farm population boom, settlers flocked to a spot, snapped up price-inflated town lots as a sure-fire investment, and built a town almost overnight. One such boom town garnered 1,800 inhabitants in a matter of months. The population fueled some sixty businesses, including eight groceries, eight hotels, five lumber

Deadwood, South Dakota in 1876. (National Archives)

113

yards, and three each of stables, banks, and hardware stores. * Easterners came to their prairie town lots, purchased sight-unseen, expecting broad avenues and brick houses, only to find sod and board shanties lining muddy paths.

So quickly were the boom towns built that the hotel rooms were mere cubicles divided by partitions fabricated from blankets or canvas. Those were the good hotels. Others were divided into two large halls serving as men's and ladies' dormitories. The quality of hotel meals varied wildly and depended entirely on the skill of the cook, often the hotel keeper's wife. Boom towns also held grist mills, harness-makers, blacksmiths, and livery stables, important both to the surrounding homesteaders and the land seekers. But when disaster struck a boom town – the railroad passed it by, it lost its bid for the county seat, or the stage line changed its route – people and businesses deserted and the town dwindled away.

Firewood in the arid southwest was sufficiently hard to get that traders found it worthwhile to bring it to market on the backs of donkeys. The patient beasts even carried feed for other livestock. (Arizona Historical Society)

Describing the trips to town, twenty miles distant, of his South Dakota boyhood, a man recalled:

'we had to get up long before daybreak to get the cows milked and turned out to pasture. Then the horses had to be fed; we put additional hay in the wagon box and some grain in a sack for them. Mother would put up a lunch for all of us as we could not afford to buy a meal.

'When we reached Huron, we would locate an empty lot, unhitch the team, and tie the horses to the wagon so that they could eat the hay. At noon we would come back, give them their feed, and eat our own lunch in the shade of the wagon. We were not accustomed to walking on the hot wooden sidewalks... '**

* Herbert S. Schell, History of South Dakota (Lincoln, NE, 1968), p. 167.
** Ruth Cook Frajola, ed., 'They went west,' South Dakota History, VI:3 (Summer 1976), p. 299.

THE VILLAGE STORE

In the earliest days of settlement, frontier farmers could rely only on what they produced themselves or what they bartered with traveling peddlers selling groceries and general merchandise off carts or flatboats. The more remote their location from village, river, or road, the higher the price a merchant could command. In fact, haggling over prices was the norm, and today's system of set prices did not prevail until after the Civil War.* In the frontier economy, where barter prevailed over cash, stores extended credit, usually interest-free, to farmers for a year or more and accepted farm produce as payment. Come autumn, storekeepers sold the accumulated farm goods at a profit to wholesalers in the population centers of the East.

Each store served as many as 400 farmers from the surrounding area. Storekeepers provided not only merchandise and an outlet for disposing of surplus farm produce, but also held customers' money for safekeeping, wrote letters for the illiterate, and served as purchasing agents for everything from insurance to newspapers from the East. In addition, they paid bills, such as medical and tax bills, for their customers and placed the amount paid on their accounts.

The earliest stores began as rough one-room cabins, no bigger than a pioneer's first home. However, stores were the buildings in a community most likely to have locks, for fear of theft. Since many of the customers came from distant farms, some storekeepers provided a yard for camping, firewood for cooking fires, and even food. In winter, customers slept inside on the floor. Families who lived nearby also made the trip to the store an all-day occasion, a chance to exchange news and browse among the wondrous array of goods. Some merchants served whiskey to encourage their customers to linger, while others resented what they called 'loungers.' **

Saturday was the most popular shopping day throughout the frontier, although some storekeepers braved the disapproval of the more religious to do business on Sunday mornings before church. Settlers organized trips to the store to coincide with militia musters and court days and stayed late to drink and socialize. A farmer in urgent need of an item expected to be served regardless of the hour, and the shopkeeper obliged rather than turn away his business. Spring and fall were the busiest seasons; settlers purchased little in the winter because the weather made travel more difficult.

The village store, because it sold general merchandise, soon came to be known as the 'general store.' It was, and is, a uniquely American institution. Today in rural America, as yesterday, if one wants to find out what is going on in the area – who needs work, has lost their dog, or has a house to rent – one asks at the country general store.

General stores carried assortments of 'penny candies' to be sold a piece at a time. Peppermint sticks and rock candy – crystallized sugar – were popular. Stores from Santa Fe to South Dakota featured a multitude of candies behind a glass showcase. No trip to town was complete without buying a treat of candy or peanuts for the children.

* Lewis E. Atherton, *The Frontier Merchant in Mid-America* (Columbia, MO, 1971), p. 54.
** Atherton, p. 22.

Inside an 1881 general store on the southwestern frontier. As in general stores everywhere, bolts of cloth line the wall (on the right). In the foreground is the display of typically unrefrigerated eggs. (Arizona Historical Society)

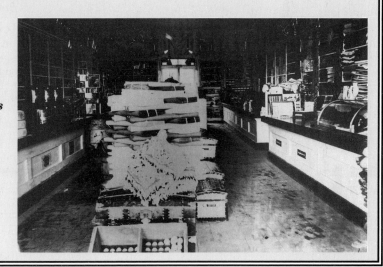

WORKING FOR HIRE

The earliest frontier families mastered many trades and provided most household and farm goods for themselves, but they were always willing to use the services of skilled tradesmen. Among their neighbors, farmers found other farmers who practiced a trade, whether blacksmith, cobbler, tanner, or teacher. They traded these skills with neighbors in exchange for labor or produce.

A man or woman, skilled or unskilled, who was willing to work for hire was always in demand on the frontier. Farmers traded heavy farm labor among themselves, but hired outsiders when possible. Farm laborers and domestic servants, so hard to find in the egalitarian West, commanded higher pay than they could in the East. Accordingly, a South Dakota home-

An 1852 blacksmith shop operated by Zuni pueblo Indians in New Mexico. Notice the large bellows used to intensify the fire's heat. (Library of Congress)

steader advised his wife, 'If you should get a job of work charge $5 per week, and if they grumble at the price tell them to do their own work...'[15] Because of the labor scarcity, even once hired, workers readily slipped away to take up better offers. Many of them hoped to gain experience and save money to take up farming of their own. They aspired to join the same economic class as their employers. A horrified Englishman reported, 'White servants are difficult to be had, and indifferent when procured, and expect at all times to be at the same table with their masters.'[16]

Skilled tradesmen had all the work they could handle. Reflecting the heavy demand for labor, the terms of hire differed from what we know today. Construction laborers expected payment in both cash and bed and board for the duration of the job. Masons expected the owner to provide men to serve as tenders. Frontier dwellers also brought a steady stream of business to blacksmiths and gunsmiths. Between them they took care of most early metal-working needs, repairing whatever metal equipment came their way. Often located alongside blacksmiths, wagon and carriage businesses served an unending stream of frontier customers. The departing emigrant needed to purchase a wagon, the newly arrived settler to have one repaired.

Men who could not or would not settle down and farm found a number of alternatives. They worked as loggers, selling firewood to steamboats or town-dwellers. They made charcoal – produced by burning wood buried in 'coal pits' – grazed herds on unclaimed land, and hunted and fished, selling hides, furs, meat, and fish in town. Some skilled tradesmen took up the traveling life, going from settlement to settlement, setting type for printers, sharpening knives and scissors, or repairing clocks and watches.

In the pine forests of the deep south, men extracted turpentine and tar from pine and sold them to the naval stores industry. They tapped pines for resin, which they distilled to yield turpentine. To extract tar, pine was burned in kilns, or in pits similar to charcoal pits. The fires required careful tending; too hot a fire would burn up the tar.

Frontier women as well found themselves compelled to make income from non-farming pursuits, or to operate farms on their own. Widows often carried on the family farm with the help of their children. Likewise in towns, women continued to run businesses after their husbands died.

Townswomen worked as schoolteachers, dressmakers, milliners, and keepers of taverns and boarding houses. Farm women turned the tasks they performed on their farms – baking bread and pies, making clothes, butter, preserves, or other household goods – to income-earning opportunities in town. Some made businesses of cooking, washing, and ironing among the male populations of mining towns: men were willing to pay well for someone else to do such work. Women of lesser means worked as laundresses, shop clerks, or domestic servants, the least respected of the 'respectable' occupations. At the bottom of the scale labored the prostitute. In a class by herself worked the midwife or medicine woman.

On the scale of non-farming aspirations, professions such as medicine, the law, teaching, and the ministry occupied top place. Next were merchants, 'mechanics' – such as millers, manufacturers, and blacksmiths – and skilled craftsmen. Parents were willing to make sacrifices to have their children enter a profession. In Kentucky in 1800, Daniel Drake's father was determined to make his initially reluctant fifteen-year-old son a doctor, though he could ill afford the cost:

> 'He courageously persevered, however, in his cherished purpose, and I had to submit; although (on his account) I would have preferred being bound to a trades man; and had actually selected a master, Mr. Stout, of Lexington, a saddler, to whom some of my cornfield companions had already gone.'[17]

Skilled and unskilled laborers completed the hierarchy. Skilled laborers included carpenters, furniture and cabinet makers, masons, wheelwrights, gunsmiths, shoe makers, bakers, butchers, tailors, barbers, plasterers, watch makers, saddle and harness makers, and silversmiths, to name just a few. Yet others made livings by crafting spinning wheels, hats, stills, iron goods, and tin goods such as chamber pots, lanterns, kettles, milk pans, cups, coffeepots, canisters, and colanders.

BUSINESS AND INDUSTRY

The initial industries of the frontier revolved around lumber and wood products. The first 'lumber yards' consisted of a two-man whipsaw team. One such team

> 'hewed out stocks enough for 1,000 feet of inch planks which we had engaged to saw for Peter Remington, a Yankee who had brought a heavy stock of goods and was in a great hurry to set them up. We were to have the planks ready by Saturday evening. We had it done a day sooner. It was for a floor and counter; and he gave us twenty dollars to lay down the floor and make the counter.... We completed the job Saturday, and I helped mark and put up goods all day Sunday, for which I received ten dollars.'[18]

As population increased, water-powered sawmills began to operate. By the early 1790s, one county in Kentucky boasted four sawmills. The first steam-powered sawmill began operation in the early 1800s. The usual price for sawing, whether by hand or mill, was half the resulting lumber.

The plentiful white oak of the newly settled western lands gave rise to a barrel stave industry, barrels being the primary means of transporting goods to distant markets. Staves are the strips of wood that make up the barrel's wall; they are bound together by metal bands. Home-building on the frontier fostered a shingle-making industry as well. An accomplished carpenter could make shingles on site and install enough to cover 100 square feet in about a day and a half.[19] No sooner were some businesses established than their founders offered them for sale. For example, from the beginning, Kentucky newspapers advertised the sale of sawmills and salt works. Clearly the operators intended to use these businesses to finance something grander.

An early frontier gristmill. Notice, on the right, a wooden conduit carrying water from the stream to power the mill. (Library of Congress)

LEAD MINING

The eighteenth-century French inhabitants of Missouri established seasonal lead-mining enterprises. In the months before and after the harvest, men traveled to the mines to extract the ore from shallow open pits with picks and wooden shovels. The miners sold the ore to the landowner. When test pits revealed an area to have plentiful ore, a fire pit or furnace was established. The owners engaged workers to smelt the ore over wood fires, built in long, narrow pits or crude stone furnaces in later years. Next, they remelted the metal and cast it into heavy bars for shipment downriver to New Orleans. When the hard-pressed Kentucky pioneers ran low on lead during their battles against the Indians, intrepid frontiersmen traveled to French territory to replenish their supplies.

By 1800, American emigrants had introduced more efficient furnaces and made shafts and tunnels for extracting the ore from deeper in the ground. Lead mining became a full-time occupation, with miners living in cabins at the mines.

Lead miners at work in Missouri. French colonists mined lead from open pits in the 1700s. The American era saw the introduction of underground tunnels. (In Albert D. Richardson, Beyond the Mississippi, *Hartford, 1869)*

A floating mill on the Ohio River in 1791. (Library of Congress)

Flowing water powered both sawmills and gristmills. Floating mills, set on rafts, also pursued the trade. Millers hastened to set up business along rivers on the well-watered frontiers of Kentucky and Oregon. One Oregon man spent an entire winter fashioning a pair of millstones from a granite boulder that he split with steel wedges. Settlers often traveled days in each direction to patronize the nearest gristmill and waited for hours once they arrived. Because of this demand, a smart gristmill owner could rapidly expand his operation. Since the farmer paid for the milling in grain, the miller, in turn, developed commercial ties with shippers and consumers. Millers sometimes raised hogs on the lower-grade grain byproducts.

Settlers who lived along roads or rivers seized every opportunity to supplement their farm incomes. They operated ferries where roads crossed rivers, and offered refreshments and lodgings to passengers waylaid by high water. They opened stores and taverns at busy crossroads to outfit passing travelers and emigrants. The most enterprising improved a stretch of road and put up a toll gate.

Government involvement in American business is by no means a recent development. Early nineteenth-century state and local governments extensively regulated commercial activities. They set prices for toll roads, ferries, and mills, and established standards for the alcohol content of whiskey served in taverns, the salt content of preserved meat, and the construction of barrels for shipping assorted foods. But in the days before swollen government, enforcement of these regulations was sporadic.

Frontier industries of the early nineteenth century provided such necessities as lime, gunpowder, cast iron, and bricks. Westerners made lime by burning pure limestone, either in kilns, or by making huge open fires. Versatile lime served to fertilize soil, make mortar and whitewash, and remove fur from hides prior to tanning.

Gunpowder consisted of saltpeter, charcoal, and sulphur, all finely powdered in log rollers. While people made charcoal wherever trees grew, and frontier merchants sold sulphur, saltpeter was harder to come by. Saltpeter dirt – dirt containing saltpeter – occurred in certain caves. Workers dug and pulverized the dirt, then placed it in large wooden leaching vats. They then let the

Horses hauling logs to the lumber mill. No job was considered too heavy for draft animals.
(Arizona Historical Society)

resulting 'peter-beer' – nitrate – leach again, through ashes. This process yielded a potassium nitrate mixture. Next they boiled down the mixture into a mass, braving the risk of an explosion. Drying, then crushing, completed the process.

By 1793, one iron works operated on the banks of State Creek on the Kentucky frontier. The employees raised ore and cut wood for the furnace, which consumed an astonishing 100 acres of woodland a year.[20] It is little wonder indeed that open fields soon replaced Kentucky's abundant woods. Iron workers repeatedly heated and hammered the ore to remove the impurities and shape the metal. The stream's flow powered both the hammers and the bellows. The works produced pig iron and castings. More sophisticated iron works used charcoal to heat the ore. So scarce were iron nails and hinges that settlers salvaged them from burnt buildings. Three Lexington men imported iron nail rods from Maryland and produced a supply of nails, which many bought without a murmur of protest at the high price.

Lime, gunpowder, and iron were vital to frontier life, but brick was a luxury. A brick house signified prosperity and permanence, the arrival of civilization. Town-dwellers especially demanded bricks, thereby turning crude settlements into places of substance. Early brick yards produced sun-dried mud bricks, differing only in size from southwestern adobes. To make fired bricks, one needed only ample supplies of clay and firewood. Brick yards produced brick by the tens of thousands.

By the mid-nineteenth century, small local gristmills had been replaced by much larger operations. The wide acceptance in the 1840s of the grain elevator, based on a chain and bucket system, led to large-scale and centralized grain handling. Livestock sales, too, became centralized. This in turn opened the way for shady operators to make dishonest money from farmers. A sufficient proportion of grain and stock dealers engaged in slick practices to give all of them a bad name. They held one key advantage over farmers: they owned the only scales in the area. Dealers

SALT

Salt springs, or 'licks,' so called because wild animals licked the salty earth bare, were the primary source of salt in Kentucky. Salt works arose at the site of each lick. First the salt maker had to sink a well, usually between 10 and 50 feet deep. If the diggers went too deep, they risked tapping a vein of unsalted water which would dilute the salt spring and make extraction too difficult.

The process began with the man who brought water up from the source, at a rate of two buckets per minute, and added it to the 20-gallon metal pans or kettles boiling over the long fire pits. The fire trenches were lined with stones, bricks, or clay. As the water evaporated, the fire-tenders poured the strengthening brine into wooden troughs where the salt settled. They boiled the brine yet again and then allowed the salt to settle. Finally, the tenders removed the salt with a dipper and placed it in another trough to dry.

As the wood choppers cut down the trees surrounding the lick, the fires were moved closer to the receding woods and the water had to be hauled increasing distances. Some works had the water piped to the furnace in pipes made from red cedar poles. The pipes were hand-augured through 10 to 15-foot sections of cedar. Some salt works used mule power to pump up the water with a wooden pump. The mules, attached to a long pole and compelled to march in circles, had to be blindfolded to prevent motion-sickness.

A small salt works employed about eight men and could produce some 100 bushels a week using three fire pits. At one lick, 100 gallons of water yielded a bushel of salt, while at another it required 800 gallons. The operator of the works paid rent in salt to the land's owner.

Salt licks also existed across the Mississippi. Extensive salt basins provided salt in the arid lands farther west. On the arid plains, salt producers used solar evaporation as well as boiling. At a salt basin near Fort Bascom, New Mexico, laborers cut the salt into large blocks during the dry season and hauled them away for use at the fort.

A salt works under permanent roof. In building such a structure, the proprietor exhibited great confidence that neither the fuel nor the salt spring would run out.
(Library of Congress)

underweighed incoming grain and livestock, and overstated the weight of what they sold. Such abuses inspired farmers to organize cooperative elevators and stockyards.

As the nineteenth century advanced, production of myriad household needs moved out of the home and into the hands of professionals. This trend created expanded commercial and business opportunities. For example, where once pioneers invariably cooked over open hearths they had built themselves and ate off of hand-carved wooden trenchers, now all aspired to stoves and dishes imported from the east. Soap, candles, shoes – once produced in pioneer homes – likewise came to be made at factories. Beginning in 1872, homesteaders could rely on Montgomery Ward, the Chicago-based mail order company, for everything from fabric and ready-made clothing to buggies and farm wagons. A Dakota Territory homesteader, over the course of two months in 1884, did the following chores in town: he purchased seed wheat from the miller, traded his heavy breaking plow for a lighter one, got his harrow sharpened, and refilled his kerosene can. A pioneer farmer in Kentucky or Oregon would have saved his own seed from his previous crop, made his own plow, sharpened his own harrow, and shot a deer to get tallow so his wife could make candles. Perhaps he would have considered his brother pioneer in Dakota a more privileged and fortunate man; or perhaps not.

[1] Glenda Riley, 'Farm women's roles in the agricultural development of South Dakota,' *South Dakota History*, XIII:1 (Spring 1983), p. 110.

[2] Kenneth L. Holmes, ed., *Covered Wagon Women: Diaries & Letters from the Western Trails, 1840–1890* (Glendale, CA, 1983), vol. 1, p. 106.

[3] Marion Tinling and Godfrey Davies, eds., *The Western Country in 1793: Reports on Kentucky and Virginia by Harry Toulmin* (San Marino, 1948), p. 64.

[4] Peter H. Burnett, 'Recollections and opinions of a old pioneer,' *Quarterly of the Oregon Historical Society*, V:2 (June 1904), p. 172.

[5] Burnett, p. 172.

[6] Fred Lockley, 'Reminiscences of Martha E. Gilliam Collins,' *Quarterly of the Oregon Historical Society*, XVII:4 (December 1916), p. 366.

[7] Burnett, p. 177.

[8] Harvey W. Scott, 'Pioneer character of Oregon progress,' *Quarterly of the Oregon Historical Society*, XVIII:4 (December 1917), p. 248.

[9] William A. Bowen, *The Willamette Valley: Migration and Settlement on the Oregon Frontier* (Seattle, 1978), p. 65.

[10] Lansford W. Hastings, *The Emigrants' Guide to Oregon and California* (Cincinnati, 1845), p. 57.

[11] H.S. Lyman, 'Reminiscences of F. X. Matthieu,' *Quarterly of the Oregon Historical Society*, I:1 (March 1900), p. 95.

[12] Rupert Norval Richardson and Carl Coke Rister, *The Greater Southwest* (Glendale, CA, 1935), p. 245.

[13] 1862 Annual Report of the US Department of Agriculture, in Wayne D. Rasmussen, ed., *Agriculture in the United States: A Documentary History* (New York, 1975), vol. 2, p. 1015.

[14] Rasmussen, vol. 2, p. 1542.

[15] Ruth Seymour Burmeister, ed., 'Jeffries letters,' *South Dakota History*, VI:3 (Summer 1976), p. 321.

[16] Tinling , p. 65.

[17] Daniel Drake, *Pioneer Life in Kentucky* (New York, 1948), p. 237.

[18] Gideon Lincecum, 'Autobiography of Gideon Lincecum,' *Publications of the Mississippi Historical Society*, VIII (1904), pp. 466–7.

[19] Tinling, pp. 64–5.

[20] Tinling, pp. 98-9.

VI

'IN THE EVENING AN EXPRESS ARRIVED'

ON THE ROAD

Visitors from Europe frequently remarked on how willingly western Americans undertook journeys of many hundreds of miles. The visitors had not experienced frontier living, where distances were great and a simple trip to town was an all-day affair. Years of living so had conditioned Americans to an easy acceptance of long journeys undertaken in difficult conditions.

The first roads of the West followed routes that had once been game trails and then Indian paths. On these primitive roads, horses had to go single file. Blazes cut into tree trunks at intervals marked the way, and forks in the trail bewildered outsiders. Most trails crossed numerous creeks, which became unfordable whenever it rained. To make a trail into a road, fit for wheeled traffic, trees had to be cut down, leaving the stumps just short enough for wagon beds to clear them. Early road builders considered 18-inch stumps to be quite short enough.

Any low spots in the road collected water with each rain, and the traffic quickly beat such spots into a permanently muddy morass. At first, pioneers forged a new trail around the boggy stretch. Later inhabitants surfaced the swampy trails with lengths of log – a process known as corduroying – or built entire wooden causeways over the wet places. In 1851, for example, Oregon's territorial legislature authorized the laying of 10 miles of plank surfacing over the morass on the road into Portland. Even dry dirt roads developed permanent deep ruts. In summer, all traffic kicked up clouds of choking dust. In winter, the entire surface froze, ruts and mud holes alike. This actually improved the ease of travel by offering a firm road bed, until the inevitable thaw. Snow

A rest stop during a family journey by covered wagon in the southwest, circa 1890. The draft animals have been unhitched so they can graze. Dirt tracks and covered wagons remained the lot of travelers in regions not yet served by railroads. (Photo by Ben Wittick, courtesy of the Museum of New Mexico)

A typical southwestern oxcart in Jemez, New Mexico. Pioneer Jesse Applegate recalled: 'The wheels were without hub, spoke, or felloe; they were simply short sections of large trees, three or four feet in diameter, sawed off and holes made in the center for the axles. This wagon was called a truck, a very clumsy affair, which without a load, a small yoke of oxen could not draw with ease even on level ground. The friction on the spindles in the wheels, though they were well tarred, was such that, even with a load of rails requiring three yoke of oxen to draw them, the truck did not need any brake going down a steep hill. Under a heavy moving load, the spindles, if not abundantly tarred, would send forth a fearful scream with variations that could be heard for miles.' (National Archives)

A southwestern ox train. (National Archives)

presented a different challenge. Out came the sleighs, pulled by the hard-working oxen or horses.

Whether in mud, bog, or snow, wagons and stagecoaches got stuck regularly. Each spring brought anew the effort to stabilize the road surface with rock and logs to make it passable. Road engineering improved in the 1820s, but the government remained unable to fund needed grading and surfacing. County laws required both free men and slaves to work on road building or be subject to a fine. Road builders first used packed gravel to surface a Kentucky road in 1829. Gravel crushers and steam rollers prepared road surfaces in the east by the 1850s. They were slow to penetrate the West. Unadorned dirt persisted as the predominant road surface from coast to coast through the nineteenth century.

The Cumberland, or National, Road, won congressional funding in 1806, and construction began in 1811. This was the first step toward what, some 150 years later, became the mighty interstate highway system. By 1821 the National Road had evolved from a dirt track filled with 18-inch stumps to a graded and crowned road, covered with crushed gravel from its beginning at Cumberland, Maryland to Wheeling in present-day West Virginia. Recall that less than thirty years earlier, these towns had served as the jumping-off points for pioneers to travel by foot, horse, and boat to Kentucky. Laborers improved the road to Columbus by 1827, and all the way to Indianapolis by 1830. They built culverts, bridges, and retaining walls, and when they were done they had created a route all but unrecognizable to the first pioneers. According to Charles Fenno Hoffman, who traveled the National Road in 1833, however, all this work had wrought little actual improvement:

'a thin layer of broken stones is in many places spread over the renovated surface. I hope the roadmakers have not the conscience to call this Macadamizing. It yields like snow-drift to the heavy wheels which traverse it...'[1]

Decades later, the federal government funded freight wagon roads across the far West. Settlers, instead of doing unpaid road work under legal compulsion, earned much-needed extra income by seeking road-building jobs. These roads often followed early wagon routes that had originally served U.S. Army forts. Prairie road building proceeded rapidly because no trees stood in the way. Wheeled travel on prairie roads, although dusty, was relatively safe because the flat landscape and lack of tree roots presented fewer opportunities for vehicles to overturn.

Early travelers followed roads across streams without the benefit of bridges. Most stream crossings required the travelers and their mounts to wade across. Gradually matters improved. Laws required mill owners to build their mill dams wide enough to serve as bridges. The Virginia legislature appropriated funds for operating ferries on selected Kentucky waterways in the prestatehood days of the 1780s. Once Kentucky became a state, the legislature aided river travel by requiring selected channels to be kept clear of obstacles. Later, federal and state governments joined to fund projects to keep western rivers navigable.

Many early improved roads were privately operated toll roads. The local government set both tolls and ferry rates. In an early example of government assistance to business, the mandated rates were higher in less traveled areas so the operators could make enough money to stay in business. Since toll booths closed at night, people tried to save money by traveling after dark.[2] By law, neither children going to school, people going to church or funerals, nor men en route to militia musters had to pay tolls. Because toll road and ferry operators made little money, they had other sources of income, usually their farms.

Ferry boat construction, like all pioneer construction, relied on a good deal of makeshift. A newly arrived Oregon emigrant in 1843 found work building a ferry for one of his neighbors:

'He first caulked the openings between the planks in the bottom of the boat, and then poured in hot pitch. As it was a large boat, he used a bushel or two of literature he

A ferry takes a covered wagon across a river west of the Mississippi. One ferryman pulls the cable, the other wields an oar. In the background, the livestock have to swim. (Library of Congress)

found in the old house. Tracts and other pamphlets that had been left there by the missionaries were forced into the cracks with a chisel and hammer.'[3]

Livery stables served an important function in travel by road. They arose in every town and provided a place for settlers who could afford it to put up and feed their horses on their trips to town. Settlers of more modest means just brought along the necessary hay and feed. Livery stables also kept small fleets of horses and rigs for hire. They supplied drivers at no additional cost, because that way their horses and wagons stayed in trusted hands.

* * *

Stagecoach lines offered regular transportation of passengers and mail over established routes. They reached across the continent by the 1850s. The most famous stagecoach design, the flat-topped Concord, came into use in the 1830s. Like today's automobiles, the coaches were seen as extensions of the drivers' personalities; the drivers named their coaches and painted the exteriors with distinctive colors and finishes.

Like flatboat men and steamboat captains, stagecoach drivers took their place in contemporary legend as dashing and colorful characters. But they had to manage their teams competently, since their livelihood depended upon their horses' wellbeing. Although drivers flourished and cracked their whips to encourage the horses, they rarely actually struck them. Drivers did take risks in order to live up to their legends, sometimes racing other coaches at breakneck pace. Inevitably, states began to pass safety laws prohibiting such practices. At best, coach passengers faced jolting, dust, and the possibility of overturning. They expected to assist in freeing a coach whenever it stuck in the mud. Under ideal conditions with fresh horses, a coach might make ten miles an hour. It beat walking, until the driver ordered the passengers to get out and help free a mired coach. John Peyton traveled the roads of Ohio by stagecoach in 1848. At that time, Ohio was far beyond the frontier phase, but even so stagecoach travel remained fraught with discom-

A bogged stagecoach, as common a sight in the 1880s as it was 50 years earlier. (Arizona Historical Society)

fort and mishap. First the driver took a wrong turn in the woods. Eventually, he admitted he was lost. Then:

> 'one of our wheels gave way.... The driver was not at all disconcerted.... Felling a small tree, he took from it a log ten feet long, one end of this was, with the assistance of the passengers, secured upon the front axle, and passed back so as to hold up the body of the coach.... This done, the passengers were coolly informed that it would be necessary for them to make the residue of the journey, a distance of twenty-five miles, on foot. To my surprise, everyone took this announcement with perfect good temper.... At the end of three miles we came upon a farmhouse, and here the driver borrowed a wheel....
>
> 'Somewhat in this fashion we made the entire journey of forty miles to Sandusky, having had three upsets and one turn-over. No lives were lost, no limbs broken, and consequently no one thought seriously of such an every-day accident.'[4]

Wells, Fargo and Company, founded in 1852, acquired its fame hauling gold in California. It also carried mail, passengers, and express packages over large areas of the trans-Mississippi. Wells, Fargo bought out its major competitor in 1866 and gained a virtual monopoly of western stage coach traffic. Its operation required scores of coaches, hundreds of mules and horses, and the building and stocking of stations at intervals of 50 miles or less.

ON THE WATER

So rugged were the early overland routes to Kentucky that there was little possibility of carrying on commerce with the home states back east. The cost alone of feeding the horses as they hauled the goods would have been prohibitive. Conestoga freight wagons plied the better roads across the mid-Atlantic states to Pittsburgh. Then the Ohio River brought people and goods downstream from Pittsburgh, but return travel against the current was too arduous to foster regular trade. Yet if they were ever to grow beyond an isolated and primitive subsistence life, the Kentucky settlers, as well as the increasing number of emigrants to Tennessee to the south and the Ohio Valley region to the north, had to establish commercial ties with the outside world. From the time of the first pioneers, men of vision focused on the Mississippi River as the conduit for this commerce. Everyone living along one of the many navigable streams and rivers west of the mountains was in contact with this great potential trade route.

There were many daunting obstacles, not the least of which was foreign control of the Mississippi's mouth. As the threat of Indian attack subsided, emigrants and traders descended the Ohio River by every type of water craft imaginable. The flagships of the early western flotilla were flatboats known as 'Kentucky flats' or 'broadhorns.' Sturdy timber beams provided a solid hull around which artisans constructed an oblong, boxlike frame. Propelled by wide oars used as sweeps, the Kentucky flats transported impressive loads and withstood battering from an unexpected shoal or log. 'We see in them ladies, servants, cattle, horses, sheep, dogs and poultry,' recalled a veteran riverman, 'and on the roof the looms, ploughs, spinning wheels, and domestic implements of the family.'[5] When crewed by experienced watermen, the 'Kentucky flats' offered relatively safe and comfortable transport. The old flatboats changed little over the decades, and they remained in use until the late 1850s.

More common were the narrow, 40- to 80- foot-long keelboats. Featuring a pointed prow front and back, the keelboats were much more maneuverable than the flatboats and drew only a few feet when fully loaded. A keelboat crew pushed the vessel out into the current and then lowered a keel through the hull to provide stability. The crew walked along the runways on either side of the center cabin while wielding poles to propel the boat. The ubiquitous keelboats carried thousands of emigrants west and brought with them an entire river culture of boisterous, hard drinking, hard-swearing crew known in their day as the 'Kaintucks.'

Less fortunate emigrants who could not secure berths on the flatboats or keelboats relied upon rude rafts fabricated from a few dozen logs with a shed roof to protect from the weather. Yet so eager were emigrants to reach the West that they pressed into service anything that could float, and many that could not. They boarded wheelboats powered by cattle, horses, or even a hand-turned crank. They embarked on sailboats, canoes, and pirogues made of hollowed tree trunks. There were many perils, about which most emigrants were ignorant. Even a flatboat, when built in a hurry out of green wood, would leak, swell, and lose buoyancy.

A guidebook published in 1801 offered advice for the would-be river traveler. First, the book explained, 'procure a boat.'[6] This was not low humor, but rather a deadly serious matter. The unwary bought too many craft unsuited for the obstacles ahead. Whirlpools, 'boils', and sucks as well as huge drifting logs and ever changing shoals menaced river travelers. More feared were sawyers, trees upside down in the water with their tops firmly embedded and their trunks protruding unseen toward the surface. The sawyers could and did rip the bottom out of any vessel whose crew failed to detect the slight but telltale disturbance beneath the surface. Equally dangerous were planters, trees driven by the current into the river bottom with their jagged tops facing upstream. The low waters of summer made the river especially difficult to navigate. The preferred time to take to the river was from fall to spring.

Fierce thunderstorms, occasional tornadoes, and hurricanes supplemented the natural dangers. Then, in December 1811, something occurred so great that it dramatically changed the very course of the river itself. A survivor recalls that at 2 a.m. a tremendous noise awakened him and he saw the river's surface violently agitated. It was the New Madrid earthquake, a powerful temblor that dropped huge chunks of the riverbank into the water and rerouted entire sections of the river. This cataclysmic event destroyed close to sixty vessels unfortunate enough to be on the river at that time. Its powerful aftershocks continued for two months.

Still, the rivers offered a much easier path west than foot trails. Although a flatboat or keelboat could float down the great river all the way to New Orleans, a return journey to Pittsburgh consumed a backbreaking three months as the Kaintucks laboriously worked against the current. Upstream travel required a sailboat to carry a cable upstream to be secured to a tree. Then the crewmen pulled their vessel up to it, and repeated the process again and again. Rather than face such labor, most rivermen sold their vessel for its timber and spent a month or more walking back north. Wealthier traders took passage on a sailing ship around Florida and up the east coast. Either choice was better than no trade at all, but was still hugely inefficient. The advent of the steamboat changed everything.

In the year of the great earthquake, a steam-powered vessel 148 feet long and 20 feet at the beam departed Pittsburgh. Its name bespoke its destination, the *New Orleans*. Her whistle terrified the inhabitants of Louisville and then made their mouths open in slackjawed amazement as she did the impossible by moving upstream against the current. The first steamboats journeyed from New Orleans to Pittsburgh in about three weeks. Entrepreneurs launched new steamboats continuously. Each year their improved engines and design shortened travel time. By the year 1820, close to seventy steamers plied the rivers. By 1860, steamboats traveled 10 miles per hour downstream and 5 miles per hour upstream. On the move only during daylight hours, a steamboat took about two weeks to go upstream from St. Louis to Omaha, a distance of more than 400 miles. Steamers carried settlers up and down river to jumping-off points for the transcontinental overland trails. The advent of the steamboat brought with it legions of wood choppers who lined the river banks. A man could make a rough living by cutting wood from the forested banks and selling it to the steamers to fuel their boilers – which consumed it at the rate of a cord every hour.

It was so very unlike the anxious travel of the turn of the century. Instead of careful vigilance against Indian attack, the traveler now could contemplate the steamboat's 'prodigious construction, with its double tiers of cabins, and its separate establishment for the ladies, and its commodious arrangements for the deck passengers and the servants.... You read.... You converse, or walk or sleep, as you choose.'[7]

Steamboats, with a flatboat hauling freight to market in the foreground. A fiddler and dancer pass the time atop the flatboat. (Library of Congress)

The aftermath of a steamboat explosion on the Mississippi River. Such explosions usually resulted from overworking the boiler, often while competing captains vied to set new speed records. (Harper's Weekly, 12 March 1859)

In fact, many of the cabins were crowded and squalid. The ladies might be compelled to retire early to their bunks so that men could avoid their own overcrowded cabin by sleeping on the ladies' cabin floor. The men's cabin floor was kept slick by a constant stream of tobacco juice. An area on the deck below the ladies' cabin might have peepholes drilled through the floor above so that men could look up the ladies' skirts. A comb and a towel, suspended from strings, were provided for common use by the passengers. Only in the 1830s did steamboats begin to offer private staterooms, although few passengers could afford them. Passengers paid by the mile, paying a higher price for the upper deck cabins. The lower decks provided no seating, just an open area in which to mill about.

Other dangers awaited the steamboat passenger in the form of snags and boiler explosions. Ever competitive, steamboat captains raced one another, causing the straining boilers to explode. Passenger Edmund Flagg wrote in 1837 of an ongoing race between his steamer and another, due to 'a private pique existing between the pilots of the respective steamers.' As the larger boat attempted to ram Flagg's smaller boat, the passengers assembled on deck, 'some pale with apprehension, and others with firearms in their hands...prepared to render back prompt retribution.' The pilot of the would-be ram, fearing death by gunfire, reversed the wheel and averted collision at the last possible moment.[8]

Not a moment too soon, in the late 1830s states enacted laws prohibiting racing, whether of stagecoaches or steamers. Nonetheless, during the first fifteen years of steamboat history, 41 percent of the vessels were destroyed rather than retired, mostly by fire or snagging.[9] In 1856, a woman wrote, 'The steamer struck a "snag" last night; gave us a terrible jar; tore off a part of the kitchen; ladies much frightened.'[10] Her boat was a fortunate one; it remained afloat.

The 1820s were also the heyday of canal building. The previous generation had already built some small canals to get around waterfalls. Canal supporters argued that the expense, danger, and inconvenience of road and river travel put a damper on commerce, and that farmers would produce more if they had a cheaper and more reliable means of transport. The Erie Canal, completed in 1825, carried settlers to Michigan and Wisconsin. The barges resembled large flatboats of an earlier era and moved at about two or three miles per hour. The passenger cabins reproduced the crowded conditions of non-luxury steamers. Railroads quickly superseded canals as passenger transport.

OVER THE RAILS

Horse-drawn vehicles on rails were introduced around 1795. Men had been experimenting with steam engines for wheeled vehicles since 1786, although many viewed their attempts as sheer lunacy. Not until 1827 did Maryland charter the first horse-drawn railroad, the Baltimore and

Ohio (B&O). By 1830, however, the B&O had to change its plans. In just three years, to the considerable dismay of stagecoach and canal interests, steam locomotive technology had advanced to the point where it rendered horse-drawn rail cars obsolete. At first, horses pulling rail cars could outrun the earliest steam locomotives, but two years later in 1831, locomotives left horses in the dust by going in excess of 20 miles an hour.

Trains soon flew along the rails at five times the speed of a stagecoach, attaining a speed of 60 miles an hour by the start of the Civil War. However, the danger of early rail travel was notorious as collisions, derailments, boiler explosions and the like took a regular toll of passengers. One midwestern train wreck became memorialized in song:

'The mighty crash of timbers   The dead and dying mangled,
A sound of hissing steam   With broken beams and bars
The groans and cries of anguish   An awful human carnage
A women's stifled scream.   A dreadful wreck of cars.'[11]

But technology was not to be denied: the year 1830 saw twenty-three miles of railroad in operation; by 1835, railroads traversed more than a thousand miles; and by 1860 more than thirty thousand miles had been built.[12] The year 1869 marked the completion of the transcontinental railroad. It had been started in 1862, under the belief that it was necessary to the defense of the Pacific coast states. Its completion both symbolically and literally linked the east and west and further encouraged westward migration.

In the ensuing decades, railroads extended north and south from the transcontinental lines, bringing settlers and trade to the outlying territories. The railroad played a direct role in the settlement and economy of Dakota Territory. The 1860s had brought the nearest rail terminus first to St. Joseph, Missouri – the one-time trail head for the Oregon Trail – then to Marshalltown, Iowa, some 200 miles to the north. Rail service extended north into South Dakota, reaching Yankton in the far southeast corner by 1873. Trains began serving Pierre in 1880, and Rapid City – 350 miles west of Yankton – in 1886. At the same time, north–south lines were built off this main east–west route. Pioneers longed for railroads to pass near their farms and voted bond issues to induce the railroads to locate accordingly. Soon enough the settlers organized against the railroads in efforts to keep their freight charges down.

A Norwegian mother visiting her homesteading son in 1882 traveled by rail from Milwaukee to a point in northeastern South Dakota. The approximately 600-mile journey took thirty-three

A railroad bridge collapses under a train in Michigan. Although railroad carnage and mayhem were common, the speed of rail travel proved irresistible to pioneers eager to reach the territories. (Harper's Weekly, 16 July 1859)

hours. The visitor preferred the center-aisle seating arrangement of American trains to the compartments of European trains because, 'Aside from the convenience of being able to move about, this type of car also protects ladies traveling alone from unpleasant company.'[13] This suggests two possibilities: an offended woman could easily get up and change seats, or the other passengers in the car could intervene. In nineteenth-century America, one could count on strangers to help in ways that are by no means assured today.

'THAT CHARACTERLESS SHEET'

Printing presses arrived early in the history of every territory. The more primitive and isolated the life, the more one craves news from the great outside. Kentucky's first printer, John Bradford, began operations in 1787, overcoming paper and ink shortages to produce Kentucky's first newspaper – and the first west of the Alleghenies – the *Kentucke Gazette*, out of Lexington. The paper's editorials reflected the prevailing political passions of the day: separation from Virginia and attainment of statehood, access to the Spanish-controlled Mississippi River trade, and the hated federal excise tax on whiskey. The *Gazette* served also as a means of communicating through advertisements: husbands disavowed their wives' debts; creditors warned the world about the unreliability of certain debtors; people sought their lost or stolen horses; and travelers organized to cross the Alleghenies.

At the time the *Gazette* began publication, the entire nation was suffering paper shortages, which sprang in turn from a scarcity of rags, paper's main ingredient. Any such shortages hit hardest on the frontier. Rags, supplemented by flax and hemp, provided most of the fiber for paper making into the early 1800s, at which time wood pulp came into use. Today, rag is still used to make the highest quality paper.

'War News from Mexico,' an 1848 painting by Richard Caton Woodville. Even in times of peace, people strained for a glimpse of the news from back east. (Arizona Historical Society)

Most newspapers came out weekly and had only four pages. In addition to the news and advertisements, the pages contained poems, essays, and serialized novels. Trans-Allegheny pioneers frequently subscribed to eastern newspapers. Newspapers sold only a few hundred copies, but people on the frontier passed them around until they fell apart. Frontier newspapers actually sold many of their subscriptions to people back east who were thinking of emigrating. In addition to newspapers, western printers published posters, flyers, and business forms such as blank deeds. Small town weeklies today also take on such extra printing jobs. Running a frontier newspaper could be a tenuous business. Early settlers could pay for subscriptions only with farm produce, but the printer still had to buy paper and ink with specie. Newspapers were founded, then failed, with great regularity. Printing the news could be dangerous as well as precarious. Nineteenth-century editors freely expressed their opinions in print: their readers knew them personally, and when offended, threatened violence or tar-and-feathering.

THE FRONTIER NEWSPAPER IN (ALMOST) FICTION

Mark Twain captures the frontier publishers' spirit of publish and be damned:

'About this time a brick came through the window [of the news office] with a splintering crash...

'The chief said: 'That was the Colonel, likely. I've been expecting him for two days...'

'The Colonel appeared in the door a moment afterwards with a dragoon revolver in his hand.

'He said: 'Sir, have I the honor of addressing the poltroon who edits this mangy sheet?'

'You have. Be seated, sir. Be careful of the chair, one of its legs is gone. I believe I have the honor of addressing the putrid liar, Colonel Blatherskite Tecumseh?'

'Right, sir. I have a little account to settle with you. If you are at leisure we will begin.'

'I have an article on the "Encouraging Progress of Moral and Intellectual Development in America" to finish, but there is no hurry. Begin.'

'Both pistols rang out...The chief lost a lock of his hair...The Colonel's left shoulder was clipped a little. They fired again. Both missed their men this time... At the third fire both gentlemen were wounded slightly, and I had a knuckle chipped. I then said I believed I would go out and take a walk, as this was a private matter...But both gentlemen begged me to keep my seat, and assured me that I was not in the way.

'They then talked about the elections and the crops while they reloaded...'

The chief felled his man and left instructions for the afternoon's business:

'Jones will be here at three – cowhide him. Gillespie will call earlier, perhaps – throw him out the window. Ferguson will be along about four – kill him. That is all for today, I believe. If you have any odd time, you may write a blistering article on the police. The cowhides are under the table; weapons in the drawer – ammunition there in the corner – lint and bandages up there in the pigeonholes. In case of accident, go to Lancet, the surgeon, down-stairs. He advertises – we take it out in trade.' *

* Mark Twain, *Editorial Wild Oats* (New York, 1905), pp. 20-4.

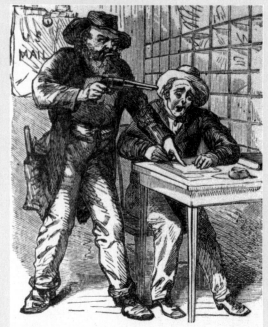

Above: A frontier newspaperman's precarious existence. He could write what he pleased... until someone took exception to it. At least he did not have to worry about being sued for libel. (In Albert D. Richardson, Beyond the Mississippi, *Hartford, 1869)*

Calling someone in print an 'inveterate liar', 'besotted blackguard', 'crawling insect', or 'black-hearted scoundrel' were among the gentler forms of invective. Frontier standards for libel were far different from those of today. Politicians, businessmen, even other editors fell prey to the rapier pen of the frontier editor. An Oregon editor wrote of a competing newspaper:

'There is not a brothel in this land that would not have felt itself disgraced by the presence of the *Oregonian* of week before last. It was a complete tissue of gross profanity, obscenity, falsehood, and meanness. And yet it was but little below the standard of that characterless sheet.'[14]

Books, neither so flamboyant nor so popular as newspapers, were among the wares of Kentucky's village general stores by 1789. The merchants imported them, usually from Philadelphia. Customers most frequently purchased Bibles, hymnals, school primers, and almanacs. Kentucky's first public library opened in Washington in 1811. Early libraries owned modest collections by today's standards. One frontier library in 1804 boasted a collection of fifty-one volumes.

The Santa Fe trade had been going on for more than a decade when an American trader imported New Mexico's first printing press in 1834. A Mexican purchased it and began publishing a weekly paper, religious tracts, and schoolbooks. The same trader also imported more than 1,000 books that year.

The boom towns of the Dakotas had newspapers almost before the towns were fairly established, the eager publishers printing the inaugural editions from their tent-offices. Townsite promoters founded many of these papers, and some proprietors received a free building and town lot to help them set up business. The papers served primarily to attract settlers from the east to a particular area. Dakota newspapers enjoyed a guaranteed income because the law required homestead claimants to publish numerous notices. Each issue carried dozens of land notices. With time, as claimants met their requirements, business dwindled and newspapers went under.

NEWS FROM HOME

In 1792, the year Kentucky attained statehood, the nearest U.S. Post Office to Kentucky stood in Pittsburgh. The postal service finally reached Kentucky in 1794, with the first post office opening in Danville. On many western routes, such as Lexington-Danville, the post rode every two weeks. Because they tried to adhere to a regular schedule, post riders made splendid targets for outlaws.

The postal service advertised contracts for mail routes. Although carrying the early U.S. mail was often dangerous and poorly paid, somebody who needed the job always turned up. As roads improved, some mail moved by stagecoach, and as steamboat traffic expanded, the steamers took on riverine mail routes, but horseback routes remained the norm. Settlement brought weekly mail, them twice weekly, thrice weekly, and daily. Complaints about the slowness of the mail were as common in 1820 as they are today.

The recipient of a piece of mail paid the postage. A printer soliciting manuscripts but loath to pay the postage advised writers to use private carriers. Settlers frequently relied on the informal private practice of sending letters along with travelers. It was to be expected that all the news-starved people along the way would read the unsealed folded sheets, so the sender avoided discussing private matters in letters. Untold numbers of letters got lost in the mishaps of the trail, and a successful exchange of letters could take many months. Travelers dropped unclaimed letters at such locations as newspaper offices, whose publishers then listed them in subsequent issues.

The first American settlers in Oregon country measured each exchange of letters in years, not weeks. A letter returning to the States over the Oregon Trail took at least a year to reach the east coast. Much transpired from one letter to the next, and the news, when it arrived, was out of date. An Oregon missionary recorded, 'In the evening an express arrived bringing letters from the US. One from home. Some of my dear friends are dead but most are living. I am not pleased with the course my brothers are persuing in regard to certain young ladies.'[15] But from Oregon, what could she do about it?

In the 1850s, mail to and from New Mexico traveled by wagon train on the Santa Fe Trail and took about a month in each direction. Between the trail head and the east coast, another two weeks elapsed. Mail deliveries arrived once a month at Santa Fe and the outlying forts. After the Civil War, the pace picked up dramatically. The mail arrived daily at Santa Fe, borne by stage-coach from the rail terminus; outlying army posts, like Fort Union, received mail three times a week. By the middle years of the nineteenth century, the U.S. post offices began offering some of services familiar to modern users. Registered letters were introduced in 1855, and postal money orders in 1864.

The federal government funded an overland stage mail route that began operation in 1858. The resulting Butterfield Overland Mail ran twice weekly between San Francisco and St. Louis via a southerly route through Texas, a distance of more than 2,500 miles. Southern interests defended the choice of this route on the grounds that its milder weather made year-round service possible. The first westward journey took twenty-five days. Despite assorted hardships and horse stealing by Comanche and Apache Indians, the mail usually arrived on schedule. The stage line also offered passenger and express package service. Where the federal government declined to fund a mail route, private mail companies took over. One of these companies established the famous Pony Express from St. Joseph to Sacramento. The riders made the journey in as little as ten days. The completion of the transcontinental telegraph lines in 1861 heralded the end of the Pony Express and reduced the importance of the overland stage routes. The government began funding daily overland mail service across the continent the same year. The stage route grew shorter as the transcontinental railroad extended farther west.

In South Dakota, postal routes radiated out from the railroad stations. Railroad stations housed post offices, and people set up post offices in their outlying homes or stores. Individual households had box numbers for addresses. The boxes consisted of simple pigeonholes in a subdivided crate set up behind the counter. Some post offices shunned boxes for the old practice of calling out the names of the lucky recipients to the assembled crowd; each then came forward for his mail and paid the postage. A typical homesteader might have to go twelve miles to his nearest post office. Like earlier times, he paid the postage when he picked up the mail. The rate doubled for home delivery, but few begrudged the cost. An express from home, or news of any sort, was most welcome to a people living so far from civilization.

[1] Warren S. Tryon, *A Mirror for Americans: Life and Manners in the United States, 1790–1870, as Recorded by American Travelers* (Chicago, 1952), vol. 3, p. 539. Scottish engineer John Macadam invented the process of surfacing roads with crushed gravel.

[2] John T. Schlebecker, *Whereby We Thrive: A History of American Farming, 1607–1972* (Ames, Iowa, 1975), pp. 88, 167.

[3] Maude A. Rucker, *The Oregon Trail and Some of its Blazers* (New York, 1930), p. 168.

[4] Tryon, vol. 3, pp. 591–2.

[5] William C. Davis, *A Way Through the Wilderness*, (New York, 1995), p. 37.

[6] Davis, p. 38.

[7] Davis, p. 57.

[8] Tryon, vol. 3, p. 573.

[9] R. Carlyle Buley, *The Old Northwest: Pioneer Period, 1815–1840*, (Bloomington, IN, 1950), vol. 1, p. 431.

[10] Cathy Luchetti, *Women of the West* (St George, Utah, 1982), p. 80.

[11] Robert C. Reed, *Train Wrecks* (Seattle, 1968), p. 31.

[12] Schlebecker, p. 93.

[13] Lorna B. Herseth, ed., 'A pioneer's letter,' *South Dakota History*, VI:3 (Summer 1976), p. 308.

[14] Robert F. Karolevitz, *Newspapering in the Old West* (Seattle, 1965), p. 134.

[15] Luchetti, p. 71.

VII

'MORE FRIENDS IN HEAVEN THAN ON EARTH': DEATH ON THE FRONTIER

By necessity, frontier dwellers treated their own ills in whatever way they could. A pioneer taken sick, injured, or wounded by Indians relied on a family member or neighbor to remove a bullet with a knife or apply a poultice (compress) of leaves or roots. Pioneers in the late 1700s did not shrink from the grisly task of treating survivors of scalping: they punched small holes all over the exposed skull, which caused a liquid to ooze out and, over the course of many months, form a new skin. That people survived scalping without falling prey to fatal infections almost defies belief, but they did. Even if a doctor lived nearby, the ailing or injured pioneer resorted first to the woman of the house, then the nearest neighbor known to have doctoring skills. Only after trying home remedies and seeing the patient grow worse did one summon a doctor.

Despite their many survival skills, pioneers exercised little control over their health. In the eighteenth and early nineteenth centuries, man had only a trifling understanding of the causes of disease. People looked on helplessly as cuts led to fatal blood poisoning, punctures to tetanus, colds to pneumonia, and poor nutrition to scurvy. A writer in 1827 decried Americans' overuse of liquor and meat, their tendency to overeat, and their low intake of fruits and vegetables. His words fell on deaf ears. Pioneers survived quite well without many things considered necessities today, but the lack of knowledge about sanitation and disease often cost American pioneers their lives. Through their own efforts they housed and fed themselves, and fought off hostile Indians, but they could not protect themselves from enemies they neither saw nor understood.

* * *

How healthy were pioneers relative to easterners, or to people today? A 1793 report named rheumatism, pleurisy, influenza, and smallpox as the most prevalent diseases of the old southwest, the area that ran from Kentucky to Mississippi. Other reports listed everything from eye strain and loss of teeth to coughs, pneumonia, death in childbirth, epilepsy, venereal diseases, intestinal worms, and dysentery. Many travelers remarked upon the unhealthy-looking sallow faces of frontier families, a condition attributed to their frequent illnesses.

While some diseases struck victims equally in the east and the west, others belonged chiefly to the frontier. Pioneers lived with fleas, bedbugs, and the mites that caused 'the itch,' or scabies. Flea bites could cause typhus. Diets lacking in fruits and vegetables gave rise to scurvy and persistent indigestion.

Nineteenth-century Americans believed, as do some people today, that their frequent colds – 'pulmonary complaints' or 'pleuritic disorders' – stemmed from chilling, exposure, and sudden changes in weather or body temperature. They thought, not without reason, that wearing dry shoes and flannel in order to retain body heat prevented colds, and that bed rest and drinking plenty of fluids cured them. However, the fluid ingested by most sufferers of upper respiratory complaints was toddy, a hot whiskey and sugar drink, a comforting, if not curative, treatment.

The settlers' homes admitted brisker drafts than the tighter homes of the east. These drafts prevented people from ever getting quite warm in winter and stirred up dust during all seasons. The inescapable dust of dirt floors or sod walls and the smoke of the cooking fire irritated the lungs.

Colds, coughs, and other contagious illnesses surely spread via shared drinking cups and eating utensils in both the home and public places. Colds sometimes lingered for months, or led to more serious illness and death.

In performing the routine tasks of their daily lives, settlers had ample opportunity to suffer an injury or meet an accidental death by drowning, falling from a horse, being crushed by a falling tree, or discharging a firearm. Accidents involving farm machinery, wagons, horses, and falls into open wells all threatened the pioneer near home. Toddlers might stumble into the large open fireplace, drown in a nearby creek, ingest a household poison, or fall into a large open basin of boiling liquid. With the nearest doctor possibly fifty miles distant, help often arrived too late.

'Bilious fever,' or ague, known today as malaria, afflicted those who lived nearest to the waterways. Pioneers occupying river bottoms and wetlands suffered greater exposure to the mosquito than did eastern city dwellers, but nobody yet understood the role of the mosquito, nor would they until 1898. Writers of the early 1800s attributed such ailments to 'noxious vapors' emitted by decaying plant matter and stagnant water. In fact, the name 'malaria' means 'bad air.' Settlers reported that they were subject to agues each year when the river flooded and then fell. Despite the palpable annoyance of mosquito attacks, they believed that the standing water deposited after the floods subsided was itself responsible for the illness. They identified the environs of mill ponds, wet prairies, and flooding bottomlands as unhealthful environments and recognized higher ground as safer. In contrast, New Mexico's reputation for healthful air rested on its dry climate: people believed that dry air was healthy because it produced no rotting vegetation.

Since the sometimes fatal fevers and chills occurred most often from July to October, a bout of illness during this period was called a 'seasoning.' The illness lasted several months and left the sufferer permanently enervated. After the first seasoning, subsequent annual attacks were less severe. Newcomers to an area, such as boatmen, fell ill more readily. In reality, the subsequent attacks of malaria became weaker as the host developed immunity. In the old northwest, reports from the 1820s claim that 30 to 90 percent of some town populations fell ill with the seasonal fevers, and that one-eighth of the entire population died of them each year. So prevalent were fevers that Kentucky's Dr. Daniel Drake published 180 pages describing the varieties of ague he had seen.

Settlers who emigrated to Oregon from the Ohio and Mississippi valleys hoped to evade malaria by relocating. The rain-soaked prairies and river valleys of Oregon, however, provided fertile breeding grounds for mosquitos. The settlers were not as afflicted by malaria as they had been back east – perhaps due to greater distances between settlements – and its incidence fell dramatically as the settlers dug ditches and drained the sodden prairies later in the century.

Oregon's Indians were less fortunate. Diseases carried in by white settlers – malaria, smallpox, and measles – decimated their population. The measles that killed Indians in great numbers spared most of the white children: the white population had a resistance to the disease that the Indians lacked. Seeing this, some Indians suspected an American plot, and others pleaded with whites to share their medicine. The Indian medicine men typically treated measles with a session in a sweat house followed by a dip in a cold stream. Having just slain the medicine man for failing to cure any of his patients, a chief approached an American woman whose children had recovered, and asked her to cure his daughter. The mother refused, saying she feared the chief would kill her too if she failed. The chief promised not to blame the woman if she failed, so the child came to stay with the American family. The mother kept her warm and gave her quantities of hot tea, and the patient recovered. In gratitude, the chief kept the family supplied with meat, nuts, and berries for years to come.[1]

Some of the illnesses reported as bilious fevers and agues may actually have been outbreaks of yellow fever or typhoid fever. Yellow fever, characterized by fever, jaundice, and vomiting, spread via the mosquito. Typhoid fever ran through entire frontier villages, probably because human wastes contaminated the water supply with bacteria. Typhoid led to fever and dysentery. The flea-borne typhus, once confused with typhoid, caused fever, weakness, and rashes.

The spread of typhoid was brought under control in later years as deep wells replaced cisterns in the West and homesteaders learned to boil their drinking water. Even in the days before the germ theory cast light on the spread of disease, some understood that dead animals and floating manure did not make for safe drinking water. People were not easily convinced, however, to abandon a hard-won water source, perhaps a hand-dug well, and dig another. On the home site itself, outdoor privies and barnyard manure piles often lay too near the shallow wells from which settlers drew their drinking water. Bacterial pollution of household wells persisted as a problem until the 1870s: knowledge of basic sanitation spread slowly.

A fatal illness prevalent in the West, milk-sickness, arose from drinking the milk of cows that had eaten poisonous plants. Even vultures or dogs who ate the meat of poisoned cattle died. The cause of this disease also remained unknown until late in the nineteenth century. Fearing contagion, people fled settlements where milk-sickness occurred. A 'regular' doctor treated milk-sickness with opium taken internally for pain, blisters applied to the abdomen, followed by cathartics and bleeding. A botanic practitioner offered a lobelia and cayenne formula to be taken internally, followed by charcoal, then spearmint oil rubbed over the stomach. Neither approach improved the dismal survival rate. Even when poisoning was identified as the basic cause, and white snakeroot as the prime suspect, researchers did not identify the specific poison, tremetol, until the 1920s.

The road west held many hazards beyond the threat of Indian attack. Advised one pioneer woman, 'No one should travle this road without medicine for they are al most sure to have the summer complaint. Each family should have a box of phisic pills and a quart of caster oil a quart of the best rum and a large vial of peppermint essence.'[2] As increasing numbers of pioneers headed west, following the established trails and camping at overused sites, they succumbed to dysentery from the sullied waters and to raging cholera epidemics. Others fell to measles, pneumonia, or 'mountain fever.' The words 'mountain fever' referred variously to malaria, typhoid, or the tick-borne Rocky Mountain spotted fever. Many migrants struggled for months with a persistent cold or cough. Those migrants who skirted the most overused portions of the trail escaped with fewer deaths from disease. One such caravan experienced only two mortalities, one by drowning and one by accidental gun discharge. Less fortunate groups suffered dozens of deaths from whooping cough, measles, and fevers. One man, leaving New England in search of a better farm, lost two of his children to an epidemic, and then his wife and remaining children drowned in a river crossing. He returned east in despair.

Those who would be pioneers, adult or child, risked finding themselves without a friend in the world, on the far side of a perilous journey months away from their former home. Stranded by illness or accident, orphans of the trail, if fortunate, were borne west by the other adults of the wagon train, and eventually adopted. Widows or widowers could take up a claim and try to prosper alone; nobody blamed them if they remarried in what today would appear to be unseemly haste.

* * *

The fragility of nineteenth-century existence began with birth, a potentially dangerous passage for both mother and child. Once safely born, a child faced a high likelihood of dying before the age of five. In some settlements, 50 percent of all deaths occurred among children under five years old.

Midwives and other women attended and assisted at most births. They possessed no formal training but much practical experience. Male doctors began taking over the midwives' function gradually, beginning early in the nineteenth century, but midwifery persisted well into the twentieth century. By the late 1820s, doctors had performed a few successful caesareans, holding out the promise of reducing deaths in childbirth. At one of the first performed in the West, on a stormy Ohio night in 1827, members of the woman's family held up blankets to keep the wind pouring through the drafty cabin walls from blowing the candles out. Even with a caesarian, a woman might survive the birth but die of infection.

In a related medical landmark, also occurring in 1827, the true role of the ovum in conception was discovered. Until then, people believed that the woman simply provided the womb in which the man's child could develop.

Despite advances in medicine, childbirth remained dangerous to life. A woman might successfully deliver numerous children, only to succumb later in life to exhaustion. On the Oregon Trail in 1851:

'August 25. I was sent for to Sister Henderson who had been sick for two days. In one hour, I was enabled to assist her in giving birth to a daughter, but the mother is so much exhausted that I fear she will not rally again.

'August 27. Sister Henderson died today at noon,...she left seven children.'[3]

Trailside births barely disrupted the routine of travel for most women. A wagon stopped for an hour or two and then went on. Yet, in the speech of the time, a woman in labor was invariably called 'sick.' However, a well-to-do woman attended by a physician in town could die as quickly as an unattended woman on the trail. Such was the fate of an officer's wife in Santa Fe:

'Monday July 15th – Mrs. Easton had a daughter born this morning...

'Monday, 22nd. At daylight this morning was called to Mrs. Easton's dying bed and remained with her till Tuesday 23rd when she breathed her last...'[4]

Lacking such diaries, simple chronologies of women's lives reveal many deaths of young women, shortly after the births of children. Wealth and privilege failed to protect Susan Shelby Magoffin, daughter of a Kentucky governor and wife of a rich Santa Fe trader, when she died at age twenty-eight, soon after the birth of her fourth child.

Midwives and experienced mothers must have known much about birth, but first-time mothers could be astoundingly ignorant by today's standards. As a newlywed on the Santa Fe Trail, the nineteen-year-old Mrs. Magoffin reported many days of illness in her diary. One of her illnesses turned out to be an early pregnancy followed by a miscarriage, but she apparently did not realize she was pregnant until she miscarried.

Marian Sloan Russell, who settled in New Mexico as a girl in the 1850s and later married a soldier, reported that during the first of her nine pregnancies she did not really believe she was to have a child until the labor pains began. This she blamed on her convent education. Her disbelief, however, on the morning she found her first infant dead in her cradle from no apparent cause, finds an echo in modern parents' experience of 'crib death,' or sudden infant death syndrome.

Children were particularly vulnerable to rapid death from dysentery and other infectious diseases. Spoiled milk frequently caused childhood diarrhea. Sometimes no disease could be blamed. One mother described in 1847 how her child weighed only six pounds at birth, failed to gain weight, and gradually faded away, surviving only a year. Even healthy children took ill and died with astonishing suddenness:

'November, 1843. I have experienced the first real trial of my life. After a few days of suffering our little Hannah died of lung fever...

'June, 1845.... I have had to pass thru another season of sorrow. Death has again entered our home; this time it claimed our dear little John...'[5]

Contagious diseases cut a wide swath through the youthful population. Diphtheria, spread by airborne bacteria, became epidemic in both the east and west, sometimes killing entire households of children and adolescents. Measles and scarlet fever also ran through the children of western communities.

* * *

Epidemic outbreaks held great terror to people who did not yet understand how the diseases were transmitted. Hundreds died in each yellow fever outbreak that struck New Orleans almost annually in the early nineteenth century. Doctors treated mosquito-borne diseases with copious bloodlettings and purges. In an Ohio yellow fever epidemic, doctors administered alternating cathartics and tonics. Quinine, a fever-reducing drug made from the bark of the South American cinchona tree, came into use for alleviating malaria symptoms in the 1840s, and is still used today. Some physicians treated agues with laudanum, and others viewed beer as a preventative. By the 1850s, Americans understood that the danger of yellow fever passed with the first frost, but they still did not connect the disease to mosquitos.

The Asiatic cholera, having traveled westward across Asia and Europe, first appeared in the United States in 1832, via a shipload of European emigrants landing in Quebec. It spread along rivers, trade routes, and overland trails and raged through cities and army barracks. The highly contagious and rapidly fatal disease was caused by bacterial contamination of water, but contemporaries believed it spread by the ubiquitous bad air and noxious vapors. A frequent treatment was hot peppers in whiskey, but victims invariably died painfully from the diarrhea and rapid dehydration. Congress, with typical effectiveness, passed a joint resolution calling for a national day of prayer and fasting. The disease abated the first winter but reappeared in the summer of 1833. In some areas, cholera outstripped all other causes of death combined. A new outbreak brought over from Europe in 1848 spread even more rapidly along the new railroad lines. By the 1850s, some wagon train doctors on the overland trails intuited the cause of cholera, warned their charges about drinking from stagnant watering holes, and called for the men to dig new wells at the campsites. But for most people, epidemic diseases mowed down their loved ones with grim inevitability. Mourned one man on the loss of his best friend:

'Thus the friends of our youth glide away one by one, and leave us behind to fight the great battle of life; and as they pass from time to eternity, we are forcibly reminded that we will soon have more friends in heaven than on earth.'[6]

Before the introduction of smallpox vaccination, pioneers practiced the only form of prevention at their command: quarantine. In 1784 Kentucky, '...there was a widow woman & family encamped a small distance below the Licks who had the small pox & were not admitted to the fort. While we lay at the river the Indians came & destroyed them.'[7]

Smallpox vaccines became widely available in the east by the early 1800s and quickly worked their way west. The earliest method, inoculation with human virus, could infect healthy people, either with smallpox itself or with other blood-borne diseases like syphilis. A safer English vaccine, using cow virus, soon replaced it. The incidence of smallpox fell dramatically through the century, but it persisted as late as the 1870s in the southwest because vaccination had not yet penetrated the frontiers. Smallpox particularly felled Indians, who were the last to receive any available vaccines.

Tuberculosis, once known as consumption, was a contagious disease that killed more people than any other disease. It did not strike the same terror in people's hearts as cholera, smallpox, and other epidemic diseases because it worked its destruction slowly. Nor did people realize it was contagious, spreading through the air or through unpasteurized milk.[8]

* * *

Nineteenth-century attitudes toward illness color our view of the state of settlers' health. Alongside alarmingly frequent reports of serious illness and death, pioneers' diaries reveal what appears to be an undue preoccupation with minor sickness. Since reports of pain and discomfort can only be subjective, we cannot know who was really unwell and who was feigning delicacy. A New Mexico post commander's middle-aged wife made frequent references to her own health. Almost every second or third day, she reported feeling sick, yet she lived to an advanced age. On the other hand, a young man who traveled to Santa Fe for his health and seemed equally preoccupied with his symptoms did not live much past forty. In all likelihood, many people suffered chronic low-level illness.

Ailing Americans occasionally sought out the healthful dry climate of New Mexico, braving the rigors of the trail for the hope of a cure. Josiah Gregg, a sickly young man suffering 'chronic dyspepsia' (indigestion), had to be carried to the departing wagon train in 1831. Within days he was riding a horse. In a dramatic turnaround, he became a Santa Fe trader and enjoyed robust health until his mysterious death years later on an expedition to California.

James Larkin, a St. Louis merchant's son, also sought a cure in Santa Fe, but continued to suffer dyspepsia and neuralgia for the remaining twenty years of his life. He died of pneumonia in his forties. At the time, neuralgia, or nerve pain, served as a general term for persistent and recurrent pain in any part of the body. When one considers the opiates and purgatives to which some Americans freely resorted for digestive ills, it is a wonder that their systems functioned at all without drugs. Addictive opiates such as paregoric and morphine cured diarrhea but caused constipation. The sufferer resorted in turn to a purgative to get the system going again, bringing back the symptoms that had sent him to the paregoric bottle in the first place. Thus it can be clearly seen how certain nineteenth-century medical practices actually caused illness. A host of minor ailments might, in being treated, cause other more serious ailments, leaving the preoccupied sufferer on a treadmill without escape.

Frontier families, mystified or terrified by mainstream medicine, remained vulnerable to quacks – or 'irregulars' – and their cures. The fact that some self-appointed doctors used common sense and effected the occasional cure served to enhance their careers and reputations. Hypo, a mental disorder peculiar to the frontier, featured a wide variety of delusions. Richard Carter, an early nineteenth-century irregular, cured many cases of the hypo. In treating a man who thought he had live ducks quacking in his stomach, Carter applied a purgative. As the man brought up the contents of his stomach, Carter deftly popped some ducklings into the basin, having first secreted them on his person. The sufferer believed himself cured.[9]

* * *

The nineteenth-century healing arts, whether practiced by laymen, charlatans, or professionals, often ran directly counter to what we know to be effective today. Pioneers who lived within reach of a frontier doctor did not always fare better than those treated by a neighbor. The prevailing wisdom of the times advised keeping the sickroom windows shut tight, denying fluids to the patient, bleeding and purging, and administering large doses of toxic chemicals. Imagine the effect of denying fluids and purging the bowels of a hapless dysentery victim. With hindsight, it appears that deaths from dehydration would have been among the most preventable if pioneers had had access to modern medical knowledge. Frontier medical practices were not, in fact, more primitive than those of the eastern cities, but spread quickly from east to west. The main difference between medical practice in the east and west was the distance one had to travel to find a doctor.

While doctors pursued their calling in the towns of the West, sold medicines, and traveled miles on horseback to distant farms to treat the injured and sick, pioneers beyond their reach resorted to a host of home cures. They knew of herb and root cures, originally developed in Europe and Asia, and passed from generation to generation. Settlers also incorporated dozens of Indian cures into their pharmacopeia. Some of these persist into modern times. For example, chamomile, used by pioneers for colic, is known today as an herbal tea that soothes indigestion. Snakeroot, walnut bark, sassafras, willow, dogwood, sheep dung, catnip, pennyroyal, nettles, rhubarb, cayenne pepper, tansy, mustard, onions, cherry bark, mullein, garlic, vinegar, and molasses were all applied by settlers either internally or externally. Settlers treated snake bites by making a cut and rubbing in salt or some other concoction, or they applied a poultice of the bark from yellow poplar roots. To relieve dyspepsia, they might resort to rubbing the abdomen with cayenne peppers soaked in spirits, followed by a drink of whiskey. Surely this treatment must have at least distracted attention from the underlying indigestion!

In 1850s New Mexico, an American mother employed a mix of homeopathic and folk remedies, almost never resorting to a doctor. She applied mustard poultices for chest ailments, tobacco smoke or a drop of oil for earache, a whole clove to an aching tooth, hot compress of hops for headache, tea or hot ginger for stomach ache, and homemade cough syrup of chokecherry bark and honey. Remedies adopted from the Mexicans included puffballs to stop bleeding, and a dirty stocking wrapped around the neck for a sore throat. The southwesterners also made a 'blood tonic' by dissolving six tenpenny nails in a bottle of vinegar. A daily dose supposedly put beneficial iron in the blood.[10]

On the Oregon Trail, a woman applied what she called 'Indian medicine,' a heated rock held to the chest to drive out a cold. She called it the best remedy she had ever known. On the Santa Fe Trail, a trader's young wife suffered frequent illnesses, including headaches, colds, and fevers. Some caused her to take to her bed for a day or two, and one fever leveled her for several weeks. She was a great believer in Dr. Sappington's Pills, a popular fever remedy that contained quinine. She also resorted to onion poultices and sweating, a Mexican practice, which employed hot foot baths, blankets, and hot drinks.

Doctors, when consulted, could choose from several systems for treating patients, among them botanic, spiritualist, Thomsonian, allopathic, homeopathic, and combinations thereof. Adherents to different schools of thought attacked one another viciously in print, and sometimes in person. Allopathic practitioners, called 'regulars,' considered themselves the mainstream and all others quacks. Allopathy involved the application of treatments designed to produce the opposite condition to the one induced by the illness. 'Regular' doctors relied heavily on bleeding and purging of already weak patients. At each session, using leech or lancet, a doctor relieved a patient of close to a pint of blood. Many patients implicitly trusted bleeding as a form of good medicine. A pregnant woman on the Oregon Trail:

'Was bled toward night. Came near fainting. Sick some.'

And the next day:

'Considerably out of health. Took a spoonful of wine, went without dinner at night. Felt better...

'Very tired.... Think bleeding did me good tho it reduced my strength more than I expected.'[11]

Another weapon in the regular doctor's arsenal was the application of poultices, called 'blisters,' of mustard or Spanish fly. He deployed these for the express purpose of raising large blisters and then rupturing them: this, no doubt opened a broad avenue for bacteria to enter the body, and probably caused some deaths by blood poisoning. The doctor also resorted to herbal remedies, sulphur baths, patent medicines, laxatives, emetics, castor oil, quinine, laudanum, opium, arsenic, vitriols, and a form of mercury called calomel. These he prescribed in excessive, often killing, doses.

Homeopathy, on the other hand, sought to counteract a condition by administering minute doses of medicines that would normally produce the same symptoms in a healthy person. Samuel Hahnemann, a 1779 graduate of European medical schools, tested homeopathic remedies and published his results in 1810. The system he propounded gained popularity in the 1840s, but it drew scathing criticisms from skeptics. One critic said, 'whosoever employeth a homeopathic doctor and is [helped] thereby hath confessed hysterics already unto condemnation.'[12] In an example of a cure effected by homeopath, a minute grain of sugar was said to have cured a contracted tendon that had deformed a toe.

Samuel Thomson, in turn, believed that heat was the source of general health, and that the application of heat and cold through steam baths and cold soaks was the answer to all ailments. He combined medicinal herbs and roots with heat to create his 'steam system of Botanic medicine.' He employed a formidable sales force to sell licenses to use his secret formulas. Thomsonianism became popular in the 1830s because people found the system relatively easy to understand, trusted herbal remedies, and feared the harrowing treatments offered by the regulars. A Thomsonian practitioner treated dyspepsia with alternating steam baths and cold vinegar rubdowns, accompanied by numerous doses of secret formula No. 6, nerve powders, spice bitters, conserve of hollyhock, golden seal, poplar bark, and cayenne. A child in convulsions from a spider bite rallied to a treatment of bear's oil, three secret preparations, and lobelia.

A self-taught regular doctor, Gideon Lincecum, at his patients' request, began offering both Thomsonian and allopathic treatments. At first skeptical of botanic medicine, he became a believer:

'About the middle of the second year of my double practice, I lost a two year old child under circumstances leaving me no ground to doubt the fact that the death was occasioned by the allopathic remedies. And, while I was gazing at the twitching muscles of the dying child, I made a solemn vow to myself that I would never administer another dose of the poisons of that system.'

And poisons they were:

'I started home; and after passing through the gate into the big road, I emptied the old school medicines from my saddlebags and left them [a mixture of sulfuric acid, nitric acid, and chloride of lime] in a pile on the ground...the people reported that it boiled and smoked there for two or three days...'[13]

The eclectic system of botanic medicine grew as an offshoot of Thomson's system, founded by dissidents in his ranks. The eclectics in turn fought among themselves, leading to an 1856 incident in Cincinnati, whereby a splinter faculty group occupied a medical school building and held it with a 6-pounder cannon.

The first medical school west of the Appalachians, Transylvania University of Lexington, Kentucky, opened its doors in 1799. Only a medical school could confer the right to use the letters M.D. with one's name, but anyone who dared could call himself Doctor. Despite many attempts to pass laws regulating the practice of medicine, this state of affairs persisted until the end of the nineteenth century, by which time medical degrees had gained increasing respect.

Many of the doctors who hung out their shingles and advertised in western newspapers during the century's first half possessed no qualification beyond reading a few books or serving a brief preceptorship. A preceptorship under another doctor involved reading, mixing medicines, making pills, caring for the horses, going on calls, and assisting the doctor until he decided that the student was qualified.

With no real prerequisites for setting up practice, and doctors' fees even higher relative to other prices than they are today, towns filled up with doctors quickly. One Kentucky town of 300 boasted five doctors. However, even the most successful doctor had much money owed him but little actually paid. Often he had to accept food or other items if he was to be paid at all. To make a doctor's existence yet more tenuous, competing doctors fought duels over stolen patients, conflicting treatment plans, and reportedly, a failed fee-fixing scheme. It was not unknown for doctors to die of drink or die paupers. Wealthy planters sent their sons to medical colleges in the Northeast, so that they could treat their slaves' ailments, but for most, formal medical training was beyond reach. A self-made frontier doctor might serve his patients well, and a formally educated one might lack the ability of his untrained but talented brethren. Yet, for all their shortcomings, doctors had something to offer their patients, and more as time went on. They reduced dislocations, set fractures, amputated shattered limbs, sewed up wounds, and pulled teeth.

A Kentucky physician, Ephraim McDowell, pioneered a major form of abdominal surgery in 1809 – removal of an ovarian tumor – without the aid of anesthetics or any knowledge of antiseptic techniques. Over the course of his practice, about 62 percent of his patients survived the operation, a rate that was remarkable for the time but unacceptable today. Given that surgery was the treatment of last resort, the tumors removed were much larger than those seen today – one was reported at 61 pounds.

Not until Joseph Lister's work on germ theory and antisepsis became known in the late 1860s did people begin to understand the causes of most of their illnesses. By the 1870s, carbolic acid had come into use as an antiseptic. Some doctors still disinfected with whiskey, which at least contained alcohol. Earlier surgeons had washed their hands and instruments with warm water and soap, but some only washed up after surgery. The versatile whiskey usually served as the only available anesthetic, and some practitioners still preferred it after ether and chloroform became available in the late 1840s. Surgical patients sometimes received only small amounts of opium or laudanum to deaden the pain.

* * *

Frontier dwellers suffered from bad teeth and lost them early. They liked sweets and lacked dentists. The widely overused medication, calomel, caused tooth loss as a side-effect. Dentistry as a practice separate from medicine grew commonplace in towns throughout the West by the 1820s. Traveling dentists wandered the frontier, the largest part of their practice pulling teeth. Tooth-pulling, far from a science, involved struggle: the dentist often placed his patient on the floor and sat astride him to wrestle out a stubborn tooth. Dentists used gold or tin foil to fill cavities, and by the 1830s offered false teeth of porcelain. By 1840, some dentists used a clay-like substance to repair broken or decayed teeth. Separate dental colleges did not open until the 1840s.

General stores stocked spectacles of varying strengths. A person with vision problems tried them on until he found some that seemed to help. Lacking the precisely calibrated lenses of today, people with defective vision suffered further from headaches and eye strain.

When the army posted surgeons to the frontier, they willingly treated civilians, and the settlers preferred them to private doctors. So respected were army personnel that civilians even sought medical care from non-medical officers. An army quartermaster in New Mexico dispensed horse medicines to a woman suffering a digestive ailment. By rights the treatment should have killed her, but she survived and pronounced herself cured. Horse medicines were, like all medicines, obtainable at any general store.

By the 1860s, veterinary science had identified such livestock diseases as pleuro-pneumonia, Texas fever, and hog cholera. State authorities admitted that they did not understand how the diseases spread, suggesting contagion in some instances, atmospheric poisons in others. They attempted to control diseases among livestock by killing all animals in affected herds or interdicting movement of herds. Texas fever, now known to be spread by ticks, mystified scientists who observed that the disease abated in winter. The Texas cattle, themselves resistant to the disease, were driven northward each year to the railhead. The ticks carrying the disease dropped off the cattle and then attached themselves to local domestic cattle. In the eyes of the settlers, their cattle died from merely crossing the path of the Texas drives.

* * *

Western town dwellers, lacking the money to pay for doctoring, could purchase all they needed to doctor themselves. Anyone who so desired could purchase medicines, syringes, and bleeding lancets from drug stores and general stores. All were available over the counter.

Frontier doctors imported their drugs from Philadelphia or Pittsburgh. In addition to drugs, they equipped themselves with mortar and pestle, with which they laboriously pulverized the drugs, and dosage-sized powder papers to wrap them in. They owned balances for weighing the doses, splints and bandages, syringes, and instruments such as tooth-pulling forceps and obstetrical tools. The stethoscope, invented in 1817, started seeing wide use in the 1830s.

Doctors frequently operated their own pharmacies. The famous Daniel Drake opened a pharmacy that boasted the West's first drugstore soda fountain in 1816. Like general stores, pharmacies carried other items besides drugs: paints and dyes, 'medicinal' wines and liquors, surgical instruments, perfumes, and horse medicines. American pharmacists trained through apprenticeships until the 1850s, when pharmacy schools began operating in the United States.

Patent medicines, while not actually patented, enjoyed wide popularity and rendered profits to the 'doctors' who made them, the salesmen who peddled them, and the newspapers that

Doctor's office in the southwest, circa 1880, with buggy and bicycle ready for the next summons. (Arizona Historical Society)

advertised them. Early patent salesmen were adept at getting attention at militia musters and court days with their 'snake oil' for aching joints and their cures for female troubles, coughs, or worms. Later, traveling medicine shows featuring music, magic tricks, and testimonials entertained crowds of frontiersmen and enriched their sponsors. The patents could be habit-forming, as many contained alcohol or opium. Some contained an excess of mercury and were downright dangerous. Others were actually effective, Dr Sappington's quinine-containing fever pills being an example.

By the 1870s, some aspects of medical practice began to assume the shape of modern medicine. Bloodletting had fallen out of favor, and surgeons practiced antiseptic techniques. Doctors used cool drinks and baths to bring a fever down, alleviated coughs with hot drinks and compresses, and prescribed fresh air and balanced diets for many ills. Even so, sheer inexperience and incompetence could fell an unsuspecting patient. Patients died of such treatable ailments as appendicitis because inexperienced doctors feared to operate until it was too late. Some resorted to whiskey to steady their nerves, and one surgeon got so drunk that he continued to operate after the patient had died.

* * *

Henry Hoyt first practiced medicine in the late 1870s in Deadwood, South Dakota, and then in New Mexico and Texas. In his day, a would-be doctor spent one year of preceptorship under another doctor, a year as a hospital intern – at that time called a steward – and two years at a medical school. The young Hoyt, restless and out of money, left Minnesota with only one year of medical school remaining, to practice on the frontier.

In 1877, Hoyt rented a hotel room in Deadwood, bought a scale to weigh gold dust, and placed an advertisement in the newspaper. His room was one of the hotel's cubicles, partitioned from the others by canvas, and sparsely furnished with two beds, two chairs, and a washstand. Many a morning he carried a snoring 'room mate' to a bed in another room so he could open his 'office' for business. After riding out ten miles to treat a prospector's bullet wound, and being paid with a generous quantity of gold dust, he found the dust was phony when he tried to spend it. Thereafter, he learned how to test it with acid before accepting payment.

Young Hoyt traveled to the southwest on horseback later the same year. In New Mexico and Texas he dispensed smallpox vaccines and treated a young woman struck down by the disease. Lacking a full supply of medicines, he applied a paste of gunpowder and water to the furiously itching blisters, and the improvised cure proved effective in preventing scarring. In gratitude, her family made him an honored guest at her debutante ball.

Settlers had little cash to spare for medical care and were reluctant to summon a doctor. After a couple of years in the southwest, Hoyt, like many frontier doctors, was having trouble making ends meet by practicing medicine, so he took on the job of riding a mail route, and later worked as a cowboy and a bartender. In Las Vegas, New Mexico, where he tended bar, numerous doctors, including one homeopath, plied their trades. Rather than compete, Hoyt tried his hand at running a gambling hall (which broke him), surveying, and serving as assistant postmaster. As a non-drinking bartender and a non-gambling casino owner, he defied the conventions of the West. The bar owner found that his profits soared because the bartender wasn't drinking them up.

Finally, Hoyt heard of an opening in Bernalillo, where an older doctor planned to retire. He borrowed money to acquire a stock of drugs and rented a two-room adobe in the town center. Discovering that the local doctor prescribed only quinine, castor oil, and large quantities of the local wine, Hoyt introduced such previously unknown practices as catheterization for bladder ailments, and fresh air and change of altitude for pneumonia patients. He observed that pneumonia patients died at high altitudes and recovered if brought down to a lower elevation.

Skilled at using whatever he had at hand, Hoyt splinted fractures on remote ranches by making casts of adobe mud. During a mumps outbreak, he prescribed hot compresses made from the ever-popular Mexican beans to be applied to the sufferers' swollen jaws. The patients did not always carry out his instructions to the letter: 'In a few days I had numerous calls and reports of "no better." I started out and found...? A nice little flat bag of raw beans fastened to each jaw!'[14]

Hoyt continued to supplement his income by selling medicines and serving as the postmaster. He then won the contract to treat the railway workers, who provided him with ample work because of the poor sanitation in their camps.

Like any other young man on the frontier, the doctor always carried a .45 caliber Colt revolver. His profession did not shield him from the violence of western life. One day as he watched one of the many public hangings of his frontier sojourn:

'...my reverie was cut short by a series of shrieks, evidently feminine, from one of the passengers. The driver plied his whip and the bus dashed up to the curb with a woman struggling with a man and screaming, "Let me go! Take me home! I will never live in this God-forsaken country!" I stepped to the bus, introducing myself to her companion as a physician, and together we carried the woman into the hotel, where I soon quieted her with an opiate.'[15]

All the opiates in the world could not alter the accuracy of her instincts. Her first sight of her new community, a hanging body, brought home forcefully the precariousness of frontier existence. Her husband ignored her entreaties to return to Arkansas. Some years later he left her a widow after a drunken man gunned him down in the street.

1   Fred Lockley, 'Reminiscences of Martha E. Gilliam Collins,' *Quarterly of the Oregon Historical Society*, XVII:4 (December 1916), pp. 369–70.
2   Kenneth L. Holmes, ed., *Covered Wagon Women: Diaries & Letters from the Western Trails, 1840–1890* (Glendale, CA, 1983), vol. 1, p. 119.
3   *Covered Wagon Women*, vol. 2, p. 266.
4   *The Daybook of Anna Maria Morris 1850–1858*, Special Collections, University of Virginia, Charlottesville, VA.
5   Cathy Luchetti, *Women of the West* (St George, Utah, 1982), pp. 138–9.
6   W.W.H. Davis, *El Gringo: New Mexico and her People* (New York, 1857), p. 294.
7   'A Sketch of early adventures of William Sudduth in Kentucky,' *Filson Club History Quarterly*, II:2 (January 1928), p. 46.
8   William A. Bowen, *The Willamette Valley: Migration and Settlement on the Oregon Frontier* (Seattle, 1978), p. 19.
9   Richard Dunlop, *Doctors of the American Frontier* (New York, 1962), p. 177.
10 Marian Sloan Russell, *Land of Enchantment: Memoirs of Marian Russell along the Santa Fe Trail* (Evanston, 1954), p. 54.
11 Luchetti, p. 64.
12 Madge E. Pickard and R. Carlyle Buley, *The Midwest Pioneer: His Ills, Cures & Doctors* (New York, 1946), p. 217.
13 Gideon Lincecum, 'Autobiography of Gideon Lincecum,' *Publications of the Mississippi Historical Society*, VIII (1904) pp. 502–3.
14 Henry F. Hoyt, *A Frontier Doctor* (Chicago, 1979), p. 239.
15 Hoyt, p. 227.

VIII

'PLENTY OLD ENOUGH'

Work distinguished a frontier childhood from childhood in the east. A farming family's survival depended on the labor of every family member. Hardly a chore existed that children could not or did not do. Parents assigned chores to children as young as the age of three. From that age, children grew in independence as parental supervision decreased.

Newborn babies on the early frontier shared their parents' bed, the warmest and safest place in the house. They soon moved to a nest in a bureau drawer or a cradle. Playpens and cribs were absent from the pioneer cabin. The child nursed on demand, often for two or three years, until the mother became pregnant again. Later in the century, the nursing period dwindled to about a year, and bottle-feeding gradually became more available. Until bottle feeding spread, a mother with insufficient milk who could not find another woman to take over nursing saw her infant starve. Frontier toddlers of both sexes wore a sack-like dress – often literally made from a flour sack – with a drawstring neck until they were weaned. Their ringlets were uncut.

By mid-nineteenth century, the more settled areas of the country embraced a new concept of childhood as a state distinct from adulthood. Childhood, at least among the middle and upper classes, became a time when children attended school and were sheltered from work. Books of advice about child-rearing proliferated. Only the children of the poorest families faced a childhood of hard labor. Farther west, education still took a back seat to farming work. Public schools, or any schools at all, remained few and far between.

Fathers called first upon their sons to work in the fields, but daughters also plowed, drove horse-drawn equipment, planted seed, weeded, and harvested. Children took care of livestock, tended vegetable gardens, gathered wild plants, hauled water, and scavenged for buffalo chips or firewood. They went on errands to borrow, return, or retrieve things from neighbors. Even very young children crawled along the crop rows to pull off worms and insects. Boys drove away or shot crows and squirrels that raided the fields. On rainy days or in winter, a multitude of indoor tasks awaited. Girls as young as five helped care for younger children. Milking cows was one task reserved for girls and strictly forbidden to boys.

The young Daniel Drake of Kentucky worked in the fields, cut firewood, and hauled corn a day's ride to the mill. He carried the sacks of corn on his horse but was too small to lift a sack back on board when it fell off. He waited for hours until a man came along to help him. Like most farm children, he rode horses capably at a young age and went in search of straying livestock. He helped his mother in all manner of housekeeping tasks, including cooking, making brooms, doing the laundry, making soap, and dressing the younger children.

The young Martha Gilliam of Oregon, whose father had died in the Cayuse war, recalled:

> 'My brother Marcus and I had to do the farming. I was going on ten years old so I was plenty old enough to do my share of supporting the family. I drove the oxen and Mark held the plow...'[1]

Farm and town children contributed cash to the family in numerous ways. They hired themselves out as herders for neighbors' flocks, or sold eggs from chickens they tended. On the Great Plains of the 1870s, they gathered buffalo bones for sale to the eastern fertilizer industry. In towns, children clerked for stores, took in laundry, cooked and cleaned for pay. Stagecoach drivers and ferry pilots as young as fourteen were not unknown in the West. In mining towns, boys hunted for game and sold the meat, while their mothers and sisters baked, cooked, and washed clothes for the miners. The more prosperous town families hired household help, cutting down the amount of work required of both wives and children.

Few frontier parents bound their children out to serve apprenticeships to tradespeople. Tradesmen wanted the help they could get from apprentices, but pioneers wanted their children to be independent farmers or professionals. Lacking parents to look out for their interests, orphans became apprentices so they could learn a trade while earning their keep. Because it was so dangerous, the Pony Express tried to recruit orphans to serve as its relay riders.

Growing up on the frontier fostered an unusual independence in young people, often to their parents' dismay. In 1850, an Oregon pioneer reported that her three teenaged sons had gone to California seeking gold. They returned unsuccessful, and three years later moved to land at some distance from their mother's farm. They were aged seventeen, nineteen and twenty when their mother wrote despairingly:

> 'My boys lives about 25 miles from me so that I cannot act in the capasity of a mother
> to them... you know my boys is not old enough to do with out a mother.'[2]

Even the most attentive parents at times subjected their children to the hardships of frontier life; isolation, exposure to winter cold and rain, and hunger. Less conscientious parents overworked their children, neglected them, beat them in drunken rages, or abandoned them. On an isolated homestead, the parents' word became law, and whether they were benign or brutal despots was a matter of fate. No power intervened between abusive parents and their children. Furthermore, no shame attached to the nineteenth-century parent who resorted to the rod to impose discipline; indeed most considered it their duty to beat down impertinence and stubbornness. A harried mother – a deeply religious woman – wrote one day of her seven-year-old, 'It is as if he was almost possessed with some demon, he is so noisy.' A few weeks later, when the boy refused to say 'please,' both parents 'used the rod till we feared to longer.' It took them nearly two days of confining the boy to bed, interspersed with beatings, to break him to their will.[3]

The prevalence of whipping as a form of child discipline dwindled both at home and in school as the nineteenth century went on. Instead, parents relied on withholding affection, shaming the child, sending him to bed without supper, making him sit in the corner, or other alternatives to beating, which came to be seen as a last resort. The most important goal of early discipline remained that of breaking the child's will, replacing willfulness with obedience. A minister wrote of confining and starving his fifteen-month-old child for more than twenty-four hours in order to train him not to fling his food onto the floor. His basic premise was in fact quite admirable, one that modern parents would do well to heed: 'There can be no greater cruelty than to suffer a child to grow up with an unsubdued temper.'[4] Today, such severity at such an early age can only be termed abuse: 150 years ago it was a standard child-rearing method that one parent saw fit to publish as an instructive example. Such instances notwithstanding, visiting Europeans viewed American parents as lax and permissive.

When both parents died or became disabled, either the oldest sons or daughters ran the household and kept the family intact, or the children were parcelled out among neighbors and relatives. Orphans did not always find care and kindness at the hands of their guardians. Some were underfed, overworked, and beaten. When an immigrant girl's mother died on the trans-Atlantic voyage, the other passengers stole her food and let her go hungry until she finally appealed to the captain. Children also ran away to try their own hand at survival, sometimes successfully. Often

Children of south-western settlers. The girl is riding side-saddle. Children were once generally assumed to be capable of handling horses and guns without adult supervision. (National Archives)

a restless man dragged an unwilling wife and children from one frontier to the next, regardless of the hardship. His children lost their attachment to home as a specific place, embraced mobility and adventure as a way of life, and ran off. Scores of impoverished boys joined the cavalry to fight Indians, drawn by the romance of it, and teenaged girls joined traveling theater troops. Running away to join the circus, a popular fictional plot turn, had a surprising basis in reality.

In enduring the hardships of the frontier, youngsters gained in independence and competence. They rambled over the countryside on foot or horseback, sometimes in the course of doing such chores as bringing in the cows for milking. Frontier children, in company with their numerous brothers and sisters, possessed simple homemade toys and made playmates of the farm animals and dogs. The Applegate brothers' favorite 'simple homemade toy' was a cast-lead working model of a cannon, about a foot long. Like boys everywhere, they were enthralled by explosives and firearms, and used much powder testing the range and accuracy of this artillery piece. The 'toy' would have been quite lethal had one of the balls ever found its mark. Eventually, the patriotic boys melted it down for bullets during the Cayuse war of 1847. A Dakota father made for his children an equally useful but more innocuous toy, a small wooden wagon, which the children used for both farm work and play. Children went skating and sledding, and played formalized games that were known throughout the country, such as hide-and-seek, blind man's bluff, and tag. Organized ball games, precursors to baseball, helped pass the time during school recesses.

People of all ages on the frontier liked a competition, and participated from childhood. They competed in shooting squirrels or killing snakes, running races or jumping. Both boys and men played marbles, the boys frequently losing theirs to older opponents. In later years, they competed at croquet and baseball, both popularized after the Civil War. Many western communities organized baseball teams for both adults and youths. Bicycling and roller skating attracted numerous devotees in the West, beginning in the 1870s. By 1884, Pierre, South Dakota boasted three roller skating rinks.

One group of American children in New Mexico played regularly with neighboring Mexican children, building forts and defending them from imaginary Indians. They improvised gambling games together and won trinkets from one another, and even invented a macabre game based on bones from an old graveyard. Their parents put a stop to both the gambling and the grave-robbing as soon as they discovered them.

Not nearly the child-centered commercial extravaganza it is today, Christmas was a religious holiday on a par with Thanksgiving. Schoolchildren of the southern frontier followed the Scottish tradition of blockading the schoolhouse and locking out the schoolmaster just prior to Christmas in order to get him to grant a vacation.

* * *

In the early days of settlement, parents paid for their children's education and viewed it as optional, to be undertaken only in the rare hours that children could be spared from farm work. Some children attended only in winter, and even then, only if the weather permitted. The settlers could not spare much money to pay for teachers and schoolbooks, thereby enduring a shortage of both. Rarely did a teacher last more than one session. Some families sent their children to board with a family near a distant school. Whereas boys attended school much more frequently than girls, none usually attended for more than a few sessions. When they could not afford to establish a school, parents taught their children to read and write at home, using whatever books or periodicals they could get, making their own ink and pens. If necessary, they made do with the Bible, a flat piece of wood, and charcoal. The education-minded Reverend Ezra Fisher gathered his children nightly around the fireplace. They sat on benches or blocks of wood while Fisher used the light of a pitch pine knot to read out the words for the children to spell. One far-sighted Oregon farmer, who had accumulated several hundred dollars, summoned his children to ask if he should build a new home to replace their poor log cabin or purchase 'Harper's Complete Library.' The children opted for the books, carefully read and remembered them, and passed them down to the next generation.

Frontier parents, nevertheless, often fell short as teachers, as demonstrated by this letter from a Dakota homesteader to his family back east:

'Want you to doe some better Spelling, hardly make out your letter. Can read poore writeing but the Spelling gets away with me.'[5]

Before the gradual spread of public education, several families jointly hired a teacher, agreed on rules of student behavior and what should be taught, and provided room and board for the teacher in one of their homes. Like physicians, anybody so inclined who could read and write could be a teacher. Boys and girls as young as fifteen fulfilled that role. Literate drunkards, intoxicated before noon each day, might also fill a teacher's shoes. The ease with which one could become a teacher stood in contrast to the difficulty of holding the job and getting paid. A teacher might be dismissed on the thinnest of pretexts, and at times the parents could not come up with the money to pay the salary. In later years, county school boards set standards for hiring teachers, but there were as many standards as there were counties.

The grandiloquently named 'Jefferson Institute' was one of Oregon's first schools. It was a simple log cabin with long benches made of plank facing the walls. Here sat the children using as a desk wide boards set into the wall. The teacher handed out pens made of sharpened goose quills, using ink made by squeezing the juice from oak balls and letting it stand in iron filings. The first pencils were lead bullets hammered flat and long. Writing paper came from the Hudson's Bay Company, and the Bible, along with whatever other books could be scrounged, served as texts. During a daily recess the teacher segregated the sexes, sending the boys to play games with knitted balls on one side of the cabin while the girls jumped ropes made of braided rawhide on the cabin's other side.

Early in the nineteenth century, men more commonly filled the post of teacher in frontier schools. At that time, men received more education than women, and they were better able to impose discipline on unruly older students. However, there were not a lot of older pupils to instruct since most frontier students did not attend school past the primary grades. Women began entering the profession in greater numbers after 1830 and came to dominate the field by the 1870s. Educational opportunities for women had expanded greatly, and school boards could get away with paying them less than they paid men. As the one-room schoolhouse for all age groups gave way to separate classrooms for each grade, female teachers took over teaching the easier to handle primary grades. In 1884, a young man wishing to teach school received this advice from Dakota:

'Hardly think you can get a school here...thare is more Red Headed old maids here than you can shake a stick at in a week, came here to get married and failed...the School Boards have a slew of Old Maids hanging on their coattails.... Wait untill we have a Siclone [tornado] thare will be a better demand for men teachers.'[6]

Although teachers did not have to be highly educated to find employment, their duties extended well beyond teaching. The teacher served as school custodian, cleaning the schoolhouse, shoveling snow, chopping firewood, carrying in the wood or coal, and starting the fire. The child living nearest the school brought the drinking and hand-washing water. John Muir, teaching school in Wisconsin, invented a device to start the fire in the schoolhouse stove each morning so he could remain in bed longer.

The spellers and readers used in schoolhouses varied from student to student, as there were rarely enough of one title to go around. Popular titles of the early nineteenth century included Webster's 'Spelling Book,' and McGuffey's readers. Both spellers and readers attempted to provide moral education in the form of fables and aphorisms. In contrast to the formal examinations and grade reports of modern times, teachers gave prizes, usually books, to the best students, and encouraged competition among students in such skills as spelling.

Lacking spellers and readers, an Oregon school, run by a pious man, resorted to religious tracts:

'As soon as a child could spell out words, however indifferently, he or she was required to read religious tracts, which were intended to make the child realize it was wicked and in danger of punishment. These tracts were alarming, more alarming, and most alarming. They were our first, second, and third readers.'[7]

The children of Mays Lick, Kentucky, first attended school, two years after the village's founding, in a neighbor's cabin presided over by a Scottish schoolmaster who made liberal use of a hickory switch. Later, the settlers pitched in to build a 16 by 20-foot log schoolhouse. Daniel Drake attended intermittently from age five to age nine, by which time he had barely learned to write. Here as elsewhere, children typically recited their lessons in ragged unison, or all shouted out their different lessons at once. They ate a midday meal brought from home, and then played together in

An idealized image of a colonial schoolroom around 1776. The rough benches, the mix of all ages in a single room, and the general chaos prevailing behind the teacher's back were all characteristic of frontier schools. (Library of Congress)

the surrounding woods, climbing trees and running races. All ages attended together. Adults who decided late in life to pursue learning sat on the split-log benches with the children and recited their lessons. Ordinarily, teachers employed thrashing to maintain order, and some won fights with the bigger boys among the students in order to stay in control. Young scholars frequently engaged in fighting and foul language. One frontier teacher, Gideon Lincecum, a man of little learning and many brief careers, faced forty-five students, both children and adults, who had already abused and run off one teacher. They

> 'had been born and raised to the age I found them among the cows and drunken cow-drivers on the outer borders of the state, and they were positively the coarsest specimens of the human family I had ever seen. I saw very distinctly that no civil or ordinary means would be applicable to their condition.'[8]

Accordingly, after observing 'many curious and disgusting occurrences,' Lincecum drew up laws and held trials to keep miscreants in line. The student juries at first tended to sentence their peers to thrashings that would reduce a grown man to tears, but they grew more lenient as the school became more orderly. One of the worst miscreants, inspired by the school's mock trials, went on to be an accomplished attorney.

Lincecum himself had attended school in an old log cabin for just five months when he was fourteen years of age. At first humiliated by the younger boys who could already read, he worked hard to catch up:

'There I sat in a sea of burning shame, while the clatter and glib clap of tongues rattled on. I soon accustomed myself to this method of studying aloud and felt myself very much at home.... The teacher soon told me to bring paper and ink to school.... He marked a place on the writing bench that was to be called mine.... I felt very proud of my writing place, though it was nothing more than a wide two inch plank laid on some slanting pins or pegs, driven into two inch auger holes, in one of the pine logs that was a part of the wall of the house.'[9]

A schoolhouse built on the edge of the woods was called a 'forest school,' and one on a tapped-out field a 'field school.' The one-room schoolhouse, typically drafty and primitive, lacked even an outhouse; the children trotted off to the woods. The sod schoolhouses of the plains shared this lack of facilities and were damp and stifling to boot.

The pursuit of literacy began with the alphabet, then syllables, words, grammar, spelling, and penmanship. Spelling became yet another competitive obsession on the frontier, extending beyond the schoolhouse. Public spelling bees were widely attended social events, featuring intense rivalries among schools and individuals, with spectators rooting for their families and villages. When large blackboards came into use, schools held ciphering contests. The study of mathematics went beyond basic arithmetic to encompass such items as weights and measures, simple and compound interest, square and cube roots, and proportions. Higher mathematics was reserved for the academy students.

Enterprising individuals opened schools in private homes, churches, or dedicated schoolhouses, charging by the student or the subject. In addition to the basic subjects, some offered surveying and the classics to boys, sewing, French, music, and deportment to girls. Others ventured to offer philosophy, geography, and astronomy.

The wealthier settlers sent their children of both sexes to private academies and their sons to college. Given that early academies opened and closed their doors with unsettling speed, many parents opted to hire private tutors. The academies provided a more advanced course of study, including foreign languages and higher mathematics. Many were church sponsored and enforced high standards of behavior and exacting admission criteria. Unlike the country schools, academies strictly segregated the sexes. Alternatively, some parents preferred to send a promising youth to study a profession. At age fifteen, Daniel Drake had barely mastered reading, writing, and arithmetic yet displayed an aptitude for study. His father decided to pay $400 to a doctor who provided four years of room, board, and medical training. So at what today would be considered a tender age, young Drake left home for good to learn to become a doctor.

In the trans-Mississippi West, public education lagged well behind settlement, not reaching some areas until the 1920s. New Mexico had only five public schools in 1870. By 1880, that number had grown to 162 schools, open only five months a year, and attended by only 13 percent of the school age population.[10] Most typically, those who could afford it, such as army officers, sent their older children from New Mexico to schools in St. Louis or points eastward.

Catholic and Protestant missions did much to promote literacy on the trans-Mississippi frontier, often being the first to establish schools in a new territory. Marian Sloan was one of the five American and ninety-five Mexican girls attending a Catholic school in the 1850s in Santa Fe. She was the only non-Catholic among them. The girls all wore long-skirted uniforms and deported themselves in orderly contrast to the chaotic field schools of the early frontier. In addition to reading, writing, and arithmetic, the girls did fine needlework. Boys attended a separate but affiliated school nearby. American children in the Spanish southwest quickly learned a few words of Spanish, and many became fluent. When Sloan grew up and married, her own children attended school, beginning in 1876. The settlement built a log schoolhouse, which at first operated only three months a year.

Tabitha Brown, a sixty-six-year-old widow who traversed the Oregon Trail in 1846, conceived the idea of a charity-run boarding school for orphans of the trail. The school, built on donated land, housed thirty orphans and accepted paying students to help support the indigent ones. Oregon's first public school opened in 1851. In 1861, a Jewish school opened in Portland, joining the Methodist sponsored schools that had been operating in Oregon for some years. The year 1869 saw the opening of the first public high school in the state. Oregon settlers found that the winter and spring rains caused flooding, which prevented their children from getting to school during the very time when farm work slackened.

In the Dakota Territory, the first public schools did not open until 1865. Prior to that time, private schools served about half the potential students in the territory. The first private school opened in 1860 for a three-month term, and settlers built the first permanent schoolhouse in 1864.[11] By 1870, thirty-four public schools had opened, and 508 were in operation by 1880, serving 42 percent of the school age population. These schools opened only five months a year.[12] A Dakota youth from a remote homestead, wishing to get an education beyond primary school, worked and lived at a farm closer to town so he could attend eighth grade.

Children of the northern great plains faced dangerous weather when they attended school in winter. Blizzards and extreme cold caused deaths among children who became lost in the snow on the way to or from school. Little else distinguished the rural schools of late nineteenth-century Dakota Territory from the schools of a century earlier. A Dakota schoolteacher was more likely to be a young woman, the schoolhouse windows glazed, and the fuel for the stove coal, but outdoor plumbing still prevailed, and only children who could be spared from farm work attended. All ages still studied together in one room under one teacher, and children carried their lunches to school in open pails. When immigrant children from northern Europe attended, they quickly learned English because it was expected of them. Schools, in bringing together children from isolated farmsteads, helped to erase cultural differences among immigrants and forge an American community. It was a task teachers were proud to perform.

[1] Fred Lockley, 'Reminiscences of Martha E. Gilliam Collins,' *Quarterly of the Oregon Historical Society*, XVII:4 (December 1916), p. 366.
[2] Kenneth L. Holmes, ed., *Covered Wagon Women: Diaries & Letters from the Western Trails, 1840–1890* (Glendale, CA, 1983), vol. 1, p. 151.
[3] Cathy Luchetti, *Women of the West* (St George, Utah, 1982), pp. 72–3.
[4] Carl N. Degler, *At Odds: Women and the Family in America from the Revolution to the Present* (New York, 1980), p. 93.
[5] Ruth Seymour Burmeister, ed., 'Jeffries letters,' *South Dakota History*, VI:3 (Summer 1976), p. 321.
[6] 'Jeffries letters,' p. 322.
[7] Maude A. Rucker, *The Oregon Trail and Some of its Blazers* (New York, 1930), pp. 169–70.
[8] Gideon Lincecum, 'Autobiography of Gideon Lincecum,' *Publications of the Mississippi Historical Society*, VIII (1904), p. 459.
[9] Lincecum, p.455.
[10] Elliott West, *Growing Up With the Country* (Albuquerque, 1989), pp. 189–91.
[11] Herbert S.Schell, *History of South Dakota* (Lincoln, NE, 1968), p.102.
[12] Elliott West, pp. 189–91.

IX

'A GRAND FANDANGO'

Living miles apart from the nearest neighbors, settlers craved company, welcomed visitors, and frequently went on all-day Sunday visits to friends and neighbors. They spoke freely with one another about their concerns and seized upon travelers as a conduit for news from the wider world. Those travelers leaving journals describe to a man the great curiosity of the voluble frontiersmen. More than a few Englishmen remarked upon the rapid-fire stream of questions directed at them by their chance hosts and tavern-mates.

Pioneers gathered together for all manner of work, turning it into an occasion for sharing food, drink, and conversation. It took only two or three families to make up a pleasant party for work or celebration. House and barn raising, harvesting and threshing, squirrel hunting, and the 'husking bee' or 'corn husking frolic' all served as reasons to gather. At such occasions, whiskey flowed freely and the host family provided a meal. Wool and cotton picking frolics or quilting bees drew groups of women. Said an Iowa woman, '...I do hate to sit down alone to pick wool so I will invite about a dozen old ladies in and in a day they will do it all up.' Afterward she reported, 'they seemed to enjoy themselves fine. Had a fine chicken dinner...and now my name is out as a good cook so I am alright for good cooking makes good friends.'[1]

Corn husking frolics usually occurred in the evening. Like other such occasions, the work provided an excuse for the men to indulge in the competition they so enjoyed. The arriving men each took a swig of whiskey and organized into two teams, arranged on opposite sides of a rail, to race through the work. While the women gossiped and prepared the supper, the men drank, worked, and argued over perceived irregularities by the opposing team.

> 'It was there that I first learned that competition is the mother of cheating, falsehood and broils. Corn might be thrown over unhusked, the rail might be pulled toward you by the hand dextrously applied underneath, your feet might push corn to the other side of the rail.... If charged with any of these tricks, you of course denied it...the chorus of voices on a still night might be heard a mile.'[2]

Whiskey was the essential drink of pioneer life. Convention required pioneer hosts to offer whiskey to all visitors, and failure to do so was a breach of etiquette that drew comment. Daniel Drake's father made a sure investment when he traded a horse for 100 gallons of whiskey. At a fine profit he sold off smaller lots of whiskey to his neighbors. Men chewed tobacco and spit constantly in any public place, thoroughly wetting down the floors on which they stood. Frontier women often smoked pipes and took snuff, a stimulant as powerful as tobacco. In the Spanish southwest, Mexican men and women alike smoked slender cigarettes hand-rolled in corn husks.

Pioneers took entertainment wherever they could find it. They made cruel sport of wild animals, delighting in the struggles of the beasts that preyed on their farm animals. Combining predator control with amusement in eighteenth-century Kentucky, a pioneer settlement:

> 'Had a good many traps round from the Station to catch wolves in, and caught a great many. Dick Piles run a ring around the neck of a wolf with his knife, drew its skin

over its eyes, and let it go. 'Twas said he skinned another alive and let it go.... The fort yard was a great place for wolf baiting. Caught a Painter [panther] once and put it into an empty crib till we should put in a wolf.... Caught a turkey buzzard and put in, but they wouldn't fight or do anything. The wolves used to come and take the pigs and things close around the Station, before we put out so many traps.'[3]

Cruelty to animals for amusement continued across the country and through the decades, taking such forms as bear-baiting, gander pulling, cock fights, and dog fights. All such events, whether animal fights or human competitions, drew an intense round of wagering. Cock fighting and dog fighting, although illegal in most states, continue to this day. Most country dwellers know of someone who raises fighting cocks or pit-fighting dogs, known as 'pit-bulls.'

The towns and villages drew settlers to market days and court days, when they took the opportunity to socialize and compete. People even wagered on the outcomes of court cases. Villagers often got up a dance for the amusement of the judge and attorneys when the circuit court came to town. Mock trials, or moot courts, served as both a public entertainment and an arena for fledgling attorneys to sharpen their skills.

When people gathered in the villages for musters, court days, or marketing, the men drank and engaged in fighting and bloody sports. Fights knew no rules and featured biting, throttling, and eye gouging, the activity that easterners believed distinguished barbaric frontiers people from civilized Americans. The climactic moment of a gouging contest came when the victor gained sufficient control over his opponent to insert his thumb into the eye socket and gouge out the eye. Rumor abounded in the east that one half of all Virginia and Kentucky men had lost an eye to gouging. Although this was a gross exaggeration, gouging was common. Presumably contestants only lost once during a lifetime.

As the frontier grew more settled, animal baiting and fighting – while never totally abandoned – began to give way to horse races, target shoots, and games and athletic contests, such as foot races. Horse and foot races had long been a staple of frontier life. While betting remained the norm, honorably paying one's bets did not, particularly on the lawless leading edge of the frontier. Henry Hoyt, a doctor in 1870s New Mexico, told of a stranger in town who challenged all comers to a foot race, a fairly typical frontier occurrence. Hoyt accepted the challenge and proved to be the faster runner. The stranger, however, was an unusually poor loser. He turned up that night at the saloon and tried to shoot Hoyt, killing instead an unfortunate Mexican bystander.

In western saloons and forts, the inhabitants enjoyed playing cards, billiards, checkers, dominos, and backgammon, all accompanied by wagering. Like gamblers today, some wagered only what they could afford to lose, and others gambled away their every penny. Gambling parlors saturated the West, featuring such card games as faro and monte. The river boat gambler was more than a legend. He loomed large throughout the frontier, haunting steamboats and pool halls, emptying pockets wherever people gathered. Professional gamblers employed all sorts of trickery to induce players to part with more money than they intended. In one such ruse, a swindler pretended to be drunk and eager to gamble away large sums of money: seeing the chance for easy winnings, the unwary player found himself fleeced by an opponent who was not so drunk as he had seemed.

The monte tables of Santa Fe lured the experienced and the naive to financial ruin. Monte was a game of Spanish origin, strictly a game of chance where players bet on the color of the cards about to be turned up. Faro operated in much the same way. A certain Mexican lady, Dona Gertrudes Barcelo, enjoyed infamy as a monte dealer whom men could not resist. Santa Fe trader Josiah Gregg described her thus:

'There lived (or rather roamed) in Taos a certain female of very loose habits.... Finding it difficult to obtain the means of living in that district, she finally extended her

Miners parting with their gold at a frontier faro table. (*Harper's Weekly, 3 October 1857*)

wanderings to the capital. She there became a constant attendant on one of those pandemoniums where the favorite game of monte was dealt.... At last her luck turned, as gamblers would say, and on one occasion she left the bank with a spoil of several hundred dollars! This enabled her to open a bank of her own, and being favored by a continuous run of good fortune, she gradually rose higher and higher in the scale of affluence, until she found herself in possession of a very handsome fortune.... She still continues her favorite "amusement," being now considered the most expert "monte dealer" in all Santa Fe. She is openly received in the first circles of society...'[4]

The years only added to her renown. A trader's wife called her:

'a stately dame of a certain age, the possessor of a portion of that shrewd sense and fascinating manner necessary to allure the wayward, inexperienced youth to the hall of final ruin.'[5]

Santa Fe enjoyed such a reputation for debauchery that the occupying US Army quickly moved its headquarters away from the city for the sake of the soldiers' morals. Most of the American women who came to Santa Fe in the decade following the Mexican War were the wives of soldiers, government officials, or traders. Under the protective escort of their husbands they occasionally attended the fandango – as the Mexicans' dances were called – but generally Americans considered the fandangos too wild and debauched for their ladies. Instead, the ladies presided over whatever respectable entertainments New Mexico could offer. Visits, dinner parties, games of whist (the forerunner of bridge), musical evenings and dancing, debating societies, horseback riding, and winter evening sleigh rides made up the social round. Army units organized bands to give regular concerts. In New Mexico and elsewhere on the frontier, army forts became magnets for the social life of surrounding communities, giving dances, concerts, plays, and other entertainments. Some soldiers sought out Indian women for sexual liaisons; others courted and married settlers' daughters.

Frontier social life, both east and west of the Mississippi, relied heavily on dances. Settlers organized dances on any pretext; to 'warm' a new house or mark an election, for example. Entire families traveled many miles to attend a dance, and stayed all night. Early country dances featured a fiddle and a harmonica playing the popular folk tunes of the time. Towns hosted more elaborate dances and costume balls. Communities that lacked a musician or religious denominations that frowned on dancing held events called 'play parties.' Such parties, peculiar to the late nineteenth-century frontier, provided an excuse to gather and socialize. They featured food and party games set to music – such as 'Skip-to-my-Lou' – and died out as the community acquired theaters and other entertainments.

The Hispanic New Mexicans, just like American pioneers, enjoyed gambling, card games, cockfights, and fandangos. They welcomed Americans to their fandangos, as long as the men left their guns outside. Fiddles, guitars, and drums provided the music. American guests commented on the colorful dress and dance halls filled with cigarette smoke:

> 'I went & found it a grand Fandango – Every one was there almost (except the decent American ladies) – officers, gents, gamblers & all with their mistresses. Champagne &c. flowed in abundance & the party was a lively one.'

> 'Had a barroom attached to the large dansing room, where much liquor was drank, & a Monte Bank attended by a woman was in full operation. A gent asks any lady to dance.... The music consists of a couple of fiddles, & I believe a guitar – & also one of the musicians singing with the music.'

> 'The women...wear their fine shawls, partly thrown over their heads, & quietly smoke their cigaritos. Waltzing forms the chief part of their dansing.... After the dance the gents take their partners out & treat them to a glass of wine or candy.'[6]

Fiddles, with various other instruments, provided the main accompaniment to dances throughout the nineteenth century. A good fiddler found a welcome everywhere, and a stranger who could play his fiddle well received the warmest hospitality. Henry Hoyt and his friends, on the trail from

Frontier saloon and dance hall. (In Albert D. Richardson, **Beyond the Mississippi,** *Hartford, 1869)*

A 'musical evening' in a southwestern home. (Arizona Historical Society)

Dakota to New Mexico Territory, one night made camp near a ranch and broke out their fiddles. Soon their playing brought the desired invitation from the ranch house, where they enjoyed soft beds and a good meal.

Music of all sorts provided an important source of relaxation throughout the West. People in the most straitened circumstances somehow managed to import pianos to such places as Texas or South Dakota. Other musicians soon gathered, and in no time at all formed bands or held musical evenings. Dakota Territory settlements peopled by Bohemian and Scandinavian immigrants organized brass bands. The melodeon provided musical entertainment on the later frontiers. Settlers brought this small bellows-operated keyboard to New Mexico, and later to Dakota. In Dakota, the family that owned a melodeon often loaded it on a sleigh or wagon to play it at social gatherings. Singing schools, specializing in hymns, drew many adherents. Their popularity reached from the early Kentucky frontier to Dakota in the 1880s.

Traveling menageries and performers, such as magicians and ventriloquists, appeared in frontier towns from the early 1800s. Circuses, traveling wax figure exhibits, and drama troupes followed. The circus as we know it today originated in England in the eighteenth century. The first circuses in the United States were stationary establishments in the east. The traveling circus, a horse-drawn caravan of equestrian, aerial, and animal acts, grew in popularity during the 1800s. Circus caravans offered free tickets to homesteaders who fed and lodged the troupe and animals. As the railroads extended their range, circuses grew larger and traveled greater distances. For young people living on isolated homesteads, circuses represented the pinnacle of exciting entertainment. A man recalling his 1880s Dakota boyhood cited his greatest youthful disappointment, arriving at a circus only to find that the price of admission was ten cents more than he possessed.

The Fourth of July held the place of honor among frontier holidays. Picnics and barbecues featured food, drink, and speech-making. Here was an irresistible opportunity for politicians to

An 1875 hunting party organized by Dakota Territory soldiers. (National Archives)

mount the stump and pontificate. Diversions of all sorts were welcome. One Dakota event hired Indians to perform one of their traditional dances. Parades, concerts, games, and races soon became part of the July Fourth celebration. Settlers also made parties or picnics out of such activities as fishing, berry-picking, taffy-pulling, or sledding. Organized camping trips were common in the latter half of the century, surprising among people who had recently spent months emigrating in a covered wagon.

Growing frontier towns soon provided the full array of entertainments available back east. Lexington, Kentucky boasted an amateur theater before 1800. The first play in Natchez, Mississippi was performed at a tavern in 1806. Debating and literary societies arrived with increasing civilization. Schoolhouses, having often been built by local volunteers, welcomed community activities, including amateur plays, concerts, spelling bees, parties, debates, and political meetings. They frequently hosted lyceums – from the word meaning a public lecture hall – for both entertainment and enrichment. A lyceum in rural Dakota in the 1880s featured recitations by children, songs by local singers, and heated debates. A group of urban sophisticates in Santa Fe, however, practiced debating with a new twist:

> 'There had been a debate previous to the party – the Literati Club, & afterwards the Empire Club – whose members are fined if they speak any sense.'[7]

'Americans of all ages, all conditions, and all dispositions constantly form associations,' observed Alexis de Tocqueville at mid-century. He attributed this tendency to Americans' dependence on collective action to achieve any goal. De Tocqueville pronounced it an endemic attribute of democracy. Whatever the underlying cause, organizations of all sorts did indeed proliferate in western communities. Secret fraternal organizations, temperance unions, civic improvement associations,

THE ORDER OF THE PATRONS OF HUSBANDRY

The grangers movement began in 1867 with the founding of the Patrons of Husbandry. The founder, a Mason, modeled the Patrons after that order and intended it to serve farmers nationwide as a social, educational, and fraternal organization complete with secret rituals and passwords. Patrons'membership rapidly outstripped that of other farming societies. The Patrons actively recruited members and admitted women to full membership.

Local chapters were called Granges. Members joined as Laborers and Maids, and aspired to move up through the ranks as Cultivator and Shepherdess, Harvester and Gleaner, Husbandman and Matron. The ambitious male Patron aspired to the highest local rank, Master.

While focusing primarily on farmer education, granger chapters also took positions on such political issues as currency, trade, and railroad regulation. The Patrons were the first to argue that railroads were public utilities that ought to be regulated.

Local chapters quickly organized into buying and selling cooperatives with varying degrees of success. Most of the cooperative stores and grain elevators failed because they were unable to compete with established merchants or extend the credit that farmers needed.

county agricultural societies, and baseball clubs multiplied alongside churches and schools.

Secret fraternal societies, or lodges, replete with rituals and initiations, were particularly popular. Some of the initiations resembled twentieth-century collegiate pranks. The basic function of most such organizations was to provide a chance for men to get together and socialize. Fund-raising and good works justified the lodges' existence. Two such lodges were the Anti-Horse Thief Association and the Society of Masons. The Society of Masons, formed in 1717 by the British, was originally an organization of cathedral builders. As the number of working masons dwindled, the society opened to the general population and spread to the New World. The Patrons of Husbandry became the first such organization to admit women as full members.

Churches held fairs and festivals to raise money. These fairs sold refreshments and handcrafted items and offered amusement booths similar to those found at county fairs. Volunteers organized Sunday schools, formed reading circles, and raised funds for public libraries. By the time homesteaders came to Dakota in large numbers, social life quickly took on a shape not far different from what exists in rural America today. Bowling alleys, a fixture in many modern rural towns, began doing business in western towns prior to the Civil War. A version of the pastime had long been established in Europe and colonists perpetuated it in the New World.

Some elements of frontier social life – open whiskey consumption, bloody sport, eagerness to participate in group activity – have fallen into disfavor among modern Americans. By and large, however, a modern gregarious person set down at a corn-husking bee or fandango would find the social scene familiar and quite comfortable.

[1]   Cathy Luchetti, *Women of the West* (St George, Utah, 1982), p. 138.

[2]   Daniel Drake, *Pioneer Life in Kentucky* (New York, 1948), pp. 55–6.

[3]   John D. Shane, 'Interview with pioneer William Clinkenbeard,' *Filson Club History Quarterly*, II:3 (April 1928), p. 105.

[4]   Josiah Gregg, *Commerce of the Prairies* (New York, 1970), p. 78.

[5]   Stella M. Drumm, ed., *Down the Santa Fe Trail and Into Mexico: The Diary of Susan Shelby Magoffin, 1846–1847* (New Haven, 1926), pp. 119-21.

[6]   Barton H. Barbour, ed., *Reluctant Frontiersman: James Ross Larkin on the Santa Fe Trail, 1856–57* (Albuquerque, 1990), pp. 98, 102, 108.

[7]   Barbour, p. 106.

X

'ALL DOING THEIR DUTY'

The issue of slavery – whether or not one human being ought to own another – divided Americans from the beginning of their history as a nation. On the frontier, this division fell along geographic lines, with the plantation economy of the southern seaboard spreading into the southern Mississippi valley. Further north in Kentucky and Missouri, slavery was present but less pervasive. When new territories opened for settlement across the Mississippi River, slave owners and abolitionists vied for control because they expected that each territory would eventually become a state. At that point, whether the state was free or slave-owning would upset the delicate congressional equilibrium between the rival ideologies.

Nineteenth-century Americans were not a particularly tolerant lot. They felt contempt for people who did not share their beliefs about slavery, for people of different religions, for people who were recognizably different, such as Mexicans and Indians, and for people of differing European origins. Wrote a pioneer of German stock, 'She is of Irish descent And you know the Irish are Not very Cleanly.'[1]

Individuals who opposed enslavement of negros did not necessarily oppose enslaving Indians. Nor did the debt peonage system among the Mexicans of the southwest, by which the wealthy virtually enslaved the poor, cause much moral distress to the conquering Americans. Some thought of it as no more than a convenient, low-cost alternative to slavery.

The small community of Mays Lick, Kentucky offers a microcosm of interlocking prejudices. The New Jersey-born founders of the village held no slaves, some because of conviction, others possibly because they couldn't afford them. The emigrants from Virginia and Maryland brought one or more slaves, depending on how many they could afford. Typical was a former Marylander who owned only two slaves and worked the land as a tenant farmer. Daniel Drake, son of a New Jersey family, even looking back as a well-educated adult, expressed deep disapproval of the Marylanders. He described them as morally inferior, cruder, and more ignorant than the New Jersey and Virginia emigrants. Furthermore, he condemned them because often they fed their slaves poorly, inflicted brutal punishment, and usually badly overworked them. The prejudice of the New Jersey emigrants extended to religion as well. As part of the Baptist majority, they viewed the Methodist camp meetings of the Maryland and Virginia emigrants as ignorant and disorderly. In this they were typical of southern Baptists, to whom Methodists appeared as fanatics.

The classless society of the late 1700s frontier quickly stratified into rich and poor, particularly in the slave-holding south. Slave ownership, size of land holdings, and wealth distinguished the planter class from the farmer class. The farmer class in turn divided along the lines of land ownership and tenancy. Planters viewed as 'poor whites' those farmers who owned no slaves or who worked alongside the two or three slaves they owned. Social stratification grew ever more entrenched as the wealthiest settlers made private land deals with corrupt government officials, buying large tracts of public land at favorable prices before they officially went on sale.

The Spanish southwest offered even more numerous opportunities to hate one's neighbor. In New Mexico, American settlers lived among both rich and poor Mexicans, the settled pueblo-dwelling Indians, and nomadic hostile tribes. They found the Mexicans' Catholicism suspect, and feared and hated the Mormons whose communities lay to the northwest in Utah. Of Mormons met on the Santa Fe Trail, Francis Parkman admitted his apprehension: 'these unwelcome visitors had a certain glitter of the eye, and a compression of the lips, which distinguished them...'[2]

Free men and women on the frontier rarely chose to work as domestic servants or hired laborers. The very thing that lured them west, inexpensive land, gave them an alternative to laboring for others and allowed them to aspire to their own homes and farms. Thus, settlers who did not own slaves did not have much recourse to hired help. In the West cheap land went hand-in-hand with scarce labor. Well-to-do Americans looked down on the servant class. Poor Americans struggled mightily to avoid joining it. This divide, however, held true only at the two extremes of the economic spectrum. The inclusive middle class contained doctors who tended bar, barbers who carried the mail, and ministers who turned their hands to the plow. Frontier professionals did not commonly shun laborers: those who did risked being accused of 'putting on airs.'

Perhaps because they had traveled so far and shared the same trials to reach their new homes, the first Oregon settlers established a more egalitarian society than those found on other frontiers. Writing about the character of Oregon's first pioneers, a settler recalled, 'Social life was free and easy, where there were no classes, and no social gradations.'[3] On the other hand, another pioneer reported that a gulf opened between old settlers and recent arrivals based on their differing economic concerns. Inevitably, class consciousness grew when the early missionary households of Oregon hired servants from the Sandwich Islands, present-day Hawaii, to assist with domestic and farm work. The islanders, encouraged by their own chiefs, shipped out on European trading vessels to seek their fortunes in the wider world. Some sought the religious teachings of the missions. In one mission household, a female house servant – a Hawaiian Christian named Hannah – did the washing and cooking, while her mistress, Mrs. Gray, did the ironing, sewing, baking, and preserving. Mrs. Gray considered her servant a poor worker and vented her pique in her diary:

> 'Have been a good deal tried with Hannah to day. I told her to night that if she remained here she must do as I told her. She has disobeyed me two or three times today & has been very lazy.'[4]

In the Spanish southwest, the conquering Americans found that they could hire Mexicans for domestic work. They could also import Negro slaves or enslave captured Indians. An American wife in New Mexico, whether married to a wealthy trader or an army officer, spent her days primarily running her household and visiting. Running the household involved supervising the servants, purchasing supplies, and sewing. Susan Magoffin, nineteen-year-old wife of a wealthy trader, thus described her household duties: 'I commenced my daily task – the superintending of the general business of house-keepers, such as sweeping, dusting, arranging and re-arranging of furniture, making of beds, ordering dinner, &c. &c. &c. This part being completed, I took up my sewing.'[5] Mrs. Magoffin also prided herself on her ability to drive a hard bargain with the Mexican youngsters who peddled vegetables in Santa Fe.

American ladies complained about the quality of domestic servants more than they praised them. Then as now, attitudes toward entire groups became hardened based on unpleasant experience with individuals. At first Susan Magoffin wrote that her Mexican servants 'remain perfectly submissive, and indeed it is a pleasure, when an underling is so faithful, to do them any little favor. Mine is a quiet little household, the servants are all doing their duty...'[6] Later she complained, 'Nothing hurts me more than to have a cross, ill-tempered servant about me.... The only way to treat a turbulent domestic, is to look above them too much to answer them back, or even to hear their impudence, till it becomes correctable by the rod.'[7]

Lydia Lane, an army wife who hired a series of Mexican cooks, baby nurses, and laborers, complained of their lack of skill and motivation in all but a few cases. And further, she concluded,

'As has always been my experience in travelling, the domestics were useless. Kit and Marie, the Mexican nurse, were at once overcome and unable to do anything.'[8]

Class consciousness ran high among nineteenth-century Americans, and pioneers were no exception. Women in the most isolated circumstances, longing for the company of other women, still shunned those whom they considered 'beneath notice.' Several frontierswomen forming a study group advertised in the village newspaper for women to attend an organizational meeting. They were appalled when some dance hall girls and prostitutes showed up. Rather than bar them from the group outright, the organizers changed the rules to require so much homework that the undesired ones, who after all did have full-time jobs, dropped out.[9]

When it came to the plight of their own race and kind, settlers gave freely of their efforts in a neighbor's time of need, knowing they would need a return favor one day. If a man sustained an injury at harvest time, neighbors brought in the harvest. If a family produced a poor crop, neighbors made up the shortfall. Frontier women dropped everything else to go to a neighbor's childbed or sickbed. Of his South Dakota homestead childhood, Guy Cook recalled, 'The fact is we had more to eat when there was sickness in our home than at other times because the neighbors brought in plenty of food.'[10]

Pioneers valued and practiced hospitality to strangers of their own kind as well. They shared their food and roof with passing travelers, who made their beds on the floor if necessary. Army wives, too, offered hospitality to all American travelers passing through their posts. As a matter of course, any friend or stranger who stopped by when a meal was about to be served was invited to share. Visitors observed the convention of hailing the householder while still mounted and not alighting until invited to come in. If someone driving a wagon to town came upon a neighbor on foot, he invariably offered a ride.

One Dakota homesteader planned to come home from church with two guests and alerted his mother to prepare for them. Instead he brought along four visitors who stopped for the night. The men were given dinner, then sent to sleep on a neighbor's floor. The first visitors were preparing to sleep two to a bed, when a family of five new emigrants, whom the hosts had expected several days earlier, finally arrived in the midst of a torrential rain. They in turn received food and coffee and all bedded down on the floor. The next morning the hostess served them their breakfast in shifts. It was far from rare for a small house already occupied by a large family to welcome simultaneously several parties of guests, even for extended visits.

When pioneers joined forces to tackle difficult jobs, – house-raising, fence-building, harvesting, threshing – they were showing a spirit of cooperation. They were also acting out of necessity and self-interest. To pioneers willing to brave the hazards of the frontier, the reward was land ownership and economic independence. Yet to achieve these goals, they required the help of neighbors. While many surely enjoyed their neighbors' company when working together, they kept mental tallies of who did how much for them, and how much work they in turn owed the others.

* * *

In Mays Lick, Kentucky, most of the earliest citizens were Baptists. They wasted no time in erecting a log meeting house and engaging a parson from Washington, 8 miles distant, to lead worship and teach catechism. In Washington, settlers erected the Baptist church on land donated by the preacher.

The farmers of the south were usually Baptists while wealthy planters adhered to Presbyterianism or Methodism. The Methodists took the duty to evangelize their faith seriously and sent out circuit riders on grueling schedules. It was all in a day's work to be drenched regularly by storms or half-drowned by fording overflowing streams while traveling on horseback to the next congregation.

Methodists sent missionaries to Oregon country when it was still an isolated outpost. In 1846 the Reverend Ezra Fisher found only two American families living in Astoria, so the audience for his sermons was small. To add to his family's discouragement, even by his mission's second year there was neither word nor remittance from the Home Mission Society back in Illinois, the group that supposedly was sponsoring him. Fisher's family lived in an abandoned cabin without windows and wore the clothes in which they had crossed the Oregon Trail. There was no variety of food, and a severe winter killed all but two of Fisher's twenty head of cattle. Still he persisted, and favorable reports from missionaries like him helped encourage emigration.

Many subsequent parties formed traveling groups based upon shared religious affiliation. The requirements for a typical group included the injunction that 'every man carry with him a Bible and other religious books, as we hope not to degenerate into a state of barbarism.'[11] In the hope of spreading their version of the gospel, a Methodist missionary opened a school in Catholic New Mexico shortly after the United States annexed the territory. Likewise, the Methodists sent preachers out to the early prairie settlements. The first Methodists arrived in the Dakotas around 1860. The Baptists and Congregationalists also enjoyed expanding communities on the prairie frontier as settlement increased. The farmers who emigrated to Oregon, when they sought church affiliation at all, became Methodists or Baptists. Those who gravitated to Oregon's towns tended to be northeastern and New England natives. Their families provided the congregations for Presbyterian and Congregationalist churches.

Protestant denominations strictly forbade tobacco use and alcohol consumption among the clergy. Beyond that, becoming a member of the Presbyterian clergy required an education, and Presbyterian ministers did not go to the frontier until hired by an established congregation. Baptist and Methodist clergy, on the other hand, did not have to be educated, but they did have to undergo conversion by divine intervention, and have a gift for swaying people through preaching. Unlike Presbyterian ministers, Baptist and Methodist preachers went west to seek converts. By the 1830s, however, they too had to attend seminaries, and the divine aspect of their calling subsided in importance. Churches sought to regulate the behavior of their congregants as well. The congregation, by majority vote, could expel members for drunkenness, cursing, wife and child abuse, fighting, and larceny. As the nineteenth century opened, the Baptists and Methodists officially opposed slavery. By the 1840s, the churches had split over the issue into northern and southern organizations.

Farmers refrained from field work on Sunday, keeping it as a day for attending church and making visits. A sizeable portion of the early settlers did not view church affiliation as important. Fewer than 10 percent in early Kentucky actually belonged to a church. The other 90 percent, if they observed the Sabbath at all, treated it as a day of rest and relaxation. Accordingly, politicians did not find it to their advantage to make much of religion or to call upon God in their speeches. In fact, some states enacted laws forbidding ministers from serving in the state legislature.[12]

The first major revival meeting convened in Kentucky in 1800. Methodists and Baptists alike flocked to revivals in the ensuing years. Such multi-day meetings, often interdenominational and conducted without official church sanction, continued in the West for several decades, moving west of the Missouri River by the 1850s. They followed a prescribed course whose purpose was the conversion of sinners through exhortation followed by divine intervention. Citizens cleared areas in the woods for the meetings, and built permanent camps with sheds and tents for the worshipers and ministers. The meetings also served as social gatherings and a welcome break from toil.

The conversions featured extravagant shows of religious fervor, including rolling on the ground – hence 'holy rollers' – spasmodic jerking, known as the 'jerks,' and speaking in tongues. Even barking was taken as a sign of religious ecstasy, although one observer noticed a group of meeting-goers in the woods practicing their barking. This is not to suggest that all such displays were insincere: frontier camp meetings provided a necessary emotional release and fulfilled a spiritual need as well as a social one. By mid-century, the revival meetings no longer elicited such displays, although some worshipers shouted, wept, or swooned.

Camp meetings drew their share of miscreants who smuggled in liquor and looked for amusement. Misbehavior at the meetings remained a matter of concern in later years. An Iowa farm wife attending a camp meeting in 1841 reported, 'There are 4 young men and two girls going with us, but I made them promise there should be no sparking ...'[13] Just in case, camp meeting grounds featured broad aisles or rail fences down the center to divide the sexes.

A Catholic population, of French or Spanish descent, preceded by many decades the largely Protestant Americans into lower and upper Louisiana, as well as the Spanish southwest. Catholics of Irish and German descent populated the frontier from the east, and the first Catholic see of the American West was established in Kentucky in 1808. When American settlers began crossing the Mississippi River to settle in the French territories of Upper Louisiana – present-day Arkansas and Missouri– a Catholic community had been in place for at least fifty years. In New Mexico Territory, a Catholic community had existed for 200 years. In the early years of American settlement, the Protestant settlers relied upon Catholic priests to perform their marriages.

A shortage of clergy on the remotest frontiers led some couples to cohabit until a minister happened along. Cohabitation might be a matter of choice, but burials could not wait for the circuit rider to make an appearance. Burials took place quickly in the days before embalming, and they were ordinarily done at home, a prayer said without the presence of clergy. People established family burial plots on farms, and community plots near churches. The religious funeral ceremony waited until the circuit rider arrived. Funerals became another reason for gathering and consuming food and drink, a necessary social outlet.

When pioneers died along the overland trails, their traveling companions buried them immediately. Coffins were rare on the trail, and the emigrants wrapped the dead in a sheet if they could spare one. The pioneers attempted to cover the grave with rocks or logs to keep wild animals from digging up the bodies. If a person died on board a ship, the body was dropped overboard after the service. On army bases in the arid Southwest, the scarcity of wood led to soldiers being buried in coffins made of packing crates.

* * *

In the first three years of Kentucky settlement, men outnumbered women three to one. One pioneer reported that in 1789, there was 'but one married man in our eight – rest of us were young men.'[14] Such a ratio was common on all frontiers, particularly in the towns. Because of the shortage of women, the initial weddings performed in Harrodsburg featured brides of ages fourteen and fifteen. Early marriages prevailed on other frontiers as well. State laws setting the female age of consent as low as ten persisted almost to the twentieth century. Only late in the nineteenth century did most states raise the age to fourteen or sixteen.

Oregon, which attracted a high proportion of families, still drew two adult men to every adult woman through its early years of settlement. The rigorous overland journey and the distance from home discouraged many women from attempting the move. Further, the occasional attempts that Indians made to purchase white women engendered the belief that women were in perpetual danger of being kidnapped if they traveled the trails west. Thus the women of Oregon, like all frontier women, found themselves in high demand. Wrote a delighted Oregon sixteen-year-old, 'There is a great many young men loves me.'[15] She soon made her fateful choice, married at seventeen, and died in agony at twenty, trying to deliver twins. Given the scarcity of women, a frontier woman who outlived her husband had every chance to remarry and was indeed expected to do so. In early Kentucky, after a man named Spahr fell to Indians, a neighbor reported, 'Cassidy lived with Spahr. Expected him to marry the widow Spahr, but he didn't; Wells took her.'[16] Contrast this with the widower of the unfortunate Oregon woman: he had to search for five years to find another wife.

Courting couples did not have to be chaperoned and took some physical liberties with the privacy accorded them. If a suitor called at a young woman's home, her parents obligingly made themselves scarce. Given all this freedom, premarital pregnancies were extremely rare, because the social stigma attending them was so great. Courtship in the civilized prairie settlements required that couples go out together, whether to a church social, or just a horseback or buggy ride over the fields. These rides afforded considerable privacy, yet they were recognized as a privilege not to be abused.

A wedding provided a great opportunity to gather and socialize. Some considered a fiddler more important to the proceedings than the minister. Feasting and dancing lasted for days. Traditionally, the groom and his friends rode from his father's house to the bride's, arriving at noon. After the vows and much dancing, the bride's friends put her to bed upstairs, and the groom's friends then did the same for him. The well-wishers burst into the bridal chamber at frequent intervals throughout the night to encourage them. The next day the feasting moved to the groom's family home. Finally, when the couple moved to their own cabin, friends carried on a 'shivaree,' an occasion full of jollity and practical jokes.

Virtuous women, that is, those who confined their sexual activity to their marriage bed, aroused the protective instincts of the rudest frontiersmen. Men treated them with respect, seldom insulting or importuning an unaccompanied woman. There can be little doubt that women on the frontier were scarce, and therefore valued. Their economic contribution to the pioneer farming household, their ability to do the necessary work, was essential to survival. Popular belief held women to be innately morally superior. However, once married, did their husbands accord them the same respect in practice that strangers did in theory, and did they take their wives' hard work for granted? Consider the words of the U.S. Secretary of Agriculture in 1862:

'In plain language...a farmer's wife, as a too general rule, is a laboring drudge; not of necessity...but for want of...consideration...

'Many a farmer speaks to his wife habitually in terms more imperious, impatient, and petulant than he would use to the scullion of the kitchen or to his hired man.'[17]

He went on to observe that even men of means put all their money into more land and denied their wives the comforts that money could buy. The discontents of pioneer wives at times appear strikingly similar to the complaints of modern wives. Wrote a missionary in Oregon around 1840:

'Have felt the past week several times as if I could no longer endure certain things that I find in my husband.... What grieves me most is that the only being on earth with whom I can have much opportunity for intercourse manifests uniformly an unwillingness to engage me in social reading or conversation.'[18]

Protested a southwestern wife in 1864:

'my companion is at Bill Hoovers store playing drafts...it seems to me that he would rather be their playing them than to be at home with me and his little boy...'[19]

Divorce records in western states show that some men came west and then divorced wives who had refused to accompany them. Certainly a great number of wives came west only with the greatest of reluctance, their husbands having imposed the decision on them. Such women saw it as a cruel tearing up of roots, not as an opportunity to enjoy greater freedom. Emigrating to the West forced women out of their traditional home-based role into other lines of work. They cannot be blamed for their failure to see liberation in having to walk behind a plow as well as tend to all their usual work. Nevertheless, many wives loved the frontier life and exulted in new-found abilities and opportunities. A woman who helped build her new house explained it thus: 'I laughed whenever I paused for a few minutes to rest, at the idea of promising to pay a man fourteen or sixteen dollars per day for doing what I found my own hands so dexterous in.'[20]

Divorce grew easier as the nineteenth century wore on, especially in the western states. Each divorce required an act of the state legislature, and most such acts passed quickly and routinely. In fact, South Dakota became known for granting easy divorces to all petitioners without informing their absent spouses. By mid-century, women petitioned for the majority of divorces. Western divorces often allowed both parties to remarry, which was unusual in the east. For most, however, divorce remained a serious matter compared to the way we view it today. When a young Oregon woman of the 1850s, whose husband would not work to support the family, first spoke of divorce to her parents, they wept at the humiliation of it and begged her to reconcile with her husband. They finally relented and helped her hire a good lawyer. Frontier conditions made it all too easy for a man to abandon his family and disappear into a new life in another territory. For a woman to flee anywhere but back to her parents remained difficult. Although marriages broke apart for most of the usual reasons, infidelity on the frontier was relatively unusual: an activity that required secrecy was nigh impossible when settlers' knew one another's personal business.

The isolation of the frontier put married women at the mercy of violently abusive husbands. Escape was not always possible. The Sloan family, on an 1856 passage over the Santa Fe Trail, happened upon a downtrodden pregnant woman at a lone cabin in Kansas. She came to them and asked the travelers to let her leave with them. At that moment her husband came and drove the would-be rescuers off with curses and threats. On their return trip, they passed by the same site and saw the cabin deserted, and the nearby graves of the woman and her infant, dated only a few weeks after they had last seen her. Did her husband kill her or did she die giving birth?

Less mysterious was the death of an Oregon woman. Adam Wimple, a man in his thirties, killed his fourteen-year-old bride within a year of their 1850 marriage. A visitor arrived the morning of the murder and observed:

'Mrs. Wimple's face was all swollen and her eyes were red from crying. Wimple saw they noticed it, so he said "Mary isn't feeling very well this morning."'

After the murder and Wimple's capture, a family friend asked him why he had killed his wife:

'He said, "Well, I killed her. I don't really know why."'[21]

The early 1800s saw the persistence of large families, eight or ten children being not uncommon. Over the course of the ensuing century, the birth rate fell across the country, but less so on the frontier. It is apparent that couples practiced some form of contraception, that they could and did limit the size of their families despite the opposition of public opinion. Few people wrote openly in letters or diaries about what was considered a most delicate subject, but some expressions of unwillingness to endure additional pregnancies survive:

'There wasn't no quarrel with Willie, no words. I was his good wife in every respect – but I wasn't going to have no more babies...

'Then we went to visit...my niece over Saturday night. I didn't carry no paraphernalia because Willie promised to behave hisself. He didn't, and that's where our troubles commenced.'[22]

The passion with which marital and medical advisers inveighed against the withdrawal method indicates that it must have been popular. American couples were also aware of the so-called 'safe period,' or rhythm method, but common knowledge on the timing of ovulation was quite shaky and subject to error. Douches and condoms became generally available by the second half of the century.

Beginning in the late 1830s, women in large numbers – particularly married women – resorted to abortion when all else failed, despite the existence of considerable public sentiment against the practice. Abortions performed by professionals were more available in cities, but women in rural and frontier areas knew how to terminate pregnancies. They took toxic drugs, injected water into their wombs, or resorted to instruments, often with the full knowledge of their husbands. One woman, dying from an abortion gone amiss, told her doctor that she had aborted herself more than twenty times during her marriage. Professional abortionists advertised in terms of 'restoring menstrual flow,' but most women knew to what they referred. In the post-Civil War years, encouraged mostly by the medical profession, laws proliferated making abortion a crime. The earliest laws made it a crime only after quickening – the point about midway through pregnancy when the fetus first moves – but soon the laws covered the entire course of pregnancy.[23]

Despite the existence of writings idealizing women as innocent of sexual feeling, most people knew women to be as sexually desirous as men. Efforts at limiting sex within marriage were due less to lack of wifely interest than to the desire to limit the number of pregnancies: at some point, a wife decided that she simply could not endure another one. One wonders, however, given the amount of work frontier families had to do and the crowded cabins in which they lived, where they found the time, energy, and privacy to produce such large families.

[1]   Lillian Schlissel et. al., *Far From Home: Families of the Westward Journey* (New York, 1989), p. 89.

[2]   Francis Parkman, *The Oregon Trail* (New York, 1949), p. 284.

[3]   Harvey W. Scott, 'Pioneer character of Oregon progress,' *Quarterly of the Oregon Historical Society*, XVIII:4 (December 1917), p. 249.

[4]   Clifford Merrill Drury, ed., *First White Women Over the Rockies* (Glendale, CA, 1963), vol. 1, p. 257.

[5]   Stella M. Drumm, ed., *Down the Santa Fe Trail and Into Mexico: The Diary of Susan Shelby Magoffin, 1846–1847* (New Haven, 1926), p. 112.

[6]   Drumm, p. 111.

[7]   Drumm, pp. 174–5.

[8]   Lydia Spencer Lane, *I Married a Soldier* (Albuquerque, 1964), p. 79.

[9]   Sandra L. Myres, *Westering Women and the Frontier Experience, 1800–1915* (Albuquerque, 1982), p. 209.

[10]   Ruth Cook Frajola, ed., 'They went west', *South Dakota History*, VI: 3 (Summer 1976), p. 292.

[11]   'Documents,' *Quarterly of the Oregon Historical Society*, III: 4 (December 1902), p. 392.

[12]   Harriette Simpson Arnow, *Flowering of the Cumberland* (Lexington, KY, 1984), p. 309.

[13]   Kenneth L. Holmes, ed., *Covered Wagon Women: Diaries & Letters from the Western Trails, 1840–1890* (Glendale, CA, 1983), vol. 1, p. 199.

[14]   John D. Shane, 'Interview with pioneer William Clinkenbeard,' *Filson Club History Quarterly*, II: 3 (April 1928), p. 101.

[15]   Schlissel, p. 16.

16 Shane, p.22.

17 Wayne D. Rasmussen, ed., *Agriculture in the United States: A Documentary History* (New York, 1975), vol. 2, p. 1023.

18 Cathy Luchetti, *Women of the West*, (St George, Utah, 1982), p. 70.

19 Myres, p. 173.

20 Myres, p. 161.

21 Fred Lockley, 'Reminiscences of Martha E. Gilliam Collins,' *Quarterly of the Oregon Historical Society*, XVII: 4 (December 1916), p. 371.

22 Ruth B. Moynihan et. al., *So Much to be Done: Women Settlers on the Mining and Ranching Frontier* (Lincoln, NE, 1990), p. 170.

23 For in-depth discussion see Carl N. Degler, *At Odds: Women and the Family in America from the Revolution to the Present* (New York, 1980).

'NOT A VERY BRILLIANT BODY': FRONTIER GOVERNMENT

COURT DAYS

American pioneers were an exceedingly litigious lot. Apparently, rampant lawsuits are not just a modern scourge. One county with a population of 4,000 men, women, and children generated 192 cases during a three-month period in 1790. Civil suits contesting only a few dollars occurred regularly, and being sued was not the traumatic event it is today. The father of Daniel Drake provides an early example. In his first year in Kentucky, he rented a horse, which soon died. The horse's owner sued Drake, and both parties hired lawyers. A jury ruled against the owner.

The most frequent civil lawsuit involved debt collection and was heard by the quarterly county circuit courts. The twice yearly superior courts heard larger civil suits, land title disputes, and criminal cases, which most often involved horse theft or manslaughter. Dealing in contraband whiskey or cutting timber from government land also numbered high among the prosecutions. Jurors rarely convicted an illegal timber cutter because settlers felt that absentee landowners had less right to the timber than did the actual residents of an area.

In later years, disputed land claims remained the most important source of litigation, but collection of Civil War pensions ran a close second. In every territory, people desired certain plots of land more than others. Late-arriving settlers sought to wrest them from earlier claimants by means both legal and illegal, but equally dishonorable. Simple 'claim-jumping' involved running the previous claimant off at gunpoint, or occupying his claim while he was absent on an errand. Where claimants were able to organize effectively, they in turn ran off the claim-jumper. When a legitimate settler killed a claim-jumper, he was unlikely to be prosecuted.

To wrest a claim away by legal means, one looked for a technical violation of the terms of homesteading and took the claimant to court. Such a violation might consist of not planting enough acreage. A legal challenger entered the land he wished to dispute and measured the acreage planted to see if it fell even a little bit short. If it did, the challenger might accept a payment for dropping the matter. Such underhanded challenges frequently met with success in court, so a claimant did well to pay off the challenger.

On certain days, the circuit-riding justices of the peace came to town to try any pending litigation. The term 'circuit court' arose from the early practice of judges and attorneys riding a judicial circuit covering a vast territory. Each town held regular court days when litigants and spectators gathered. In New Mexico, a judicial party rode the district court circuit twice yearly, in spring and fall. The territorial governor, the judge, the U.S. marshal, and the U.S. attorney went together by horseback, as few of the roads were carriage-worthy. They stayed at hotels or billeted at villagers' houses. At one stop, the court officers were compelled to share with three strangers a room containing only three narrow beds. At table, they had to share the inadequate supply of forks, passing them from one diner to another. They made the best of conditions, spending their evenings in conversation and song, and attending the occasional dance or party arranged in their honor.

The New Mexico village court room of the 1850s was a roughly furnished room with a dirt floor. The surroundings and proceedings resembled those of frontier court rooms elsewhere in the country, but the presence of a sworn interpreter made clear that one was on newly annexed foreign ground. The pueblo Indians, who had long coexisted with the Spanish-speaking inhabitants, seemed naturally to fall under the jurisdiction of American courts. A murder trial in Santa Fe focused on four pueblo Indians who had executed two of their own for what the Americans deemed 'the imaginary crime of witchcraft.'[1] After hearing copious testimony from all witnesses, the court decided it held no jurisdiction over the case after all and freed the defendants.

Lawyers gravitated to the county seats and territorial capitals of the frontier where they found plenty of work involving deeds, surveys, and disputed land claims. As many as half a dozen lawyers might practice in a county town of 300 people. To qualify as a lawyer, one 'read the law' under another lawyer for a year or two, paying tuition to the lawyer and doing menial chores, and then applied to a judge for admission to the bar. Men with political and social aspirations pursued admission to the bar as a means of climbing the social ladder. Politics was also considered a respectable leisure-time pursuit for a wealthy man. One lawyer who arrived in Oregon during the early pioneer days reported, alas, that 'this is, as yet, no country for lawyers' because the territory had the 'most peaceable and quiet community in the world.'[2]

In the days before a territory became a state, the maintenance of public order remained a tenuous idea dependent on the persistence of sheriffs and the quality of the individual territorial governors and judges. The first emigrants to Oregon selected a popular former fur trapper named Joe Meek to serve as sheriff. His courage was soon tested when the community issued a warrant to arrest a man for fighting:

'Meek went to Dawson's shop, where he was at work at his bench with his jack-plane. Meek walked in, and said laughingly, "Dawson, I came for you."'

Courtroom conduct, Kansas, circa 1857. In this US District Court, the spectators sit on planks laid across stumps and stones. The judge, a South Carolinian, shows his regard for the defense attorney's oratory by reading his hometown newspaper, the **Charleston Mercury.** *The District Attorney turns his back to warm his feet on the stove. Despite the court's obvious bias against the abolitionist defendant, the jury demonstrated characteristic frontier independence by voting to acquit. (In Albert D. Richardson,* **Beyond the Mississippi,** *Hartford, 1869)*

Dawson refused to go, and Meek insisted. At that, Dawson tried to strike Meek with his jack-plane, but the sheriff wrenched it away:

> 'Dawson at once turned around and picked up his broad-ax; but at the moment he faced Meek he found a cocked pistol at his breast. Meek, still laughing, said: 'Dawson, I came for you. Surrender or die!'"[3]

Dawson surrendered to force majeure and so justice was served.

The more remote the frontier, the less stringent the qualifications for legal practitioners. Tales abound of illiterate hard-drinking judges, political appointees who knew little of the law and practiced a highly individual brand of justice. They threatened to jail unfavorable witnesses, or sent lawyers outside to solve the case with a fistfight. In contrast to the courtroom of today, casual behavior and dress of judge, lawyers, defendants, and jurors alike was the norm.

The marginal judicial talent of the frontier came up against a population that possessed more than its share of fugitives from justice. Outlaws moved westward, drawn by the looser bonds of government and law, hoping to evade punishment and practice their chosen trades – highway robbery, livestock theft, and various swindles. Such men rarely hesitated to kill in the course of a robbery. In some frontier territories, outlaws imposed a virtual reign of terror over law-abiding settlers. Just retribution for their crimes was far from certain, but when it fell it was swift.

Settlers frowned less on a homicide than they did on horse theft. The loss of a horse or cow could mean loss of livelihood, and in turn life. A dispute between men that led to a shooting was viewed more as a private matter, provided no one was shot in the back. Such disputes were similar to duels, a time-honored way of settling differences. A man who killed in order to steal, however, was marked for death. To the struggling pioneer, theft of hard-won property was the greatest crime.

Conventions existed for the honorable handling of stray animals found on one's property. One was expected to publicize a description of the stray. It remained an easy matter, however, to ride a stolen horse away and sell it quickly. In the 1790s, the law did not always execute horse thieves, but sometimes cut off their ears or branded their faces, marking them for life as horse thieves.

Travelers were particularly vulnerable to robbery. Stagecoach hold-ups occurred on every frontier. Some say that the term 'hold-up' derived from the highwayman's command to 'Hold up your hands.' Knowing that most men carried weapons, outlaws expected armed resistance. By this common salutation, the robber meant to prevent a passenger from reaching for his gun to defend his valuables. River pirates also waylaid and plundered travelers, abandoning their victims on a deserted bank or killing them. Their heyday began with flatboat traffic on the Ohio and Missis-

For fear of highway robbery, stagecoaches traveled under armed guard on the frontier, a man 'riding shotgun' next to the driver. Stagecoach robberies persisted in the southwest until late in the nineteenth century, forcing operators to provide their own protection. (Arizona Historical Society)

sippi rivers and ended with the advent of steamboats. Among their methods for capturing flatboats were to overtake them in faster boats, lure them to shore with a phony distress call – as Indians had lured emigrants – or pose as pilots above hazardous stretches of river. The slowness of frontier communications allowed pirates to operate with impunity from the same site for many months: a trader setting off down the river could be missing a long time before his colleagues began to worry. By then it was far too late.

Should a criminal be so unlucky as to be captured, he had ample opportunity to escape. Should he come to trial, conviction was as unlikely as it is today. Obtaining a conviction in a criminal case tried before a jury was a particular challenge. Jurors often based their verdicts on popular opinion of the litigants. Unlike today's jurors, they sat in thinly populated areas and knew personally all the principal actors in a case. In a New Mexico courtroom in the mid-1850s, one jury not only acquitted the defendant, but fined the district attorney for having the temerity to prosecute. As the court adjourned, a juror picked the pocket of a court official.[4]

Jails were scarce, inadequate, and easy to escape. Therefore, punishment rarely took the form of a jail term. The US Attorney for New Mexico, serving 1853 to 1856, described the jail at Taos, a room off the courtroom:

> 'a prisoner confined there would be about as safe as when picketed out on the Plaza...the door, instead of being locked, was securely fastened with a twine string.'[5]

An Oregon man, who had helped his brother temporarily elude capture after committing a murder, received a sentence of three years in the penitentiary:

> 'but as there was no penitentiary and they didn't want to build one for the exclusive benefit of Hiram Everman, they decided to sell him at auction...Hiram was sold the day his brother was hung.'[6]

Everman served three years' punishment as an indentured laborer. Another man in the same community, who had killed his wife, was sentenced to hang, but the lack of a jail to hold him until the appointed day presented a problem. He stayed at the home of the sheriff under the watchful eye of four guards. The sheriff's wife cooked for the condemned man as well as her own family. The man escaped once but a posse brought him back.

Instead of imprisonment, whipping, branding, confinement to a pillory, hanging, and even castration were handed down and quickly administered in the closing years of the eighteenth century. Whipping became rarer as the nineteenth century went on. Frontiersmen often punished horse theft, counterfeiting, and slave stealing with hanging. If, on the other hand, they felt the victim of the crime deserved his fate, they found the accused innocent. If they found the defendant guilty, frequently vigilantes cut off his route to an appeal by inflicting punishment immediately.

Likewise, when a jury's guilty verdict was overruled on a technicality, an outcome ardently sought by lawyers, the vigilance committee did the will of the citizenry nevertheless. When an acquittal outraged the community, the secret committee met at night, passed judgment, and sent the vigilantes to the jailhouse, where the jailer knew better than to protest or resist. Depending on the offence, the vigilantes beat the offender, tarred and feathered him, ran him out of town, pushed him down a hill in a barrel, or summarily hung him. Rarely, a sheriff tried to hold off the mob at gunpoint and insist on official justice taking its course. His success depended both on his ferocity and his standing in the community. Even among lynch mobs, a code of behavior could be observed. The New Mexico physician Henry Hoyt told of a man knocking down and kicking a murderer as vigilantes led him to the gallows. The other men forced him to desist.

Vigilantes formed posses to pursue and apprehend horse and cattle thieves or murderers, and they expected to exchange gunfire before capturing their men. Hundreds of vigilance committees formed in frontier communities. Otherwise law-abiding citizens tried to impose order by this extralegal means because they decried the lack of an effective criminal justice system. They deterred some crime by warning thieves and giving them a chance to leave voluntarily. Those who refused to leave, or who returned after being run off, faced summary execution. At times innocents were put to death by vigilantes on suspicion without evidence: innocence, not guilt, had to be proven. More often, solid evidence existed. These citizens' committees usually disbanded once they eliminated the worst criminals, but some, drunk on their successes, became self-appointed morality patrols, harassing petty offenders or people they deemed undesirable. Thus, vigilante justice on the frontier was both necessary and dangerous to liberty. Such is the trade-off of any form of social control.

When a miscarriage of official justice led to conviction of the innocent, little could be done. In an early Kentucky murder case, an innocent man was convicted because he was caught in the act of pulling the knife from the wound. The guilty party left messages exonerating the jailed man before he fled, but to no avail. A woman of ill repute offered to marry the condemned man, as that would have prevented the hanging, but he refused, and so he hung.

American settlers in New Mexico lived in fear of theft from the beginning. Almost every diary from the conquest onward mentions money stolen from wagons along the Santa Fe Trail, or houses robbed in the occupants' absence. The situation grew worse before it got better, and even law-abiding men went everywhere armed with revolvers. Nobody took any but congratulatory notice when citizens seized matters in their own hands: 'Lt OBannon having meat stolen...put arsenic in a piece of mutton, & it was stolen last night. Unlucky thief who eats it.'[7] New Mexico's infamous Lincoln County War, a murderous feud between rival cattle ranchers, marked the late 1870s as a particularly bloody period in the territory's history. The penetration of the railroad in 1879 brought even more outlaws to the region.

Colorful images of outlaws and desperados exaggerate the real situation found on the western frontier. Nevertheless, crime was a common occurrence with the first, and often only, line of defense being armed self-defense.

ON THE STUMP

Most permanent settlers, once they had met their primary goal of securing a piece of land, next wanted to live in an organized county. Most, but not all, particularly in the case of an 1843 Oregon community. Some eager would-be lawmakers forced through unpopular local bills banning the distillation or sale of liquor and related 'good' government measures. Only then did they concern themselves about how to enforce the law, given that 50 out of 102 voters had opposed the formation of their government. With unintended understatement, a pro-government man recalls that 'There were so many of our people who were conscientiously opposed to the organization of any government that we found it a delicate matter to use force against men whose motives we were sure were good. Still, government had to be practically enforced.'[8]

Early county governments levied taxes while providing little in the way of law enforcement, but they did offer a place to record and keep track of land ownership, debts, brands and earmarks, and related legal matters. Politically appointed county clerks took care of all such business. Justices of the peace, lifetime political appointees, comprised the county courts and met at intervals to govern the counties. The county courts regulated the operation of ferries, mills, and taverns, setting prices and decreeing even the strength of the grog sold. In this the counties continued the regulatory tradition in effect before the Revolution; that of prescribing the details of how business

The first legislature of Kentucky convenes. Most of the representatives wear buckskin hunters' dress. A similar mix of buckskin and formal dress prevailed in Dakota Territory's legislature more than 70 years later. (Library of Congress)

should be conducted. Rounding off the ranks of county officials were sheriffs and surveyors. In post-Revolutionary days, men voted only for legislators, who in turn decided all else.

In the early 1790s, Mason County, Kentucky levied taxes per man, per animal, per slave, and per acre. The funds went for public buildings, roads and bridges, public salaries, payment of bounties on wolves, and support of the indigent. The latter ranks often included those wounded or left destitute by Indian attacks. Tax collectors, ever considerate, traveled the early counties to save settlers the long trip to the county seat. Lotteries provided an alternate source of funding for public buildings, public works, charitable enterprises, and even churches. After the Homestead Act went into effect, local governments initially collected very few tax dollars, because land remained tax-exempt until the owner attained full title. Until then, the homesteader paid taxes only on the improvements – fences, houses, barns, equipment.

American settlers in Oregon's Willamette Valley formed a provisional government in 1843, three years before the United States took official possession. Largely a law-abiding group, the farmers organized to maintain order and to protect their land claims. They had taken up unoccupied land at will, free of charge, but realized that it could just as easily be taken away if no authority prevented it.

New Mexico presented a unique challenge in which the United States had to govern a largely Spanish-speaking population. The annexation treaty permitted Mexican inhabitants of the new territory to retain Mexican citizenship. The U.S. court ruled that those who so chose actually retained dual citizenship and could vote in U.S. elections. The territorial legislature had delegates of both nationalities and conducted its business in two languages. Most of the delegates spoke Spanish while the territorial governor gave his speeches in English. Translators worked side by side with the politicians to assist mutual comprehension.

In all other respects, the New Mexico legislature was thoroughly American. Observed the sitting U.S. attorney in 1857:

'Those who were candidates for office in either House and their friends began the system of electioneering so prevalent in other sections of the Union; and the few days that intervened...were spent in wire-pulling, log-rolling, and all the other strategic movements known in modern politics.'9

One piece of legislation, involving the lucrative contract for printing up the new laws, nearly brought the government to a standstill. A stubborn faction held up the proposed contract because,

'They could not obtain it for their own friends, and determined to prevent any body else getting it.'[10] The dissenting delegates wanted to award the contract to a printer whose newspaper had supported them during their campaigns for office. They attempted to skirt their rivals by meeting twenty minutes earlier than the session's normal opening to pass their chosen contract. Having done this, they adjourned and went home. Twenty minutes later, the regular session met, and in the dissenters' absence, passed the original contract. Such episodes only confirmed the following observation: 'I attended the meeting of the Senate of N.M. which closed this evening. It is not a very brilliant body.'[11]

In the 1860s, during Dakota Territory's early days, government had but a tenuous hold. Corrupt politicians ran amuck in the wide open, thinly settled territory. So blatantly did they buy votes, accept bribes, and stuff ballot boxes with votes from under-age or deceased voters, that in 1864 a disgusted Congress threatened to annex the territory to Nebraska.

Deadwood, South Dakota, a rough miners' boom town, operated without official government. The miners had flocked there on report of gold, ignoring the fact that the gold lay on land ceded by treaty to the Sioux. Since the miners were there illegally, the army, unable to keep them off, refused to become involved in their disputes. This forced the gold-seekers to mount their own response to contested claims. Like the orderly settlers of Oregon more than three decades earlier, the miners formed their own government, which included a system of mining districts to regulate claims. Even the scofflaw seeks legal recourse when he perceives a threat to property.

The perceived need for social organization and laws encouraged the ardent few to enter politics. Some did so out of a sense of civic responsibility, many more saw a chance for personal advantage. By 1820, a new tradition of going on the campaign trail began. Candidates stood on tree stumps to give their speeches, giving rise to the expression 'stumping' for office. Like the modern politician, a frontier politician could win votes by calling attention to his humble origins and telling jokes. A charming personality or heroism at war could make up for a lack of political experience. Would-be voters expected their candidates to provide barbecues and whiskey at campaign stops. Voters can still attend candidate-sponsored barbecues – minus the whiskey – in rural America today.

On the appointed day, men arrived on horseback at the nearest village to cast their votes, whispering – or shouting – their choices to a clerk stationed on the courthouse porch. At times, groups of partisans gathered to intimidate men who arrived to vote against their cause, and fights broke out. In communities lacking a courthouse, the vote took place at a settler's house. Like everything else, the first ballot boxes were makeshift affairs fabricated out of packing crates or cigar boxes.

The sort of pioneer who tried to stay a step ahead of civilization cared not at all about government, except to evade its grasp. But the true settler took a passionate interest in politics, for the chance to socialize, the hope of influencing local events, and because he cared about his nation. An Oregon pioneer recalls that issues of religion and social values caused little controversy. 'Only on political questions was real difference of opinion asserted,' he explained, and this

A frontier polling place, complete with whiskey vendor. Sixty years would pass before women appeared at American polls. (In Albert D. Richardson, Beyond the Mississippi, Hartford, 1869)

stemmed from the national schism over slavery. 'The Kansas-Nebraska struggle in politics was fought in Oregon as in Massachusetts and Missouri – even though we were at a continental distance from the scene of conflict.'[12]

One of the first acts of Oregon's citizen-founded provisional government was a rather crude attempt to distance the settlers from the slavery question. In the words of one settler who heartily disapproved of the measure to ban negros from Oregon:

> 'the full measure of their wrath fell upon the poor negroes...any negro bond or free so unfortunate as to be found in this land of liberty is to be flogged a certain number of stripes.'[13]

In keeping with the aphorism that all politics are local, across the country settlers called political meetings to decide county borders and county seats, or to consider bond issues for railroads. Towns battled for the advantage of being named the county seat. In Dakota in the 1880s, citizens resorted to stealing county records from one town and moving them to another. Still others stuffed ballot boxes, bought and sold votes, and corrupted the election in whatever way they could, all to gain the economic advantage of county government. In this the common citizen only echoed the corruption at the highest levels of government. In an 1883 scandal, the territorial governor of Dakota and a band of his cronies held up applications and extorted payments from citizens desiring to organize into counties.

Corruption among public officials was perhaps even more blatant and expected than it is nowadays, but pioneer Americans did not lapse into today's despair and apathy as a result. Instead, they busily set about trying to turn the situation to their advantage. In their thinly populated settlements, they took seriously their participation in government, and they believed each person had both influence and the obligation to use it. Generally, settlers craved law and order, but many willingly disregarded it when it suited their convenience. They employed every means at their disposal, honest or corrupt, to make local governments promote their economic interests. The frontier had always required its inhabitants to take matters into their own hands, and so they entered the political rough and tumble with zeal.

1   W.W.H. Davis, *El Gringo: New Mexico and her People* (New York, 1857), p. 329.
2   'Documents,' *Quarterly of the Oregon Historical Society*, III:4 (December 1902), p. 426.
3   Peter H. Burnett, 'Recollections and opinions of an old pioneer,' *Quarterly of the Oregon Historical Society*, V:2 (June 1904), pp. 167-8.
4   Davis, pp. 358–9.
5   Davis, p. 310.
6   Fred Lockley, 'Reminiscences of Martha E. Gilliam Collins,' *Quarterly of the Oregon Historical Society*, XVII:4 (December 1916), p. 370.
7   Barton H. Barbour, ed., *Reluctant Frontiersman: James Ross Larkin on the Santa Fe Trail, 1856–57*, (Albuquerque, 1990), p. 116.
8   Burnett, p. 167.
9   Davis, p. 251.
10 Davis, p. 288.
11 Barbour, p. 119.
12 Harvey W. Scott, 'Pioneer character of Oregon progress,' *Quarterly of the Oregon Historical Society*, XVIII:4 (December 1917), p. 249.
13 Maude A. Rucker, *The Oregon Trail and Some of its Blazers* (New York, 1930), p. 229.

EPILOGUE

'It is said that they are an idle, dissolute, quarrelsome, insolent set of adventurers, who were too vicious or too poor to live where they were born, and have therefore fled from the society of honest, civilized men.' — Harry Toulmin, 1793

The people who settled the American West had the freedom to go to a new country. There they might find riches or they might come to rest in an unmarked grave. Pioneers confidently believed that the rewards outweighed the risks. They left everything familiar behind to take a chance on a new life. By grasping freedom they let go of security. In heading west, a person might walk away from the consequences of past mistakes, but by crossing the frontier he forfeited the chance of assistance if he stumbled. Whether he stepped surely or mis-stepped, found fortune or misfortune, had something to do with character and skill and everything to do with chance.

American society is a mobile society. To move away from one's home town in search of a better life, to rise above the circumstances of one's birth, is to be typically American. The letters, the memoirs, the feats of the pioneers themselves testify to this characteristic. The frontier offered a chance to make one's fortune – for fortune is what we have always wanted – and drew young men and women away from their place of birth as surely as careers and corporate transfers do in the modern world. Hardship on the journey was hardly worth considering; pioneers walked if the road required it.

The idyllic rural multi-generational family with deep roots in the land is a modern fantasy. The pursuit of land on the frontier split families up. Pioneers sought a place where they could farm their own land alongside their children, but they left their own parents behind to do so. With the exception of the infrequent letter from home bringing news months old, once they departed for the West they severed family ties. On the frontier, long hours of work and short periods of schooling bred capable, independent children. Some loyally served their family farms well into adulthood; others took off early and never looked back.

Along with their feather beds and seed corn, pioneers brought with them the skills to provide themselves with both the necessities and an array of comforts. Most adults of the American West, and many children, could shoot, field dress, skin, and butcher an animal. They planted crops, built houses, and produced cloth. They crafted furniture, and indeed the very tools they used. Yet the settlers abandoned handmade goods for manufactured as soon as merchants imported goods from the east and extended credit. To American pioneers, success meant enough money to pay somebody else to do the time-consuming work of basic production.

Most anyone who could work, learn, and adapt, could survive and prosper in the West. Anyone willing to venture their time and money on a frontier farm or business stood to gain. Then as now, nobody was just a farmer; all had other jobs or businesses as well. Even in the absence of any other skills, willingness to perform manual labor – whether hewing building timber or cutting firewood for steamboats – earned a productive niche. Still, the West also had its share of ineffectual dreamers who found in the frontier not wealth, but a broader canvas on which to paint their failures.

* * *

A person who was content with little could live out the dream of an independent existence, untroubled by neighbors or government. But most pioneers wanted to be part of a community as soon as possible. Wherever Americans gathered, they quickly organized, for work or play, politics or salvation. In pioneer communities where people lived always under the eyes of their neighbors, those who gave as good as they got earned respect. The community shunned those who did not.

From the beginning, Americans were accustomed to government regulation, and sought more of it when it suited their ends. They wanted the government to give them free land, and many otherwise honest people happily defrauded the government to get more than their share. They entreated the government to send the army west, not just to defend them, but to help them pursue their blood feuds against the Indians. Then as now, Americans looked to government to help them when they failed, and blamed the government for their failures. Then as now, they countenanced corruption when it worked to their benefit, and decried it when they suffered as a result.

Frontiersmen from all walks of life – farmers, doctors, outlaws – were quick to give and take offense. They brawled, duelled, shot at presumed enemies on sight, and when all else failed, resorted to Americans' natural proclivity for the lawsuit. In addition, there always has existed a class of people who want only what they can take by force or guile from someone else. A widely scattered populace offered tempting targets. However, that populace usually carried firearms and this, no doubt, deterred some crimes. It is difficult to evaluate whether western settlers felt safer or more menaced than Americans today. Whereas the precarious life of the early Kentucky pioneer, with its ever-present Indian threat, surpassed the dangers confronted by subsequent pioneers, it may find an analog in the modern inner city.

* * *

One major factor distinguished the pioneer's world from the modern. Disease was a far more serious threat, a lurking presence through all of life, the one thing beyond all control. Little understood, diseases seemed to come out of the blue to strike people down, carrying off child after child with chilling regularity. Pioneer Americans appear fatalistic to modern eyes. They show an astonishing disregard for what we would call basic safety precautions. They carried loaded firearms, raced horses and vehicles to destruction, and behaved in countless ways that now seem reckless. Perhaps they tempted fate because they knew they could not evade it. American pioneers knew existence to be tenuous and themselves to be at fate's mercy. What they clearly possessed was an acceptance of events they neither could foresee nor control and the will to keep trying when misfortunes dashed their hopes. Their persistence and determination to succeed led them to the western lands, where they defined the frontier spirit by their willingness to try and try again.

BIBLIOGRAPHY

GENERAL

Atherton, Lewis E. *The Frontier Merchant in Mid-America*. Columbia, MO, 1971.

Atherton, Lewis E. *The Southern Country Store: 1800–1860*. Baton Rouge, 1949.

Axelrod, Alan. *Chronicle of the Indian Wars*. New York, 1993.

Bartlett, Richard A. *The New Country: A Social History of the American Frontier, 1776–1890*. New York, 1974.

Bidwell, Percy W. and John I. Falconer. *History of Agriculture in the Northern United States, 1620–1860*. Washington, 1925.

Bruce, Dickson C., Jr. *And They All Sang Hallelujah: Plain-Folk Camp Meeting Religion, 1800–1845*. Knoxville, 1974.

Chapel, Charles Edward. *Guns of the Old West*. New York, 1961.

Degler, Carl N. *At Odds: Women and the Family in America from the Revolution to the Present*. New York, 1980.

Dunlop, M.H. *Sixty Miles From Contentment: Traveling the Nineteenth-Century American Interior*. New York, 1995.

Dunlop, Richard. *Doctors of the American Frontier*. New York, 1962.

Gates, Paul W. *The Farmer's Age: Agriculture 1815–1860*. New York, 1960.

Hawke, David Freeman. *Everyday Life in Early America*. New York, 1988. Covers the colonial period and provides historical antecedents of frontier ways.

Horsman, Reginald. *The Frontier in the Formative Years, 1783–1815*. New York, 1970.

Karolevitz, Robert F. *Newspapering in the Old West*. Seattle, 1965.

Luchetti, Cathy. *Women of the West*. St. George, Utah, 1982.

Merk, Frederick. *History of the Westward Movement*. New York, 1978.

Myres, Sandra L. *Westering Women and the Frontier Experience, 1800–1915*. Albuquerque, 1982.

Rasmussen, Wayne D., ed. *Agriculture in the United States: A Documentary History*. 4 vols. New York, 1975. Reprints of historical laws, early government reports, letters, and articles.

Reed, Robert C. *Train Wrecks*. Seattle, 1968.

Schlebecker, John T. *Whereby We Thrive: A History of American Farming, 1607–1972*. Ames, Iowa, 1975.

Shannon, Fred A. *The Farmer's Last Frontier: Agriculture, 1860–1897*. New York, 1945.

Thwaites, Reuben Gold. *Early Western Travels, 1748–1846*. 32 vols. New York, 1966. Reprints of contemporary journals. Bradbury, John, 'Travels in the interior of America in the years 1809, 1810, and 1811,' vol. 5. Cuming, Fortescue, 'Sketches of a tour to the Western country,' vol. 4. Michaux, François André, 'Travels to the west of the Allegheny Mountains... in the year 1802,' vol. 3.

Tryon, Warren S. *A Mirror for Americans: Life and Manners in the United States, 1790–1870, as Recorded by American Travelers*, 3 vols. Chicago, 1952.

Twain, Mark. *Editorial Wild Oats*. New York, 1905.

West, Elliott. *Growing Up With the Country*. Albuquerque, 1989.

Wooster, Robert. *The Military and United States Indian Policy 1865–1903*. New Haven, 1988.

BIBLIOGRAPHY

KENTUCKY AND OLD NORTHWEST

Beckner, Lucien. 'Rev. John Dabney Shane's Interview with Mrs Sarah Graham of Bath County,' *Filson Club History Quarterly*, IX:4 (October 1935) pp. 222–41. Reverend Shane interviewed numerous early Kentucky pioneers in their old age. The Filson Club reprinted these memoirs in various issues of their journal.

Birkbeck, Morris. *Notes on a Journey in America*. London, 1818. By an Englishman looking for land to settle in the old Northwest.

Buley, R. Carlyle. *The Old Northwest: Pioneer Period, 1815–1840*. 2 vols. Bloomington, IN, 1950.

Channing, Stephen A. *Kentucky: A Bicentennial History*. New York, 1977.

Chartrand, Rene. *Uniforms and Equipment of the United States Forces in the War of 1812*. Youngstown, NY, 1992.

Collins, Lewis. *History of Kentucky*. Covington, KY, 1882.

Dicken-Garcia, Hazel. *To Western Woods: The Breckinridge Family Moves to Kentucky in 1793*. Cranbury, NJ, 1991.

Drake, Daniel. *Pioneer Life in Kentucky*. New York, 1948. An excellent first-person account of the author's boyhood in Kentucky, from 1788 to 1800.

Eckert, Allan W. *The Frontiersmen: A Narrative*. Boston, 1967.

Fearon, Henry. *Sketches of America*. London, 1819. An English traveler's account.

Irvin, Helen Deiss. *Women in Kentucky*. Lexington, KY, 1979.

Lester, William Stewart. *The Transylvania Colony*. Spencer, IN, 1935.

Muir, John. *The Story of My Boyhood and Youth*. New York, 1913. The author's family sailed from Scotland to settle in central Wisconsin. He remained on the family farm from 1849 to 1860.

Nelson, Paul David. *Anthony Wayne: Soldier of the Early Republic*. Bloomington, IN, 1985.

Pickard, Madge E. and R. Carlyle Buley. *The Midwest Pioneer: His Ills, Cures & Doctors*. New York, 1946.

Rothbert, Otto A. 'John D. Shane's interview with Colonel John Graves of Fayette County,' *Filson Club History Quarterly*, XV:4 (October 1941) pp. 238–47.

Shane, John D. 'Interview with pioneer William Clinkenbeard' *Filson Club History Quarterly*, II:3 (April 1928) pp. 95–128.

'A Sketch of early adventures of William Sudduth in Kentucky,' *Filson Club History Quarterly*, II:2 (January 1928) pp. 43–70.

Smith, John F. 'The salt-making industry of Clay County, Kentucky,' *Filson Club History Quarterly*, I:3 (April 1927) pp. 134–41.

Thruston, R.C. 'Letter by Edward Harris, 1797,' *Filson Club History Quarterly*, II:4 (October 1828) pp. 164–8.

Tinling, Marion and Godfrey Davies, eds. *The Western Country in 1793: Reports on Kentucky and Virginia by Harry Toulmin*. San Marino, 1948. An eighteenth-century English clergyman described the region for future emigrants.

U.S. Federal Writers Project. *Military History of Kentucky*. Frankfort, KY, 1939.

MISSISSIPPI VALLEY

Arnow, Harriette Simpson. *Seedtime on the Cumberland*. Lexington, KY, 1983. Focuses on Tennessee history and culture.

Arnow, Harriette Simpson. *Flowering of the Cumberland*. Lexington, KY, 1984. Focus on Tennessee, as stated above, with good detail on whiskey making and the Mississippi River trade.

Crete, Liliane. *Daily Life in Louisiana, 1815–1830*. Baton Rouge, 1981.

Davis, William C. *A Way Through the Wilderness*. New York, 1995.

Dick, Everett. *The Dixie Frontier*. New York, 1948.

Ekberg, Carl J. *Colonial Ste. Genevieve: An Adventure on the Mississippi Frontier*. Gerald, MO, 1985.

Lincecum, Gideon. 'Autobiography of Gideon Lincecum,' *Publications of the Mississippi Historical Society*, VIII (1904) pp. 443–519. Lincecum lived in Mississippi during the early and middle 1800s. A lively and colorful account.

Moore, John Hebron. *The Emergence of the Cotton Kingdom in the Old Southwest: Mississippi, 1770–1860*. Baton Rouge, 1988. Good detail on slavery practices, cotton culture, and town descriptions.

Skates, John Ray. *Mississippi: A Bicentennial History*. New York, 1979.

Stoddard, Amos. *Sketches, Historical and Descriptive, of Louisiana*. Philadelphia, 1812. The author served as military governor when the United States assumed control of the Louisiana Purchase.

PACIFIC NORTHWEST

Boag, Peter G. *Environment and Experience: Settlement Culture in Nineteenth-Century Oregon*. Los Angeles, 1992.

Bowen, William A. *The Willamette Valley: Migration and Settlement on the Oregon Frontier*. Seattle, 1978.

Burnett, Peter H. 'Recollections and opinions of an old pioneer,' *Quarterly of the Oregon Historical Society*, V:2 (June 1904), pp. 151–98.

'Documents,' *Quarterly of the Oregon Historical Society*, III:4 (December 1902) 390–426.

Dodds, Gordon B. *Oregon: A Bicentennial History*. New York, 1977.

Drury, Clifford Merrill, ed. *First White Women Over the Rockies*, vol. I. Glendale, CA, 1963. Features letters and diaries by missionary women in Oregon from the 1830s.

Glen, Julia Veazie. 'John Lyle and Lyle Farm,' *Quarterly of the Oregon Historical Society*, XXVI:2 (June 1925), pp. 130–50.

Hastings, Lansford W. *The Emigrants' Guide to Oregon and California*. Cincinnati, 1845.

Henderson, Sarah Fisher et. al. 'Correspondence of the Reverend Ezra Fisher,' *Quarterly of the Oregon Historical Society*, XVI:1 (March 1915), pp. 64–104.

Holmes, Kenneth L., ed. *Covered Wagon Women: Diaries & Letters from the Western Trails, 1840–1890*, 11 vols. Glendale, CA, 1983. An excellent collection.

Lockley, Fred. 'Reminiscences of Martha E. Gilliam Collins,' *Quarterly of the Oregon Historical Society*, XVII:4 (December 1916), pp. 358–72.

Lyman, H.S. 'Reminiscences of F. X. Matthieu,' *Quarterly of the Oregon Historical Society*, I:1 (March 1900), pp. 73–104.

Molson, Mrs William Markland. 'Glimpses of life in early Oregon,' *Quarterly of the Oregon Historical Society*, I:2 (June 1900), pp. 158–64.

Parkman, Francis. *The Oregon Trail*. New York, 1949. First published in 1847 after Parkman, just out of college, went adventuring on the trail.

Rucker, Maude A. *The Oregon Trail and Some of its Blazers*. New York, 1930. Contains the 1914 memoir of Jesse A. Applegate, who arrived in Oregon as a child in 1843.

Schlissel, Lillian et. al. *Far From Home: Families of the Westward Journey*. New York, 1989.

Scott, Harvey W. 'Pioneer character of Oregon progress,' *Quarterly of the Oregon Historical Society*, XVIII:4 (December 1917), pp. 245–70.

Worster, Donald. *Rivers of Empire: Water, Aridity, and the Growth of the American West*. New York, 1985.

NEW MEXICO

Barbour, Barton H., ed. *Reluctant Frontiersman: James Ross Larkin on the Santa Fe Trail, 1856–57*. Albuquerque, 1990. By a health-seeker from a well-to-do St. Louis family.

Davis, W.W.H. *El Gringo: New Mexico and her People*. New York, 1857. Davis served as U.S. attorney to New Mexico Territory from 1853 to 1856.

Drumm, Stella M., ed. *Down the Santa Fe Trail and Into Mexico: The Diary of Susan Shelby Magoffin, 1846–1847*. New Haven, 1926. By the young wife of a wealthy trader.

Foote, Cheryl J. *Women of the New Mexico Frontier 1846–1912*. Niwot, CO, 1990.

Gregg, Josiah. *Commerce of the Prairies*. New York, 1970. Gregg began as a health-seeker and ended up as a Santa Fe trader in the 1830s. He first published this memoir in 1844.

Hart, Herbert M. *Old Forts of the Far West*. New York, 1965.

Hoyt, Henry F. *A Frontier Doctor*. Chicago, 1979. Reprint of first-person account of events in South Dakota, Texas, New Mexico, and elsewhere during the 1870s and 1880s.

Lane, Lydia Spencer. *I Married a Soldier*. Albuquerque, 1964. Southwestern army life in the 1850s–1860s.

Moynihan, Ruth B. et. al. *So Much to be Done: Women Settlers on the Mining and Ranching Frontier*. Lincoln, NE, 1990.

Murphy, Lawrence R. 'Rayado: Pioneer settlement in Northeastern New Mexico, 1848–1857,' *New Mexico Historical Review*, XLVI:1 (January 1971), pp. 37–53.

Myres, Sandra L., ed. *Cavalry Wife: The Diary of Eveline M. Alexander, 1866–1867*. College Station, TX, 1977.

Richardson, Rupert Norval and Carl Coke Rister. *The Greater Southwest*. Glendale, CA, 1935.

Russell, Marian Sloan. *Land of Enchantment: Memoirs of Marian Russell along the Santa Fe Trail*. Evanston, 1954. The writer first arrived in New Mexico as a child during the 1850s.

Sunseri, Alvin R. *Seeds of Discord: New Mexico in the Aftermath of the American Conquest, 1846–1861*. Chicago, 1979.

Westphall, Victor. 'The public domain in New Mexico, 1854–1891,' *New Mexico Historical Review*, XXXIII:1 (January 1958), pp. 24–52.

MANUSCRIPT

The Daybook of Anna Maria Morris 1850–1858, Special Collections, University of Virginia, Charlottesville, VA. She was the wife of Gouverneur Morris, who held a military command in New Mexico. The entries are both monotonous and revealing.

SOUTH DAKOTA

Burmeister, Ruth Seymour, ed. 'Jeffries letters,' *South Dakota History*, VI:3 (Summer 1976), pp. 316–23.

Dick, Everett. *The Sod-House Frontier, 1854–1890*. New York, 1937.

Frajola, Ruth Cook, ed. 'They went west,' *South Dakota History*, VI:3 (Summer 1976), pp. 281–305.

Hampsten, Elizabeth. *Settlers' Children: Growing up on the Great Plains*. Norman, OK, 1991.

Herseth, Lorna B., ed.'A pioneer's letter,' *South Dakota History*, VI:3 (Summer 1976), pp. 306–15.

Lee, Robert. *Fort Meade & the Black Hills*. Lincoln, NE, 1991.

Riley, Glenda.'Farm women's roles in the agricultural development of South Dakota,' *South Dakota History*, XIII:1 (Spring 1983), pp. 83–121.

Schell, Herbert S. *History of South Dakota*. Lincoln, NE, 1968.

Tallent, Annie. *The Black Hills*. St Louis, 1899. Tallent settled in the Black Hills in the 1870s.

Trumbo, Isreal. 'A pioneer's letter home,' *South Dakota Historical Collections*, VI (1912), pp. 201–3.

Wessel, Thomas R., ed. *Agriculture in the Great Plains, 1876–1936*. Washington, 1977.

INDEX